D1158314

Conceptual Foundations for Therapeutic Recreation

edited by

David R. Austin, Ph.D., CTRS, FALS
Indiana University

John Dattilo, Ph.D., FALS
University of Georgia

Bryan P. McCormick, Ph.D., CTRS
Indiana University

Conceptual Foundations for Therapeutic Recreation

edited by

David R. Austin, Ph.D., CTRS, FALS
Indiana University

John Dattilo, Ph.D., FALS
University of Georgia

Bryan P. McCormick, Ph.D., CTRS
Indiana University

 Venture Publishing, Inc. • *State College, Pennsylvania*

Copyright © 2002

Venture Publishing, Inc.
1999 Cato Avenue
State College, PA 16801
Phone: (814) 234-4561; Fax: (814) 234-1651

No part of the material protected by this copyright notice may be reproduced or utilized in any form or by any means, electronic or mechanical, including photocopying, recording, or by any information storage and retrieval system, without written permission from the copyright owner.

Trademarks: All brand names and product names used in this book are trademarks, registered trademarks, or trade names of their respective holders.

Production Manager: Richard Yocum
Manuscript Editing: Michele L. Barbin, Valerie Paukovits
Cover Design and Illustration: Echelon Design

Library of Congress Catalogue Card Number 2002104096
ISBN 1-892132-30-3

Table of Contents

Chapter 2
Behavior Modification in Therapeutic Recreation:
Observing Behaviors and Applying Consequences.......... 31
John Dattilo, Ph.D., FALS, and Brent Wolfe, M.A., CTRS

Chapter 3
Social Support in Therapeutic Recreation 49
Bryan P. McCormick, Ph.D., CTRS

Chapter 4
Self-Determination and Enjoyment
in Therapeutic Recreation 73
John Dattilo, Ph.D., FALS, and Douglas Kleiber, Ph.D., FALS

Chapter 5
Control: A Major Element in Therapeutic Recreation 93
David R. Austin, Ph.D., CTRS, FALS

Chapter 7
An Overview of Therapeutic Outdoor Programming 133
Alan Ewert, Ph.D., FALS, Alison Voight, Ph.D., and
Brady Harnishfeger, Ph.D.

Chapter 8
Increasing Cultural Competence
in Therapeutic Recreation 151
Deb Getz, Re.D., CTRS

Chapter 11
Therapeutic Recreation Education: A Call for Reform ... 207
David R. Austin, Ph.D., CTRS, FALS

Chapter 12
A Call for Training in Physical Activity 225
David R. Austin, Ph.D., CTRS, FALS

Chapter 13
Making Presentations Related to Therapeutic Recreation .. 235
Richard Williams, Ed.D., CTRS, and John Dattilo, Ph.D., FALS

Chapter 14
Some Tips for Students about Attending Conferences ... 253

Youngkhill Lee, Ph.D., CTRS, Janet A. Funderburk, M.S., CTRS, and David R. Austin, Ph.D., CTRS, FALS

Chapter 15
Professionalism 265

David R. Austin, Ph.D., CTRS, FALS

Chapter 16
A Third Revolution in Therapeutic Recreation? 273
David R. Austin, Ph.D., CTRS, FALS

Chapter 17
This I Believe... About Therapeutic Recreation 289

Chapter 18

Preface

Conceptual Foundations for Therapeutic Recreation is intended for students and practitioners in therapeutic recreation. Instructors who teach upper-level undergraduate courses and graduate courses in therapeutic recreation can use this book to help students formulate a conceptual basis for their practice and develop themselves as professionals. Practicing therapeutic recreation professionals will find this book offers them information intended to encourage them to become more reflective practitioners.

Our intention was to provide a user-friendly book. The chapters are written in clear, understandable prose. Reading comprehension questions at the conclusion of every chapter direct readers and provide discussion questions for instructors.

This book is different from others. First, it provides empirically based theoretical perspectives on topics that have never been given thorough coverage in the therapeutic recreation literature. For example, concepts such as control, self-determination, social support, therapeutic relationships, and conceptual models are covered. These key concepts are critical to therapeutic recreation practice.

Second, this book offers easily accessible overviews of timely topics. Such topics include cultural competence, evidence-based practice, therapeutic outdoor programs, and healthcare in America.

Third, this book offers historical and philosophical perspectives never before found in the therapeutic recreation literature. In addition to a chapter on the history of therapeutic recreation, two chapters offer philosophical statements from current national therapeutic recreation leaders ("This I Believe…"), and provide insights about those therapeutic recreation leaders who have advanced the profession ("Leaders in Therapeutic Recreation").

Fourth, three chapters offer practical professional information. Topics such as giving professional presentations and attending professional conferences offer insights to those experiencing these professional activities for the first time. In fact, seasoned professionals will likely find useful concepts in these chapters as well.

We wish to express thanks to colleagues who joined us in authoring chapters for *Conceptual Foundations for Therapeutic Recreation*. We also wish to express appreciation to Dr. David Compton for allowing us to use materials on curriculum reform from his book, *Issues in Therapeutic Recreation*. Particular appreciation goes to the staff of *Palestra* for allowing authors of tributes that appeared in *Palestra* to include material from those tributes within their presentations of therapeutic recreation leaders.

David R. Austin
John Dattilo
Bryan P. McCormick

Chapter 1

Conceptual Models in Therapeutic Recreation

David R. Austin, Ph.D., CTRS, FALS

The increasing centrality of conceptual models in therapeutic recreation is attested to by the growth of literature on conceptual models that has occurred in recent years. In addition, a number of sessions at therapeutic recreation conferences and workshops have been devoted to the presentation of conceptual models. Why is this?

Bullock and Mahon (1997) have stipulated that the development of models is essential for all helping professions. Establishing a basis for scholarship and practice is critical to the evolution of any profession. In an emerging profession, such as therapeutic recreation, the publication and presentation of conceptual models has marked a significant advancement. These conceptual frameworks have given direction to the profession both in terms of raising relevant questions for examination by scholars and offering guidelines for practitioners. In short, conceptual models in therapeutic recreation have provided both philosophical and pragmatic orientations to advance both the theory and practice of the profession.

Also another important role for conceptual models in therapeutic recreation is that they define the profession for the public. Austin (1998) has written:

> Conceptual models of therapeutic recreation provide explicit frames of reference to describe…professional practice. They are means for us to articulate what is distinctive about our profession. In this day of healthcare reform, it is especially critical that we are clear about our mission to clients and policy makers. (p. 109)

In another source, Austin (1997) has underscored the critical importance of clearly and concisely defining the therapeutic recreation profession. Specifically, he focused on the need to better interpret therapeutic recreation to others in order to survive and prosper in the competitive healthcare marketplace. Austin further emphasized the need to define the boundaries of the profession, because carefully defining the profession will ultimately lead to the expansion of a focused and documented body of knowledge, provide students with a clear sense of mission and purpose, and differentiate therapeutic recreation from inclusive and special recreation. He warned that without establishing clear boundaries therapeutic recreation would be doomed to basing professional preparation and practice on murky definitions that would not offer the clarity needed to advance the profession. In sum, Austin stressed that well-defined boundaries provide clear lines of demarcation for professions. Dumas (1994) drove home this point when he stipulated:

> Boundaries enable us to set limits and to distinguish what to divide and separate. They denote the relative position of each entity within the organizational structure. Boundaries define roles, responsibilities, and prerogatives [of professions]. (p. 13)

Thus, conceptual models of therapeutic recreation play at least three large roles. First, they describe and define the profession. Second, they identify key elements for discussion and examination. And, third, they allow practitioners to practice in a reasoned manner.

Defining Conceptual Models of Practice

Because the development of formal conceptual models has been a relatively new phenomenon in therapeutic recreation, many have less than a complete understandings of them. In fact, the notion of conceptual models is recent enough that even some who consider themselves scholars have only a tenuous grasp of the nature and purpose of conceptual models. To lay a foundation for the discussion of conceptual models in therapeutic recreation, it may be instructive to examine conceptual models in general. Understanding the use of the terms *concepts* and *models* may provide a beginning point.

Concepts

Concepts are "vehicles of thought" that describe objects, properties, and events (Austin, 1999). Fawcett (1995) has defined concepts as "words that describe mental images of phenomena" (p. 2). She has gone on to state:

> The concepts of a conceptual model are so abstract and
> general that they are neither directly observed in the real
> world nor limited to any particular individual, group, situa-
> tion, or event. (p. 2)

Chinn and Kramer (1995) have warned:

> Attempting to create specific meanings of abstract con-
> cepts prematurely may interfere with exploring a wide
> range of possibility that leads to discovery. (p. 110)

Thus, concepts represent a means to communicate mental images. Within
the context of conceptual models, authors caution that concepts are abstract
in nature.

Models

Morgan (1996) has defined the term model as: "A simplified representation
of reality that explains the relationship of different concepts" (p. 29). Reed
and Sanderson (1992) defined the term model as: "A physical or symbolic
device that represents a set of ideas for the purpose of explanation" (p. 344).
Chinn and Kramer (1999) defined the term model as:

> A symbolic representation of an empiric experience in the
> form of words, pictorial or graphic diagrams, mathematic
> notations, or physical material.... (p. 53)

Riehl and Roy (1980) have used the example of a toy model of a car to
illustrate the concept of a model. The model car is, of course, not the actual
car but it represents the actual car. Similarly, therapeutic recreation models
of practice represent actual practice in the field.

Conceptual Models

Using these definitions, it may be seen that conceptual models are composed
of general and abstract notions (i.e., concepts) used to describe relationships
in order to explain a symbolic representation, or provide a picture, of a
phenomenon (i.e., model). Conceptual models, according to Reed (1998),
"present basic assumptions, boundaries, content, and context associated
with the substantive focuses of the discipline" (p. 385). Exhaustive definitions of concepts are not inherent parts of conceptual models. Instead,
conceptual models are highly abstract (Fitzpatrick & Whall, 1989). Fawcett
(1993) has stipulated that:

> Because conceptual model concepts are so abstract, not all
> of them are defined, and those that are defined typically
> have broad definitions.... (p. 12)

As Christensen and Kenney (1995) have explained, "Models are an abstract
perspective or framework representing reality" (p. 17). These authors went
on to comment that, "Models are more abstract with fewer specifically
defined concepts than theories..." (p. 17). Finally, Fawcett (2000) has
written that because the concepts are so abstract:

> Propositions that state how the concepts are empirically
> observed and measured are not found in conceptual models,
> nor should they be expected. (p. 16)

Conceptual models in therapeutic recreation offer an image or visual-
ization of the component parts that make up the discipline of therapeutic
recreation, and then describe how these parts relate to one another. Conceptual models outline the purpose and scope of practice in therapeutic
recreation. Austin (1999) has added that sound conceptual models must also
rest on solid theoretical foundations. Any complete therapeutic recreation
model of practice must be supported by theory.

Evolution of Conceptual Models of Therapeutic Recreation

In one sense, conceptual models have appeared in therapeutic recreation
since the early days of the field because even the earliest authors attempted
to convey their conceptualization of the discipline. For instance, Davis'
book *Principles and Practices of Recreational Therapy* (1936) described
recreational therapy as pleasurable, voluntary activity that provided for
emotional release. Such early efforts, however, provided only general im-
pressions of the field and made no attempt to offer a complete picture of
the profession with all its component parts as is done in the presentation
of formal conceptual models.

The inception of the first formal conceptual model of therapeutic recreation came when Gunn and Peterson's Leisure Ability Model was initially
introduced. Gunn and Peterson's practice model appeared in *Parks & Recreation* in 1977, and was more fully presented in their textbook in 1978.
The development of this model was timely because the therapeutic recreation profession was working frantically to define itself. Peterson became

a particularly articulate spokesperson for the model, and in a period when there were no alternatives, the Leisure Ability Model quickly gained acceptance within the profession. At the time the then new model was criticized by some (e.g., Austin, 1982; Meyer, 1980). Nevertheless, Gunn and Peterson's conceptual model was widely embraced by an emerging profession hungry to define itself and its practice.

More recently, in a survey of national leaders in therapeutic recreation, Hamilton and Austin (1992) found a growing dissatisfaction with the Leisure Ability Model. Since the time of Hamilton and Austin's study, the Leisure Ability Model has been revised (Stumbo & Peterson, 1998) in a effort to address concerns expressed about the model. The revision of the Leisure Ability Model is typical of the evolvement of conceptual models of practice. Conceptual models are constantly evolving as their authors attempt to refine and improve them.

In order to provide an alternative to the Leisure Ability Model, Austin developed the Health Protection/Health Promotion Model. Austin's model first appeared in 1991. In his model, Austin presented therapeutic recreation as health oriented, in contrast to the leisure orientation of the Leisure Ability Model. Other conceptual models soon followed. Among initial contributions were Van Andel's TR Service Delivery and TR Outcome Models that appeared in Carter, Van Andel, and Robb's 1995 textbook. Then, in 1998, acknowledging the critical nature of conceptual models to the development of therapeutic recreation, the editors of *Therapeutic Recreation Journal (TRJ)* initiated a series in which therapeutic recreation practice models were presented. The inaugural issue for the series appeared in *TRJ* during the third quarter of 1998. Featured in this issue were the Leisure Ability Model and the Health Protection/Health Promotion Model.

Additional models presented in the *TRJ* series were: Van Andel's (1998) TR Service Delivery and TR Outcome Models; Dattilo, Kleiber, and Williams' (1998) Self-Determination and Enjoyment Model; Widmer and Ellis' (1998) Aristotelian Good Life Model; and Wilhite, Keller, and Caldwell's (1999) Optimizing Lifelong Health Through Therapeutic Recreation Model. Concluding the series was an article by Mobily (1999) in which he critiqued the models presented in the series.

Leisure Ability Model and Health Protection/Health Promotion Model

The Leisure Ability Model and Health Protection/Health Promotion Model were the initial conceptual models for therapeutic recreation. These models have fulfilled the useful function of serving as prototypes for all others that have followed. These initial practice models have also represented the two major streams of thought that have influenced therapeutic recreation profession since its early days. The Leisure Ability Model has advanced the nonclinical "recreation for all" approach first advocated by the Hospital Recreation Section of the American Recreation Society in the 1940 and 1950s. The Health Protection/Health Promotion Model extends the clinical approach first championed by the National Association Recreational Therapists (NART) in the 1950s and which, more recently, has been associated with the American Therapeutic Recreation Association (ATRA). This stream of thought sees recreation as a tool for treatment to bring about health restoration. (For additional discussion of these two streams of thought please see Chapter 16, "A Third Revolution in Therapeutic Recreation?")

Leisure Ability Model

The Leisure Ability Model has a strong leisure orientation (Stumbo & Peterson, 1998). The mission of therapeutic recreation according to the Leisure Ability Model is the enhancement of leisure functioning. Peterson and Stumbo (2000) have written:

> Simply stated, if independent leisure functioning is the overall purpose of therapeutic recreation services, then the functional intervention component can and should address functional behavioral areas that are prerequisites to, or a necessary part of, leisure involvement and lifestyle. (p. 29)

Underlying Concepts

According to the authors of the most recent presentation of the Leisure Ability Model (Peterson & Stumbo, 2000; Stumbo & Peterson, 1998), four concepts underlie their model: (a) learned helplessness versus self-determination; (b) intrinsic motivation, internal locus of control, and causal attribution; (c) choice; and (d) flow. The notion of learned helplessness is that being able to exercise control and self-determination keeps people from feeling helpless. The concepts of intrinsic motivation, internal locus of control, and causal attribution deal with the individual being the agent of control who can produce outcomes from his or her behavior. Personal choice is closely related to the prior concepts. Having personal choice implies having the freedom to form attitudes and opinions and to act on them. The final concept of flow deals with having an optimal experience due to match between the challenge of an activity and the participant's skill level (Stumbo & Peterson, 1998).

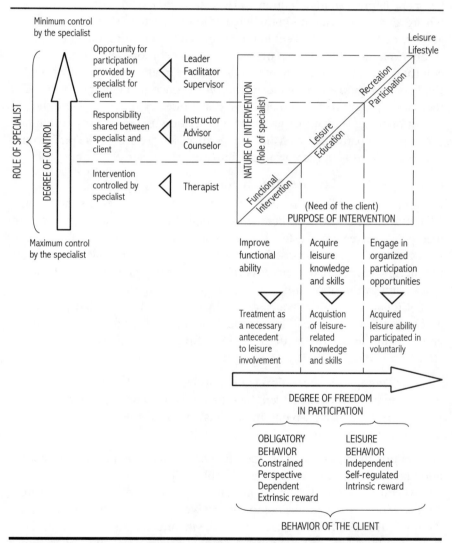

Figure 1.1   The Leisure Ability Model (Stumbo & Peterson, 1998)

Components of the Leisure Ability Model

Three major components constitute the Leisure Ability Model: functional intervention, leisure education, and recreation participation. *Functional interventions* are antecedents to actual leisure involvement. Their purpose is to improve functional ability. Within the functional intervention component the practitioner fulfills the role of a therapist who maintains the control as he or she applies an intervention. *Leisure education* deals with developing leisure awareness, gaining knowledge of leisure resources, and acquiring activity and social skills. Within the leisure education component the practitioner may assume the role of instructor, advisor, or counselor. More control is assumed by the client than within the treatment component. The final component, *recreation participation,* is concerned with provision of recreation programs for persons with disabilities or illnesses. Here the practitioner is a leader, facilitator, or supervisor who provides opportunities for recreation participation. Minimum control is exercised by the practitioner while the client is in recreation participation (Peterson & Stumbo, 2000).

Critiques of the Leisure Ability Model

Austin (1999) and Bullock (1987) have been critical of the Leisure Ability Model for the inclusion of recreation participation as a major component of therapeutic recreation. Austin (1999) has stated that the concern of therapeutic recreation is with purposeful and systematic interventions that employ the therapeutic recreation process (i.e., assessment, planning, implementation, and evaluation). It is not a primary role of therapeutic recreation professionals to provide special recreation services. Instead, general parks and recreation personnel should assume responsibility for serving all citizens, including persons with disabilities. Similar criticisms have been stated by Bullock (1987) who has written:

> Therapeutic recreation is the purposive use of recreation...
> to promote independent functioning and to enhance optimal
> health and well-being in persons with illnesses and/or dis-
> abling conditions.

He went on to stipulate: "Therapeutic recreation is not any and all recreation services for persons who are disabled" (p. 153).

Austin and Bullock, along with Yaffe, have also criticized the Leisure Ability Model for lacking a complete and well-integrated theoretical foundation. Yaffe (1998) has stipulated that the theoretical bases are too limited. Bullock (1998) has suggested that the model's theoretical concepts are not well-integrated, and it could profit from drawing upon other theoretical constructs from the disability literature. Austin (1999) has concluded that the model's "theoretical concepts seem to be incomplete and to be layered onto the Leisure Ability Model, rather than truly forming a foundation for it" (p. 154).

While originally presented in 1977, a theoretical basis for the Leisure Ability Model was not provided until 1998 (Bullock, 1998). The original Leisure Ability Model simply described the world of therapeutic recreation as the authors saw practice at the time. The model was descriptive in nature. Even though it did not possess a theoretical foundation, the appearance of the Leisure Ability Model was an important step in theory development for therapeutic recreation. As Stevens (1979) has explained:

> Descriptive theory is not only the first level of theory de-
> velopment, but it is also the most important level because
> it determines what entities will be perceived as the essence
> of the phenomenon under study. (p. 3)

All ensuing therapeutic recreation conceptual models have been influenced by the Leisure Ability Model, including Austin's Health Protection/Health Promotion Model (1991, 1998, 1999).

Health Protection/Health Promotion Model

Just as leisure is the focus of the Leisure Ability Model, health is the central concept in the Health Protection/Health Promotion Model developed by Austin (1991, 1998, 1999). Austin (1998) has stipulated:

> The purpose of therapeutic recreation is to recover following
> threats to health (health protection) and to achieve as high
> a level of health as possible (health promotion). (p. 110)

The overriding mission of therapeutic recreation is to assist persons to move toward an optimal state of health.

Healthcare is in a state of dynamic change according to Coyle, Boyd, Kinney, and Shank (1998). To use their words: "Healthcare is dramatically different today than it was ten to twenty years ago...." (p. 58) when it relied on a biomedical approach that emphasized the treatment of disease and neglected health promotion. Today's holistic, biopsychosocial perspective views illness and health as the result of both psychosocial and biological factors. The current view has moved from a disease orientation to a broader, health orientation that has concern for both health protection and health promotion (Bandura, 1997). It is the position of Coyle and her Temple University colleagues that such a dramatic change calls for new ways for approaching therapeutic recreation. The Health Protection/Health Promotion Model was formulated to provide a new means to conceptualize therapeutic recreation practice. The Health Protection/Health Promotion Model rests on the philosophical position that healthcare should be concerned with more than the absence of physical and emotional distress. In fact, this model stands for the principle that therapeutic recreation professionals should strive to help clients to enjoy the highest levels of wellness possible.

Underlying Concepts

Four major concepts underlie the Health Protection/Health Promotion Model. These are: a humanistic perspective; high-level wellness; the stabilization and actualization tendencies; and health (Austin, 1998).

The *humanistic perspective* takes a holistic view of the person. It sees humans as being actively engaged in dynamic interactions with their environments and not just reacting to external factors. Further it holds that both children and adults are capable of change and possess a tendency toward self-actualization.

The humanistic perspective has also heavily influenced the concept of *high-level wellness*. Dunn (1961) originated the concept of high-level wellness, which he defined as: "…an integrated method of functioning which is oriented toward maximizing the potential of which the individual is capable" (p. 4). Thus the notion of high-level wellness goes beyond traditional medicine's concern of solely treating disease to assisting people to reach as high a level of wellness as they have the capacity of achieving.

The *stabilizing tendency and actualizing tendency* are motivational factors. The stabilizing tendency has to do with maintaining the "steady state" of the individual. It is the motive behind health protection and "focuses on efforts to move away from or avoid…illness or injury" (Pender, 1996, p. 34). The other half of the motivational coin, the actualization tendency, drives people toward health promotion. It moves people toward "a state of high-level health and well-being" (Pender, 1996, p. 34).

The fourth, and final, concept under the Health Protection/Health Promotion Model is *health*. Pender (1996) has emphasized the stabilization and actualization tendencies in her definition of health. She has written:

> Health is the actualization of inherent and acquired human potential through goal-directed behavior, competent self-care, and satisfying relationships with others, while adjustments are being made as needed to maintain structural integrity and harmony with relevant environments. (p. 22)

Optimal health constitutes a balance of physical, emotional, social, spiritual, and intellectual health. People who are healthy can cope adaptively. They can deal with stressors they encounter in their environments. Those who achieve optimal health are free to pursue the highest levels of personal fulfillment. They typically have supportive environments that encourage healthy lifestyles. As Austin (1998) has explained: "The highest-level of wellness is gained when we exist in a 'very favorable environment' and enjoy 'peak wellness'" (p. 110).

Components of the Health Protection/Health Promotion Model

Three major components make up the Health Protection/Health Promotion Model: prescriptive activities, recreation, and leisure. These three components range along a illness–wellness continuum with poor health at one end and optimal health at the other.

When people initially encounter illnesses or disorders, they often become self-absorbed. At this time, individuals have a tendency to withdraw from normal life activities and to experience a loss of control over their lives (Flynn, 1980). These persons are located on the poor health end of the illness–wellness continuum. They are not ready for recreation or leisure. For them, prescriptive activities are a necessary prerequisite to health restoration. During prescriptive activities therapeutic recreation professionals

Prescriptive Activities	**Recreation**	**Leisure**
TR is outer-directed and is structured	Mutual participation	Self-direction

Stability tendency (TRS is active; client choice is limited)	Stability tendency declines (TRS role narrows)	
TRS-DIRECTED		
		Actualization tendency (Client has freedom of choice)
	Actualization tendency grows	
(Client control is small)	(Client role enlarges)	CLIENT-DIRECTED

Poor health in unfavorable environment		Optimal health in favorable environment

⟵————————————————————————————⟶

Figure 1.2 The Health Protection/Health Promotion Model (Austin, 1998)

provide direction and structure for client participation within a supportive atmosphere. Prescriptive activities activate clients. Being active provides the opportunity for clients, who otherwise might do nothing and might just feel sorry for themselves, to become energized, to gain control, and to resist feelings of helplessness and depression. Being active in a supportive environment allows for feelings of success and mastery. Clients begin to experience hope that they can regain control over their lives and restore their health.

Clients who are ready for the recreation component are farther along the illness–wellness continuum. Through recreation, clients "re-create" or "refresh" themselves. Clients use recreation as a means to adapt to and cope with threats to health. Many of us use similar mechanisms in our everyday lives, such as when we go for a run to cope with stress, or we take in a "feel good" movie at a time when our mood needs a boost. It is this ability of recreation to restore that allows clients to regain their equilibriums so they return to what is normal for them. Once their health is restored, they are ready to move toward growth, development, and actualization. Within the recreation component, clients begin to take greater responsibility for themselves and therefore exercise increasing control. The role of therapeutic recreation practitioners is that of joining in a partnership with their clients within a therapeutic collaboration. Practitioners are empathetic and supportive. They encourage their clients to take as much control as they are ready to assume. Ideally clients will be able to approach their recreation experiences so that they are not just participating to reach a treatment goal but because the activity has become an enjoyable end in itself.

While recreation is an adaptive device that leads to health restoration, leisure involves freely chosen and intrinsically motivated activity that leads to health promotion. Leisure is the "freedom to become." That is, the leisure experience is one freely chosen by the participant and which allows the participant to apply his or her abilities to meet a challenge, to have a growth experience, and to become more than he or she was before. Austin (1999) has explained:

> Leisure experiences contain the elements of intrinsic motivation, self-determination, mastery, and competence, which, in turn, lead individuals toward feelings of self-efficacy, empowerment, excitement, and enjoyment. Leisure experiences provide opportunities for the expression of the actualizing tendency and enable individuals to develop themselves. Leisure can play a critical part in helping clients to actualize and to move toward optimal health. (p. 161)

The role of therapeutic recreation professionals under the leisure component is to continue to be supportive of their clients but to allow them to maintain a maximum amount of control. As a matter of fact, within each component along the illness–wellness continuum (i.e., prescriptive activities, recreation, and leisure) professionals are constantly working toward having their clients assume for themselves as much control as possible. Locus of control culminates during the leisure component.

Critiques of the Health Protection/Health Promotion Model

Lee (1998) and Ross (1998), in separate critiques, concurred that the holistic approach underlying the Health Protection/Health Promotion Model is an appropriate one in today's healthcare world. Ross' central criticism of the Health Protection/Health Promotion Model was that the component parts should be defined in much more detail. Expanded discussions of this model's concepts do seem to be called for. Yet, exhaustive definitions of concepts are not inherent parts of conceptual models. Instead, conceptual models are highly abstract (Fitzpatrick & Whall, 1989). Fawcett (1993) has stipulated that: "Because conceptual model concepts are so abstract, not all of them are defined, and those that are defined typically have broad definitions..." (p. 12). In his critique, Lee raised several issues that warrant comment. For example, he stated that "there is little difference in meaning between prescriptive activity and recreation" (p. 21). In the sense that both lead to the positive outcome of health protection, Lee is correct. But the model differentiates between prescriptive activities and recreation in terms of the level of structure and control. Prescriptive activities are structured and outer directed. When clients are ready to handle more, recreation provides less structured experiences and greater client control. Another concern expressed by Lee was: "The model needs further specification in its promising concept of health" (p. 122). Health is a complex concept that should receive additional attention as the Health Protection/Health Promotion Model evolves. Additionally, Lee suggested that the model could benefit from more coverage of environmental factors as they relate illness and wellness. While Austin's model does address how the environment can affect health, greater attention to the environmental concerns could enhance the model. Finally, Lee raised the issue as to whether the humanistic perspective embraced by the model "reflects a 'victim-blaming' perspective that emphasizes individuals' 'responsibility' for problems and recovery" (p. 120). This may be construed to be a limitation of the model because there are times when individuals have little control over the situation and, therefore, little responsibility for it.

Common Elements in Therapeutic Recreation Models

Bullock and Mahon (1997, pp. 318–319) have analyzed existing therapeutic recreation practice models to identify threads, themes, or common elements. According to these authors, common elements found in therapeutic recreation models represent core beliefs and philosophical perspectives for the therapeutic recreation profession. Key elements identified by Bullock and Mahon follow.

Continuum of Growth and Intervention

Therapeutic recreation models tend to employ a continuum of services that dictates the proper intervention to match clients' functional levels or health states. Therefore, the models follow a systematic approach that focuses on the match between clients' needs and the type of interventions employed. An additional interpretation of the common element of continua in therapeutic recreation models is that therapeutic recreation interventions tend to be wide-ranging to meet a variety of client needs.

Belief in the Strengths and Abilities of the Individual

Therapeutic recreation professionals focus on clients' abilities and intact strengths. Therapeutic recreation interventions involve employing client strengths and abilities in helping clients to meet their needs. Therapeutic recreation assessments include building "strengths lists" in which client strengths and abilities are delineated. Identified strengths and abilities are then used while intervening to bring about change.

Increasing Freedom and Self-Determination

Continua, in therapeutic recreation models, tend to range from client dependence on therapists and limited client freedom of choice at one end to client independence and autotomy on the other extreme. For example, the Health Protection/Health Promotion Model portrays therapeutic recreation to be outer directed and structured for the client when the client is in poor health. At the other end of the continuum in this model the client assumes self-direction while experiencing optimal health. Dattilo, Kleiber and Williams' (1998) therapeutic recreation model has self-determination as a central feature.

Decreasing Therapist Control

A central theme in therapeutic recreation models is that as the client progresses, the therapist's control diminishes and, conversely, the client's level of control increases. Austin (2001) has stated that:

> The essential role of therapeutic recreation specialists is that of a catalyst who works in partnership with clients in order to help them to be as self-directed as possible. (p. 12)

Bullock and Mahon (1997) have written that "the sign of an effective therapeutic intervention often comes when the client no longer *needs* the therapist in the same way as before (p. 319)."

Increasing Involvement and Participation in the "Natural" Community

Bullock and Mahon (1997) have suggested that participation in the client's natural community is an end that is implied by all therapeutic recreation models, if not made explicit. They have written that:

> A part of the *continuum* of growth is that the individual becomes increasingly able to participate fully in activities, settings, and social groups of his or her own choosing, and that these choices are based upon abilities and preferences, rather than upon disability grouping or other labeling process. (p. 319)

Additional Elements

In addition to those common elements identified by Bullock and Mahon (1997), it would appear that consideration should be given to health, the environment, and the therapeutic relationship as important elements that should be found in therapeutic recreation practice models. Health, the environment, and the therapeutic relationship have been explicitly addressed or implied as elements in several models, including the Health Protection/ Health Promotion Model, the TR Outcome Model, and the Optimizing Lifelong Health Model. The authors of these models would likely argue that these concepts are vital elements in therapeutic recreation. Yet, a review of their models reveals that health, the environment, and the therapeutic relationship have not been given the level of attention that might logically be anticipated for what appear to be key concepts. In the sections that follow the elements of health, the environment, and the therapeutic relationship are discussed with the intent of raising the awareness of readers of the need to consider these elements in conceptualizing therapeutic recreation practice, and to suggest that model authors give consideration to fully including these concepts in their models.

Health

Certainly most people today would agree that health goes beyond the "absence of illness." Over fifty years ago, the World Health Organization defined health as a "state of complete physical, mental and social well-being and not merely the absence of disease or infirmity" (1948, p. 28). Yet, as Ryff and Singer (1998) have explained, today health status is still equated with the prevalence of disease and illness. Ryff and Singer have exclaimed, "there has been no discernible progress" (p. 1) in the adoption of a positive definition of health by scientists and practitioners. For instance, we continue to measure health by rates of mortality and morbidity, "not rates of wellness and positive functioning" (p. 2). They go on to state:

> Unfortunately, the medical profession and the culture that supports it has equated the task of treating human infirmity with the goal of fostering health. (p. 3)

In contrast to the traditional view of health, Ryff and Singer (1998) have suggested that what defines health are "the meaningfulness and purposefulness of patients' daily activities, and the nature and quality of their social ties with others" (p. 21). In addition to meaningful activities and personal relationships, Ryff and Singer have added feelings of self-esteem and mastery as components of health. In sum, the approach to health put forth by Ryff and Singer suggests that healthcare professionals widen their perceptions to perceive health "not as the absence of disease, but as wellness of mind and body" (p. 23). It seems obvious that the views of Ryff and Singer are in accord with prevailing perceptions by therapeutic recreation professionals, and that therapeutic recreation models could be enhanced by embracing the positive view of health advanced by Ryff and Singer.

Similarly, authors of therapeutic recreation models may wish to consider the views of Newman (1989) who has explained that illness occurs when people's needs are not sufficiently met due to stressors and more energy is needed than is available. Stressors can come from within individuals (i.e., intrapersonal) or from outside individuals (i.e., interpersonal). They are tension-producing stimuli that cause instability within individuals. Energy is then expended to cope with the stressors in order to return to stability. Health exists when needs are met and energy is not used but is accumulated. Health involves coping adaptively with threats to health (i.e., health protection) and with actualization through personal growth and development (i.e., health promotion). When needs are fully met, individuals enjoy high-level wellness. In this state of well-being all subsystems are in harmony. There are not stressors with which to cope and on which to expend energy. In sum, health exists as an adaptive process that allows adjustment to changes (i.e., stressors) in the environment, and is a state that ultimately permits individuals to strive to achieve maximum potentials. Mitchell and Cornmack (1998) have reminded us that:

> Any achievement of an ideal state of balance or equilibrium could never last for long…since we live in a world in which change is the norm…. (p. 20)

Such would be the case even under Newman's conceptualization of health. Health is not a static concept—it is dynamic. Newman's view would seem to be congruent with most perceptions of health in therapeutic recreation and appears to have a particularly good fit with Austin's Health Protection/ Health Promotion Model.

Mitchell and Cornmack (1998) have expressed a concept similar to that of Newman. They suggest that people "can only be healthy insofar as they can function and survive in the particular circumstances in which they find themselves" (p. 20). Health then, according to Mitchell and Cornmack, is the way in which "individuals respond and adapt to the challenges of everyday life" (p. 20).

The concept of health discussed by Mitchell and Cornmach (1998) appears to draw together the views of health presented by Ryff and Singer (1998) and Newman (1989). You will recall Ryff and Singer saw health as the ability to function in everyday life while experiencing meaningful activities and human relationships which produce feelings of self-esteem and mastery. Newman's concept of health involved being able to cope with stressors and then having the zest for personal growth and development. To the twin notions of relating health to everyday life and responding and adapting to challenges, Mitchell and Cornmach have added the idea that the "circumstances in which they find themselves" (i.e., environmental factors) play a role in health. This takes us to the discussion of the environment.

The Environment

From the discussion of the concept of health, it is clear that it is both people's adaptability and their environment's adaptability that can promote (or hinder) health. Mitchell and Cornmack (1998) made this point clear when they wrote:

> From this perspective, people can only be healthy if their circumstances and environment are suited to their needs. The challenge here for healthcare is to find ways to intervene at social and environmental levels to promote communities within which individuals can fulfill their potential. (p. 21)

In the past, therapeutic recreation has given insufficient attention to the environment. In assessing clients, consideration should be given not only to clients' needs, strengths, and limitations but also to the environment as well. Therapeutic recreation professionals need to ask what conditions, circumstances, and influences have affected the client negatively and which may have potential benefit in counteracting the threat to health. Christensen and Baum (1997) have identified three major aspects of the environment: (a) the physical environment; (b) the cultural and social environment; and (c) social support.

Concerning the physical environment, the question is whether it accommodates the unique needs of the client. Concern with the cultural and social environment is centered around whether the climate is one in which the client is comfortable. A final aspect is whether the environment offers the potential for social support. Is there a social network in place to provide social support for the client? Social support is a key to health because a great deal of evidence shows both direct and buffering effects of social support on both physical and mental health (Stewart, 1993; Stroebe & Stroebe, 1996). Thus the environment can be a source of resources that produce positive outcomes, as well as a source of stressors.

The Therapeutic Relationship

According to Austin (1999), the relationship between the therapist and client lies at the heart of most therapeutic recreation interventions. Austin has gone on to term knowledge of the therapeutic relationship "an essential ingredient" for the therapeutic use of self by therapeutic recreation professionals.

Therapeutic recreation professionals are blessed by enjoying unique relationships with clients. After all, therapeutic recreation practitioners do things *with* clients, not *to* them as doctors, nurses, and others often do. Choice and control are given to clients, along with opportunities that permit clients to use their capabilities. Clients come to view therapeutic recreation practitioners as their allies who guide and assist them rather than directing them. Interactions between therapeutic recreation practitioners and clients also regularly occur in a supportive and nonthreatening atmosphere. Finally, the therapeutic recreation interventions provided by practitioners typically offer hope and optimism and often lead to fun and enjoyment. Is it any wonder that, under these circumstances, clients tend to develop warm feelings for therapeutic recreation professionals?

The therapeutic relationship provides an avenue for the therapeutic recreation professional to better understand the needs, feelings, and motivations of the client. Having shared knowledge of the client's illness or disorder provides a "special kind of bond" between the therapist and client (Lyons, Sullivan, Ritvo & Coyne, 1995, p. 128) and this type of relationship creates a caring and trusting atmosphere between the therapist and client. For the client, the relationship with the therapeutic recreation professional is a means to receive social support and assistance.

Because of the relatively unique relationships that therapeutic recreation professionals tend to have with clients, it would make sense for the authors of therapeutic recreation models to include the therapeutic relationship as a concept within their models. Certainly the therapeutic relationship seems to be a key concept in therapeutic recreation.

Selecting a Therapeutic Recreation Model

Exploring a variety of conceptual models for therapeutic recreation practice should provide students and professionals insights into clinical practice. Models raise questions and reveal options that may otherwise be overlooked. It is important to understand that a variety of models are necessary because no global model fits every setting. As Mobily (1999) has correctly stated:

> Each setting has unique demands that preclude one or more
> models and invite the application of others. "Which is best?"
> is an eternal question, best answered with the remark: "It
> depends." (p. 190)

While it is true that the model must have a good fit with the setting in which the professional is practicing, it may be added that the practice model must also fit with, or match, philosophical beliefs of those embracing it. Philosophical considerations include both those of the individual and the philosophy and goals of the agency. Riehl-Sisca (1989) has reinforced this notion when she stated that selecting a model "depends upon the congruence between organizational philosophy and goals and the practice model interface" (p. 24).

Thus it is important for students and practitioners to analyze therapeutic recreation models to find the model that seems to have the best fit both in terms of setting and personal philosophy. If they are affiliated with an agency, then the organizational philosophy and goals of their agency must be considered.

Analysis of Models

As might be anticipated, there are a number of methods for analyzing models. Kenney (1999) presents five guidelines for selecting nursing models. These can be easily modified for application in therapeutic recreation. As applied to therapeutic recreation, the guidelines are:

1. *Consider personal values and beliefs about therapeutic recreation, clients, health, and environment.* Each professional or student possesses a personal perspective of therapeutic recreation, based on his or her assumptions, beliefs, and values about therapeutic recreation. The individual must, therefore, clarify his or her values and beliefs about clients, health, and therapeutic recreation practice to determine how these coincide with those represented in the model.

2. *Examine the underlying assumptions, values, and beliefs of various therapeutic recreation models, and how the major concepts are defined.* Once his or her own values and beliefs have been clarified, the professional or student needs to examine and understand the definitions of major concepts contained in the models being analyzed.

3. *Identify models that are congruent with personal values and beliefs about therapeutic recreation, clients, and health.* Are the models' underlying values and beliefs congruent with those of the professional or student? Models reflect the author's views about humans and therapeutic recreation. These directly effect how clients are approached, how information is gathered about clients, and what client outcomes are expected.

4. *Identify the similarities and differences in client focus, therapeutic recreation interventions, and client outcomes of the models.* Models are made up of concepts that have specific definitions and statements that describe how concepts are related to one another. Often specific therapeutic recreation actions and expected client outcomes are presented. By analyzing the models, professionals and students determine which offer the best "fit" with their values and beliefs.

5. *Practice applying the models to clients with different health concerns to determine which best "fit" specific situations and guide therapists' actions in achieving sought outcomes.* This step explores specific models in depth, helping determine their usefulness. The professional or student decides which models are most appropriate for each client's health concerns.

A Specific Approach for Analysis

While these five steps presented by Kenney (1999) offer useful guidelines for model analysis, they are general in nature. A more specific framework for analysis of conceptual models of nursing has been presented by Fawcett (1995). Analysis involves systematically reviewing all writings by the author of the model in order to clearly understand exactly what the author has presented about the model. As Fawcett has written: "The analysis targets the *origins* of the conceptual model, as well as its unique *focus* and *content*" (p. 52). A number of questions should be used to guide the analysis as applied to conceptual models in therapeutic recreation. Questions may be grouped under three areas: (1) the philosophical orientation of the model; (2) the unique focus of the model; and (3) the concepts and propositions of the model.

Philosophical Orientation Questions

The first questions to be asked are: What are the origins of the conceptual model? What is the historical evolution of the conceptual model? What is the author's motivation for developing the conceptual model?

Next, philosophical concepts should be examined by asking: On what philosophical beliefs and values about therapeutic recreation is the conceptual model based? What strategies for knowledge development were used to formulate the conceptual model or, stated another way, what inductive or deductive strategies were used to transform a private image of therapeutic recreation into an explicit conceptual model? What scholars influenced the model author's thinking? What worldview is reflected in the conceptual model?

Unique Focus and Content of the Model

This step in analysis involves examining the unique focus and content of the model being analyzed. The central question is: What is the unique focus of the conceptual model?

General Concepts and Propositions

Here the analysis of the content of the model is accomplished by examining the definitions and descriptions of the person, environment, health, and therapeutic recreation. Questions for analysis include: Who is the client and how is the client defined and described? How is the environment defined and described? How is health defined? Are illness and wellness differentiated? How is therapeutic recreation defined? What is the mission or goal of therapeutic recreation? How is the therapeutic recreation process described? What is stated about the relationships among the concepts of the person, environment, health, and therapeutic recreation?

This analysis might be expanded to include those elements previously identified as being commonly found in therapeutic recreation conceptual models. Therefore, in addition to the elements of the person, environment, health, and therapeutic recreation, could be added the elements of a continuum of growth and intervention; a belief in strengths and abilities of the individual; increasing freedom and self-determination; decreasing therapist control; increasing involvement and participation in the "natural" community; and the therapeutic relationship.

An Approach to Evaluation of a Model

While analysis deals with reviewing a model to gain an explicit understanding, evaluation involves making judgments based on evaluative criteria. The evaluation is based largely on the results of the analysis. Other sources of information used in evaluation may include published critiques of the model, any research based on the model, and reports of the application of the model in practice or professional preparation (Fawcett, 1995).

Questions for evaluation have been organized by Fawcett under several general headings: explication of the model's origins, comprehensiveness of content, logical congruence, generation of theory, credibility of conceptual models, and contributions to the discipline.

Explication of the Model's Origins

The initial step is to evaluate the origins of the conceptual model. Evaluative criteria include two primary evaluation questions: Are the philosophical claims on which the conceptual model is based made explicit? Are the scholars who influenced the model author's thinking acknowledged, and are citations provided?

Comprehensiveness of Content

This second step deals with how comprehensive the model is or its depth and breadth. Questions related to *depth* include: Does the model provide adequate descriptions of all major concepts (i.e., the person, environment, health, therapeutic recreation)? Do the relational propositions of the model completely link the four major concepts? Questions related to *breadth* include: Are researchers given sufficient direction about what questions to raise and what methodology to use? Do educators have sufficient guidelines on which to construct a curriculum? Do administrators have sufficient direction to organize and deliver therapeutic recreation services? Is the clinician provided enough direction to be able to make pertinent assessments, decide if a therapeutic recreation intervention is appropriate, and plan a course of action which achieves the goal specified in a variety of clinical situations?

The evaluation of the comprehensiveness of the model might be expanded by posing questions related to additional common elements found in therapeutic recreation models. Included could be questions that examine if the following are considered by the model's author: a continuum of growth and intervention; a belief in strengths and abilities of the individual; increasing freedom and self-determination; decreasing therapist control; increasing involvement and participation in the "natural" community; and the therapeutic relationship.

Logical Congruence

The third step in evaluation of a model deals with the logic of the model's internal structure. Fawcett (1995) has explained:

> The process [of logical congruence] involves judging the congruence of the model author's espoused philosophical claims with the content of the model. Critical reasoning also involves judgments regarding the worldview(s) and category(ies) of …[therapeutic recreation] knowledge reflected by the model. (p. 57)

Questions for judging logical congruence include: Is the internal structure of the conceptual model logically congruent? Does the model reflect more than one worldview or philosophical view of human beings? Are all ideas presented in the conceptual model consistent?

Generation of Theory

The fourth step in evaluation involves the relationship between models and theories. This element of evaluation is concerned with whether the model's concepts are sufficiently clear so that relatively concrete concepts and propositions of theories can be deduced and testable hypotheses formulated. The question here is: What theories have been generated from the conceptual model?

Credibility of Conceptual Models

The fifth evaluation step deals with the credibility of the model. The goal here is to determine where a conceptual model is appropriate for use in clinical settings and for which types of clients. The overriding question is: Does the conceptual model guide therapeutic interventions in any setting? Fawcett (1995) has suggested that in determining the credibility of a model the *social utility, social congruence*, and *social significance* need to be examined. Under social utility the evaluation question is: Are education and skill training required prior to the application of the conceptual model in therapeutic recreation practice? Under social congruence the evaluation question is: Is it feasible to implement clinical protocols derived from the conceptual model and related theories? Finally, under social significance the evaluation question is: To what extent is the conceptual model actually used to guide therapeutic recreation research, education, administration, and practice?

Contributions to the Discipline of Therapeutic Recreation

The final step in evaluation of conceptual models deals with the general issue of the contribution of the model to the discipline of therapeutic recreation. Fawcett (1995) has explained that each model should be evaluated on its own merits and not in comparison to other models. The evaluation question here is: What is the overall contribution of the conceptual model to the discipline of therapeutic recreation?

❋　❋　❋　❋　❋

In conclusion to this section, Fawcett's (1995) framework for analysis and evaluation of conceptual models offers practitioners and students a means to analyze and evaluate potential therapeutic recreation conceptual models. While both analysis and evaluation may be exhaustive processes, it is important for practitioners and students to examine models before adopting one. Analysis and evaluation offer means with which to closely examine conceptual models.

Conclusion

Prior to this chapter, a thorough presentation of the nature and purposes of conceptual models has been absent from the literature of therapeutic recreation. Nor has the literature provided structures to guide the analysis and evaluation of therapeutic recreation practice models. Unfortunately, without understandings of the nature of conceptual models and without systematic methods to examine them, those attempting to complete critical reviews of therapeutic recreation models have not possessed the fundamental understanding needed to make well-informed judgments. As a result of reading this chapter, it is hoped that therapeutic recreation professionals and students will understand conceptual models and will be better prepared to analyze and evaluate therapeutic recreation models.

Reading Comprehension Questions

1. Why are conceptual models in therapeutic recreation important to the development of the profession?

2. Define the term *conceptual model*.

3. Trace the evolution of conceptual models in therapeutic recreation.

4. Briefly describe the Leisure Ability Model and the Health Protection/Health Promotion Model.

5. What elements are common to therapeutic recreation models? Do you agree that health, the environment, and the therapeutic relationship should be elements in therapeutic recreation conceptual models? Why or why not?

6. Analyze a therapeutic recreation conceptual model, then evaluate it.

7. Which model (or models) best fits your personal views of therapeutic recreation? Why?

References

Austin, D. R. (2001). Introduction and overview. In D. R. Austin and M. E. Crawford (Eds.), *Therapeutic recreation: An introduction* (3rd ed.). Boston, MA: Allyn & Bacon.

Austin, D. R. (1999). *Therapeutic recreation processes and techniques* (4th ed.). Champaign, IL: Sagamore.

Austin, D. R. (1998). The Health Protection/Health Promotion Model. *Therapeutic Recreation Journal, 32,* 109–117.

Austin, D. R. (1997). Recreation therapy education: A call for reform. In D. M. Compton (Ed.), *Issues in therapeutic recreation* (2nd ed., pp. 193–210). Champaign, IL: Sagamore.

Austin, D. R. (1991). Introduction and overview. In D. R. Austin and M. E. Crawford (Eds.), *Therapeutic recreation: An introduction* (pp. 1–29). Englewood Cliffs, NJ: Prentice Hall.

Austin, D. R. (1982). *Therapeutic recreation: Processes and techniques.* New York, NY: John Wiley & Sons.

Bandura, A. (1997). *Self-efficacy: The exercise of control.* New York, NY: W. H. Freeman and Co.

Bullock, C. C. (1998). The Leisure Ability Model: Implications for the researcher. *Therapeutic Recreation Journal, 32*(2), 97–102.

Bullock, C. C. (1987). Recreation and special populations. In A. Graefe and S. Parker (Eds.), *Recreation and leisure: An introductory handbook.* State College, PA: Venture Publishing, Inc.

Bullock, C. C. and Mahon, M. J. (1997). *Introduction to recreation services for people with disabilities: A person-centered approach.* Champaign, IL: Sagamore.

Carter, M. J., Van Andel, G. E., and Robb, G. M. (1995). *Therapeutic recreation: A practical approach* (2nd ed.). Prospect Heights, IL: Waveland Press.

Chinn, P. L. and Kramer, M. K. (1999). *Theory and nursing: A systematic approach* (5th ed.). St. Louis, MO: Mosby.

Chinn, P. L. and Kramer, M. K. (1995). *Theory and nursing: A systematic approach* (4th ed.). St. Louis, MO: Mosby.

Christiansen, C. and Baum, C. (1997). Person-Environment Occupational Performance: A conceptual model for practice. In C. Christiansen and C. Baum, *Occupational therapy: Enabling functions and well-being* (2nd ed., pp. 47–70). Thorofare, NJ: Slack.

Christensen, P. J. and Kenney, J. W. (1995). *Nursing process: Applications of conceptual models* (4th ed.). St. Louis, MO: Mosby.

Coyle, C., Boyd, R., Kinney, W., and Shank, J. (1998). The changing nature of therapeutic recreation: Maintaining consistency in the face of change. *Parks & Recreation, 33*(5), 56–63.

Dattilo, J., Kleiber, D., and Williams, R. (1998). Self-determination and Enjoyment Enhancement: A psychologically-based service delivery model for therapeutic recreation. *Therapeutic Recreation Journal, 32*(4), 258–271.

Davis, J. E. (1936). *Principles and practice of recreation therapy for the mentally ill.* New York, NY: A. S. Barnes and Co.

Dumas, R. G. (1994). Psychiatric nursing in an era of change. *Journal of Psychosocial Nursing, 32*(1), 11–14.

Dunn, H. L. (1961). *High-level wellness.* Arlington, VA: R. W. Beatty.

Fawcett, J. (2000). *Analysis and evaluation of contemporary nursing knowledge: Nursing models and theories.* Philadelphia, PA: F. A. Davis Co.

Fawcett, J. (1995). *Analysis and evaluation of conceptual models of nursing* (3rd ed.). Philadelphia, PA: F. A. Davis Co.

Fawcett, J. (1993). *Analysis and evaluation of conceptual models of nursing* (2nd ed.). Philadelphia, PA: F. A. Davis Co.

Fitzpatrick, J. J. and Whall, A. L. (1989). *Conceptual models of nursing: Analysis and application* (2nd ed.). Norwork, CT: Appleton & Lange.

Flynn, P. A. R. (1980). *Holistic health.* Bowie, MD: Robert J. Brady Co.

Gunn, S. L. and Peterson, C. A. (1978). *Therapeutic recreation program design: Principles and procedures.* Englewood Cliffs, NJ: Prentice Hall.

Gunn, S. L. and Peterson, C. A. (1977). Therapy and leisure education. *Parks & Recreation, 12*(11), 22–25.

Hamilton, E. J. and Austin, D. R. (1992). Future perspectives of therapeutic recreation. *Annual in Therapeutic Recreation, 3,* 72–79.

Kenney, J. W. (1999). Theory-based advanced nursing practice. In J. W. Kenney (Ed.), *Philosophical and theoretical perspectives for advanced nursing practice* (2nd ed., pp. 327–343). Boston, MA: Jones and Bartlett Publishers.

Lee, Y. (1998). Critique of Austin's Health Protection and Health Promotion Model. *Therapeutic Recreation Journal, 32*(2), 118–123.

Lyons, R. F., Sullivan, M. J. L., Ritvo, P. G., and Coyne, J. C. (1995). *Relationships in chronic illness and disability.* Thousand Oaks, CA: Sage Publications.

Meyer, L. (1980). Three philosophical positions of therapeutic recreation and their implications for professionalization and NTRS. *Proceedings of the First Annual Post-Doctoral Institute* (pp. 28–42). Bloomington, IN: Department of Recreation and Park Administration, Indiana University.

Mitchell, A. and Cornmack, M. (1998). *The therapeutic relationship in complementary health care.* Edinburgh, Scotland: Churchill Livingstone.

Mobily, K. E. (1999). New horizons in models of practice in therapeutic recreation. *Therapeutic Recreation Journal, 33*(3), 174–192.

Morgan, S. (1996). *Helping relationships in mental health.* New York, NY: Chapman & Hall.

Newman, B. (1989). *The Newman Systems Model* (2nd ed.). Norwalk, CT: Appleton & Lange.

Pender, N. J. (1996). *Health promotion in nursing practice* (3rd ed.). Stamford, CT: Appleton & Lange.

Peterson, C. A. and Stumbo, N. J. (2000). *Therapeutic recreation program design: Principles and procedures* (3rd ed.). Needham Heights, MA: Allyn & Bacon.

Reed, K. L. and Sanderson, S. N. (1992). *Concepts of occupational therapy* (3rd ed.). Baltimore, MD: Williams & Wilkins.

Reed, P. G. (1998). Nursing theoretical models. In J. J. Fitzpatrick (Ed.), *Encyclopedia of nursing research* (pp. 385–387). New York, NY: Springer Publishing.

Riehl-Sisca, J. P. (1989). *Conceptual models for nursing practice* (3rd ed.). Norwalk, CT: Appleton & Lange.

Riehl, J. P. and Roy, C. (1980). *Conceptual models for nursing practice* (2nd ed.). New York, NY: Appleton-Century-Crofts.

Ross, J. (1998). Critique of Austin's Health Protection/Health Promotion Model. *Therapeutic Recreation Journal, 32*(2), 124–129.

Ryff, C. D. and Singer, B. (1998). The contours of positive human health. *Psychological Inquiry, 9*(1), 1–28.

Stevens, B. J. (1979). *Nursing theory: Analysis, application, evaluation.* Boston, MA: Little Brown and Co.

Stewart, M. J. (1993). *Integrating social support in nursing.* Newbury Park, CA: Sage Publications.

Stroebe, W. and Stroebe, M. (1996). The social psychology of social support. In E. T. Higgins and A. W. Kruglanski (Eds.), *Social psychology: Handbook of basic principles* (pp. 597–621). New York, NY: Guilford Press.

Stumbo, N. J. and Peterson, C. A. (1998). The Leisure Ability Model. *Therapeutic Recreation Journal, 32*(2), 82–96.

Van Andel, G. E. (1998). TR Delivery and TR Outcome Models. *Therapeutic Recreation Journal, 32*(3), 180–193.

Widmer, M. A. and Ellis, G. D. (1998). The Aristotelian Good Life Model: Integration of values in to therapeutic recreation services delivery. *Therapeutic Recreation Journal, 32*(4), 290–302.

Wilhite, B., Keller, M. J., and Caldwell, L. (1999). Optimizing lifelong health and well-being: A health enhancing model of therapeutic recreation. *Therapeutic Recreation Journal, 23*(2), 98–108.

World Health Organization. (1948). *World Health Organization constitution.* Geneva, Switzerland: Author.

Yaffe, R. M. (1998). The Leisure Ability Model: A response from a service perspective. *Therapeutic Recreation Journal, 32*(2), 103–108.

Chapter 2

Behavior Modification in Therapeutic Recreation
Observing Behaviors and Applying Consequences

John Dattilo, Ph.D., FALS
Brent Wolfe, M.A., CTRS

Knowledge of behavior modification techniques can help therapeutic recreation specialists (TRSs) deliver effective services. Unfortunately, behavior modification continues to be "grossly misunderstood" (Anderson & Romanczyk, 1999). Therefore, Cook, Tankersley, Cook, and Landrum (2000) recommended that practitioners providing services for people with disabilities receive more training in ways to effectively implement behavior modification strategies.

This chapter contains a description of various observation strategies to encourage TRSs to accurately and efficiently assess and monitor participant behaviors. Also, information is presented on possible techniques to increase behaviors that allow people to experience leisure and decrease behaviors that are impairing their ability to enjoy their lives. The information presented in the chapter is intended to act as a catalyst for effectively using behavior modification strategies that demonstrate respect and improve the lives of people with disabilities.

Observe Behaviors

When target behaviors are clearly described, systematic change to those behaviors can occur. After a target behavior has been identified in terms of observable and measurable actions, it is helpful to determine how these behaviors will be observed so that a behavior can be accurately assessed and effects of therapeutic recreation interventions determined. Development of an effective observation strategy is necessary to assess either frequency or duration of the behavior. Although there are many ways to observe and record behavior, four common methods—frequency, duration, interval, and instantaneous time sampling—are described in this chapter.

Frequency Recording

Frequency recording involves identifying a behavior to change and then counting and recording the occurrences of that behavior within an established period of time. This method is primarily used when the identified behavior occurs at a low rate and lasts for brief periods of time. Frequency recording is an appropriate method of observing behavior when the target behavior has an easily defined beginning and ending. Behaviors that have a clear beginning and ending are termed *discrete* and are conducive for the application of a frequency recording system. Behaviors, such as throwing paintbrushes, catching a ball, or sporadic verbalizations in short bursts during discussions, may be effectively measured using frequency recording. Behaviors, such as demonstrating positive social interaction skills during community outings, frequent and consistent rocking during a free-play time, or repeated temper tantrums that occur for longer periods of time, may be better measured using other methods. As an example, frequency recording would be appropriate if a TRS was conducting a leisure education class for Juan to teach him social skills. The treatment team has asked the TRS to record the number of times that Juan volunteers to make a statement in his leisure education class. The TRS could then record the frequency of Juan's volunteering during the class.

Filla, Wolery, and Anthony (1999) used frequency recording to evaluate strategies to promote conversations of nine preschool children with and without disabilities during play. Three behaviors were measured: (a) verbally initiating a conversation with a peer or obtaining the attention of a peer; (b) verbally responding within four seconds to a peer who initiated a conversation; and (c) verbally responding to a peer within four seconds of the response to an initiation. The number of times participants engaged in the behaviors were recorded. Similarly, Collins, Hall, and Branson (1997) used a frequency recording system to measure effects of an intervention designed to teach four adolescents with moderate disabilities four leisure skills (i.e., playing cards, selecting a television program, playing a sports videotape, and playing a computer game). Task analyses were developed for the leisure skills that identified the observable and measurable target behaviors. For instance, the task analysis for playing a card game was as follows: (a) cut the deck of cards in half, (b) shuffle the deck of cards, (c) put cards into one pile, (d) deal seven cards to each player, (e) wait for turn, (f) lay card or draw card, (g) continue to follow directions on card until game ends. These seven behaviors all occurred at a low rate, for a brief period of time, and were discrete behaviors. Therefore, the authors employed a frequency recording system to observe the behaviors.

Duration Recording

Another method that can be used when observing behaviors is duration recording. *Duration recording* involves recording the length of time a behavior occurs during a predetermined observation period; therefore, a TRS would determine how long the behavior lasts rather than the number of times the behavior occurs (as with frequency recording). Duration recording is employed when the target behavior occurs at a low frequency and lasts for an extended period of time. The TRS needs to have a timepiece that identifies seconds to accurately record duration. Duration recording requires that the target behavior has a definite starting and ending point (i.e., a discrete behavior). When treatment goals include increasing or decreasing the length of time a behavior occurs, duration recording is an appropriate observation method.

By way of illustration, a TRS may be interested in increasing the amount of time Mateeka spends in cooperative play with other children. Before initiating efforts aimed at increasing this target behavior, it is helpful to know the amount of time she currently spends in cooperative play. During a fifteen-minute observation period, the TRS uses a timing device to measure and record how long Mateeka remains in close proximity (defined as no further than three feet) to other participants. Therefore, if the children were sitting together playing and Mateeka sat down with the group, the TRS would start a stopwatch. When Mateeka stood up and walked away from the group, the time would stop. At the next instance when Mateeka returned to the group, the TRS would again start the watch, and then stop it when Mateeka left the group.

With the above example the TRS has two options for recording duration of behavior. The first option is to record the total time Mateeka was with the group. For this, the TRS does not clear the time on the stopwatch every time Mateeka leaves the group. The time continues to build until the end of the fifteen-minute period. The TRS could state that Mateeka engaged in the activity for a total of nine minutes and thirty seconds (9m, 30s) during the fifteen-minute time period. The second option involves viewing each instance of group participation separately. After recording the time with the group in one instance, when Mateeka left the group, the TRS would note the time duration, clear the stopwatch, and repeat this process for each interaction. The TRS could then state that Mateeka was with the group on three different occasions, (2m, 45s), (3m, 12s), and (3m, 33s) respectively, for a total of 9m 30s. Strategies to increase the length of time Mateeka engaged in cooperative play could then be determined and implemented.

Fisher, Piazza, Bowman, and Amari (1996) illustrated duration recording in their study of six youths, ages 5–17, diagnosed with severe destructive behaviors. Two target behaviors were measured using the duration method: (a) in-square behavior (i.e., having any portion of their body in a 0.7m x 0.7m square taped on the floor), and (b) in-seat behavior (i.e., buttocks having direct contact with chair). The times participants spent in their chair or in their square were recorded in ten-minute blocks. Next, preferred items or experiences were identified, such as tape-recorded music, juice, a heating pad, rocking chair, or a hug from therapist. When participants sat in the chair or stood in the square, they were allowed access to an item. The time spent in the chair or square with the item present was recorded. In addition, Piazza, Fisher, Hagopian, Bowman, and Toole (1996) conducted similar observations by recording the length of time four participants, ages 7–19, spent in their chair and in their square. When the children stood in the square or sat in the chair, they were immediately given an item of their choosing. Because the behaviors measured occurred at a low rate and were discrete, the duration method was effective in determining the length of time participants engaged in target behavior.

Interval Recording

Interval recording, another method of observation, requires that a block of time be divided into short segments of equal length. The intervals should be short enough to allow recording of separate occurrences of behavior, but long enough to facilitate accurate observation. An interval of one second does not provide a TRS enough time to continuously observe and record the behavior, whereas a fifteen-second interval does. Interval recording includes two different methods—whole interval and partial interval.

Whole Interval

Whole interval recording involves observing and recording the duration of a behavior during a short interval. With this method, for a behavior to be recorded as occurring it must happen during the entire interval, not for a portion of the time. For instance a TRS could divide a thirty-minute crafts session into 120 fifteen-second intervals. If Manuel did not talk to his peers for all fifteen seconds of an interval, the TRS would not mark that Manuel had engaged in this target behavior for that interval.

Partial Interval

Partial interval recording is similar to whole interval except with partial interval the behavior only needs to occur once during the interval for it to be recorded. For instance, a ten-minute session could be divided into a total of 60 intervals of ten seconds each, and a TRS would observe for the entire ten minutes. As the participant is observed during each of the 60 intervals, a mark is recorded if the target behavior occurred at any time during the interval. It makes no difference if the behavior occurs once or several times during an interval; it is simply recorded as having occurred during the interval. If the behavior lasts over several intervals, it is recorded in each interval that it occurs. For example, a TRS who is working with Sonja, teaching her to juggle, divides a five-minute practice time into a total of 25 twelve-second intervals, and uses partial interval recording to determine if Sonja was practicing juggling. The TRS observed Sonja for five minutes of practice time, and marked that the behavior occurred during the interval if Sonya engaged in the behavior at any time during the twelve-second interval.

Roane, Vollmer, Ringdahl, and Marcus (1998) used partial interval recording consisting of five-minute segments divided into ten-second intervals to observe ten participants with moderate to profound disabilities. During the five-minute segment, a mark was made every ten seconds if a participant manipulated certain items, such as candy, fruit, magazines, balls, or a radio. Each item was recorded separately. If a participant manipulated an item for the entire five minutes, then 30 marks were tallied; if the participant manipulated one item for one minute of the five-minute interval and a different object for one minute, then six marks were tallied for each object (i.e., 12 total). The interval recording strategy provided a chance to determine participant preferences.

Instantaneous Time Sampling

Instantaneous time sampling is yet another common method of observation. Similar to interval recording, when a TRS uses instantaneous time sampling behaviors are recorded during intervals when the participant is being observed. However, with this method it is not necessary to divide the time into shorter, equal segments because the TRS only records the behavior that occurs *at the end* of the time period. The observation periods are of equal length, but they can be separated by larger blocks of time. Due to the longer observation periods with behaviors being recorded only at the end of the period, the TRS does not need to observe participants for extended periods of time. Instantaneous time sampling is appropriate when the behavior occurs at a high frequency, and the TRS does not have time to continuously observe participants. To illustrate, a TRS may want to evaluate Samuel dribbling a basketball. Since there are nine other participants in the group, the TRS cannot devote all her attention to Samuel so she uses instantaneous time sampling to observe the frequency of Samuel dribbling. The TRS observes Samuel for five seconds at the end of every ten-minute period. A tally for dribbling the basketball is made only if he is dribbling during the five-second observation interval at the end of each ten-minute period. While instantaneous time sampling may be more practical, it does not allow for precise recording of behaviors. If Samuel was dribbling during the five-second interval, but did not dribble any other time during the observation, the TRS might present an exaggerated picture of Samuel's dribbling. It would also be possible for Samuel not to dribble during any five-second observation interval, but have dribbled several other times.

Burgio, Burgio, Engel, and Tice (1986) used instantaneous time sampling to measure the mobility and social interactions of seniors (seven women, one man) residing in a nursing home. During the 40th minute of each forty-minute interval, the staff members located a participant, recorded her or his mobility status, and whether the participant was engaged in social interaction. Instantaneous time sampling provided a way to monitor several participants' behaviors with limited personnel.

Table 2.1   Observational Strategies

Strategy	Purpose	Advantages	Disadvantages
Frequency	Know number of times behavior occurs	• Can identify low rate, brief, discrete behavior	• Difficult to observe high rate, extended behaviors • Must observe constantly
Duration	Know total amount of time behavior occurs	• Can identify total time of discrete behavior	• Difficult to observe more than one person or behavior • Must observe constantly
Interval	Estimate frequency and duration of behavior	• Can be used with any behavior • Can be used for only a portion of time	• Only provides estimate of behavior
Instantaneous Time Sampling	Estimate duration of behavior	• Can be used with any behavior • Can be used for only a portion of time • Can be used with more than one person or behavior	• Only provides estimate of behavior

Apply Consequences

Another important aspect of implementing effective behavior modification programs is the application of appropriate consequences. TRSs can apply consequences to increase behaviors of individuals with disabilities so that they can experience leisure and the associated benefits while also helping people to decrease behaviors that result in negative experiences and inhibit people from experiencing leisure. Therefore, the remaining portion of this chapter describes two consequences that increase behaviors—positive and negative reinforcement—as well as two consequences that decrease behaviors—punishment and extinction.

Positive Reinforcement

Positive reinforcement represents a powerful tool for promoting appropriate behavior and is the most commonly applied behavior modification procedure (Maag, 1999). *Positive reinforcement* involves the delivery of a consequence that makes a behavior more likely to occur more often. The behavior to be reinforced must be specific and measurable so that change can be measured. It is also necessary for the relationship among the target behavior, the delivered consequence, and the subsequent behavior to be clearly defined. For instance, Tania is a young girl who does not enjoy physical activities. Her family has communicated that they would like to see Tania engage in more physical activities since she has a low level of physical fitness. Due to the family's concerns, the TRS has taught Tania how to play several active playground games. Although she quickly learned these activities, the TRS wanted to encourage Tania to participate in them on a regular basis. Therefore, when she was engaged in a physical activity, the TRS would provide her with verbal praise. Providing Tania with verbal praise functioned as a positive reinforcer and encouraged her to continue engaging in the physical activities.

Various objects and events such as food, activities, and praise can act as positive reinforcers; however, an object is a positive reinforcer only if it increases the behavior. For example, receiving a hug for a behavior may be a positive reinforcer for some people, but not for others. Likewise, receiving free time for engaging in a target behavior may act as a positive reinforcer for some, but not for all; some individuals may not have adequate skills or confidence to take advantage of their free time. Similarly, receiving praise might serve as a reinforcer for some people, but others who want to avoid attention may view praise negatively. The actual effect the consequence has on a behavior is critical as opposed to the intentions of the person providing the consequence.

Whenever possible it is helpful to use natural reinforcers as opposed to arbitrary ones. *Natural reinforcers* are consequences that increase behaviors directly and functionally related to the task so that when behaviors occur they are naturally rewarded (Koegel, Koegel, Harrower & Carter, 1999). In contrast, an *arbitrary reinforcer* is one that is not intrinsically related to a task so that when a person exhibits a desired behavior, he or she will obtain a reward unrelated to the task or activity. For example, when teaching Yolanda to kick a soccer ball, the TRS may try to teach Yolanda to kick the ball so it goes into the goal and thereby allowing Yolanda to receive the natural reward of the ball entering the goal, rather than giving her a piece of candy each time she kicks the ball. By using natural reinforcers TRSs can create situations that do not require them to be present when a desired behavior occurs because the participant can still receive the positive consequence from the activity. Since a major purpose for providing therapeutic recreation interventions is to teach people skills that allow them to experience leisure, there is value in using natural reinforcers that are inherently present in the activity. Also, overuse of external rewards that do not naturally occur with an activity can result in a TRS directing participants' attention away from the inherent joys of the experience, and instead have them focus more on unrelated, peripheral rewards.

Kee, Hill, and Weist (1999) compared effects of two treatments on the behaviors of a ten-year-old girl with profound mental retardation. One treatment included ignoring hitting, spitting, and cursing, and applying passive restraint when they occurred as well as providing praise for positive behavior. The other treatment was removal of the individual from the situation and continued praise of positive behavior. During both phases positive verbal reinforcement was provided when the girl had not engaged in a negative behavior for fifteen minutes. Within three days of initiating the intervention that included the introduction of the time-out and continued praise for positive behavior, all three problem behaviors were occurring at lower levels than baseline and remained low for the remainder of the intervention. Similarly, Green and Reid (1999) designed a program to reduce unhappiness among three individuals with profound multiple disabilities during exercise. Participants were provided with access to preferred situations (e.g., playing with a revolving toy carousel, rocking in a hammock, listening to music) immediately before, during, and after exercise. During the first phase, participants were provided with these preferred situations for five minutes before the exercise session. During the second phase, the preferred situation was provided for 5–10 seconds at one-minute intervals throughout the exercises. In the final phase, participants were provided with the preferred situation for ten minutes following the session. The program was accompanied by decreases in indicators of unhappiness that routinely occurred during exercise routines. Participants achieved a higher level of happiness (as measured by the authors) as a result of being positively reinforced by their preferred situations.

Negative Reinforcement

According to Maag (1999), "no one behavior modification concept results in more confusion than negative reinforcement" (p. 73). As with positive reinforcement, negative reinforcement is a method that increases the strength of a behavior. *Negative reinforcement* increases the strength of a behavior by removing or postponing an aversive antecedent, contingent on the occurrence of the behavior. An aversive antecedent refers to some ongoing object, event, or situation that is present in the environment and is not desired by the individual. It is necessary for an aversive condition to exist, or have the possibility of existing, for negative reinforcement to occur. When the individual engages in a behavior that avoids or allows the person to escape from the aversive condition, negative reinforcement has occurred. Therefore, the consequence of the behavior is avoidance of or escape from an ongoing aversive condition.

A classic example of negative reinforcement involved using shock with pigeons. When shock was administered, the pigeons could eliminate this aversive event by pecking at a lever. Therefore, the pigeons were negatively reinforced for pecking the lever because in doing so they escaped the aversive shock. Negative reinforcement occurs when a behavior removes a negative situation, and as a result of this removal, the person is encouraged to engage in the behavior more. Any introduction of an aversive event as a *consequence* of behavior, such as a verbal reprimand, is *not* a form of negative reinforcement; rather, it is a punisher. Negative reinforcement results in an increase in behavior, not in reduction or elimination.

Any object, event, situation, or condition that increases the frequency or duration of a behavior is considered to be reinforcement for that behavior. Reinforcement is positive if it involves the presentation of a consequence that is desired by the participant, after the participant has engaged in the appropriate behavior. Therefore, something that is desired by the individual has been added to the situation. Reinforcement is negative if it involves elimination or postponement of something from the environment that is an aversive event to the participant after the person has engaged in the behavior. Therefore, something that is not desired by the participant has been removed from the situation. In both positive and negative reinforcement, the behavior of the individual is strengthened.

Some characteristics that apply to positive reinforcement are also applicable to negative reinforcement. One individual may consider an event aversive, but it may not be considered aversive to another. Removing an event would reward the person who views the event as aversive; however, another person who views the event as favorable would be penalized by the removal of the event. Also, a condition may be perceived as aversive for an individual at one time, but not at other times. Removal of a condition is a negative reinforcer only if it strengthens behavior. There are two major responses that can be negatively reinforced—escape and avoidance.

Escape

In the case of *escape*, the aversive antecedent is presented to the individual. When the person engages in a behavior, the antecedent is removed. For instance, when Cynthia screams, a response by the TRS that removes the screaming, such as yelling at Cynthia, will tend to recur whenever Cynthia screams. The TRS's response of yelling at Cynthia is strengthened by the cessation of Cynthia screaming resulting in the TRS escaping the negative sound. Unfortunately, the inappropriate behavior of yelling will be more likely repeated by the TRS when a participant screams in the future.

Avoidance

Another aspect of negative reinforcement is avoidance. With *avoidance*, an individual prevents the aversive condition from occurring by engaging in a behavior. If the behavior occurs, the aversive antecedent is not presented. Thus, the behavior is strengthened. If the behavior is not performed, the aversive event is presented. The aversive antecedent can be avoided if the individual engages in the behavior that prevents the aversive event from occurring. For example, Zehna knocks over some equipment and leaves the room to avoid being reprimanded by the TRS. Her avoidance of the TRS's reprimand negatively reinforces her behavior of running away.

✳ ✳ ✳ ✳ ✳

Kahng and Iwata (1998) compared self-injurious behavior when participants were (a) alone in a room without toys; (b) playing with toys; and (c) given instructions to complete a task that were followed by a gestural and physical prompt if necessary. When participants were required to complete a task, their self-injurious behaviors were maintained via negative reinforcement because the situation was considered aversive to participants. Because participants exhibited self-injurious behaviors to escape the demand condition, their escape from an undesired situation reinforced a destructive behavior and functioned as a negative reinforcer.

Because negative reinforcement requires the presence or the threat of an aversive condition, it is typically not used by TRSs. Negative reinforcement should not be employed if the same behaviors can be increased via positive reinforcement. However, an understanding of the principle can help the TRS understand why some behaviors may occur and increase without the application of a positive reinforcer.

Extinction

One challenge facing TRSs is to help people change their dangerous and disruptive behaviors that interfere with their ability to learn and enjoy life in ways that value the individual and demonstrate respect (Weiss, 1999). One way to decrease inappropriate behaviors is via extinction. *Extinction* occurs when reinforcers that originally maintained a behavior are no longer available to an individual. When a behavior is no longer followed by reinforcement, it gradually diminishes. Consider the example of Rashad who constantly tugs on the TRS's arm to get her attention. If arm tugging is the behavior the TRS is attempting to extinguish, responding to Rashad every time he tugs her arm will not extinguish the behavior. If Rashad wants attention, the TRS's response will only serve to reinforce the behavior. Ignoring Rashad's tugs may be enough to extinguish his inappropriate behavior.

When an inappropriate behavior has been selected for extinction, it is imperative that alternative positive reinforcers for the selected inappropriate behavior are not available. Alternative positive reinforcers are reinforcers other than those being withheld. If alternative positive reinforcers are not identified and controlled, then extinction is not taking place, but rather positive reinforcement of inappropriate behavior is occurring. For example, Sanchez belches often and loudly during a creative arts session resulting in the TRS speaking to Sanchez and scolding him for his behavior. After this behavior persists for several weeks, the TRS believes that giving her attention to Sanchez after he belches is reinforcing it; therefore, she decides to extinguish the behavior by ignoring Sanchez when he belches. However, after several days the inappropriate behavior has not been eliminated because it is reinforced by attention given by his classmates. In this case, alternative positive reinforcers are supporting the inappropriate behavior and should be eliminated.

Extinction is more effective if positive reinforcement is used to reward a desired behavior that can replace the inappropriate behavior. However, positive reinforcement cannot be applied immediately after the cessation of the inappropriate behavior or it will reinforce the inappropriate behavior. Reinforcement is applied after the individual engages in the desired behavior.

For example, Tania may cry continuously whenever she is not given attention by the TRS. This results in the TRS devoting most of her time to Tania, while neglecting others. If the TRS would not provide a response to the crying, Tania would eventually stop crying (unless it is reinforced by an alternative positive reinforcer). Then, after Tania stopped crying for a short period of time and started to play with a toy, the TRS could positively reinforce her toy play. It is likely that the combination of ignoring the crying (extinction) and rewarding toy play (positive reinforcement) will result in future instances of less crying and more toy play.

After an extinction procedure is initiated, it is common for the inappropriate behavior to increase. This occurrence is termed an *extinction burst* and means that the inappropriate behavior will be engaged in more often, more vigorously, or for longer periods of time by the individual in an effort to receive the reinforcer. For example, a TRS encounters Rob who engages in temper tantrums. The TRS decides to extinguish the tantrums by ignoring them. It is quite likely that the tantrums will initially increase in duration and intensity. If the tantrum increases in severity and the TRS, not being prepared to handle the increase in inappropriate behavior, then attends to it, the result is positive reinforcement of more inappropriate behavior

After an extinction program has progressed, the behavior may temporarily reappear, even though it has not been reinforced. The temporary recurrence of a nonreinforced behavior is referred to as *spontaneous recovery*. The major concern during a spontaneous recovery is that the behavior not be reinforced in any way; this would only delay the extinction process. It is important that all staff members who interact with a person understand goals for the individual so inappropriate behaviors are not reinforced.

Because extinction is a gradual process, it may not be appropriate if quicker results are desired. Also, there are some behaviors that are not prone to extinction. Self-reinforcing behaviors are particularly difficult to extinguish. As an example, Trey may spend most of a leisure education class gazing out the window. His inattentiveness is limiting what he learns from the class and the TRS chooses to eliminate the behavior; however, gazing out the window is a self-reinforcing behavior. The pleasure gained from looking out the window reinforces the behavior. The TRS may apply an alternative procedure to extinction to weaken the behavior of looking out the window, such as reinforcing behaviors incompatible with looking out the window.

Richman, Wacker, Asmus, and Casey (1998) determined effects of extinction on screaming, throwing, and finger picking of a woman with multiple severe disabilities during her free play. When demands were given to the woman, prompts were used to help her complete tasks while inappropriate behaviors were ignored. When this condition did not influence the woman's finger picking, she received reinforcement for alternative behaviors. When she attempted to pick at her finger, her hand was placed on a toy. If she freely played with the toy, she was praised (reinforcement of alternative behavior). The addition of the reinforcement significantly reduced her finger picking. This study demonstrated the effectiveness of extinction to eliminate some behaviors, but also showed the importance of providing positive reinforcement of alternative behaviors.

Punishment

Punishment, another consequence that decreases behavior, involves presentation of an aversive event following a behavior that leads to a decrease in that behavior. It is a consequence that has some negative aspects, and therefore should be used with caution and only after other courses of action have been tried and found ineffective.

It is important that positive reinforcement of acceptable alternative behavior be used in conjunction with punishment of inappropriate behavior. Prior to using punishment, desired alternate behaviors should be identified and plans made to reinforce these positive behaviors. Determinating what prompts the inappropriate behavior and what reinforcers maintain it can be helpful. Also, choosing an aversive event is an important part of punishment. It is possible that what is generally regarded to be an aversive event may not, in fact, be an aversive event for an individual. The aversive event must be powerful enough to serve as a punisher. Presenting the aversive event in a mild form with the thought that, if necessary, it can be applied in stronger forms in the future is problematic. If the event is too mild, it may not be a punisher. Gradually increasing its strength in subsequent applications may result in steady loss of its effectiveness. A better approach is to carefully determine what the strength of the aversive event should be and then present it at that level for its first, and subsequent, applications. The punisher needs to be strong enough to be effective but, at the same time, nothing is gained by using a strong punisher when a mild one will achieve the same results.

Lerman, Iwata, Shore, and DeLeon (1997) attempted to discover effects of gradually thinning delivery of punishment to five adults with profound disabilities who engaged in self-injurious behaviors. Schedules of punishment were thinned from a continuous schedule to intermittent. For all but one participant, when the schedule was thinned, self-injurious behavior increased to levels similar to those during baseline. This research demonstrated the need for punishment to be delivered continuously.

It is important for a TRS to make the punisher as brief as possible and provide minimal social interaction during its application. Frequently, people exhibit inappropriate behaviors to gain attention. If this is the case, the more attention the TRS provides the individual, the more likely the person will view the situation as reinforcing.

It is imperative that punishment is applied immediately after the behavior occurs. If punishment is delayed, there is a chance that the person will, in the interim, engage in other behaviors. If punishment is then delivered, other behaviors may be punished. In addition, the punisher must be consistently presented following each instance of the target behavior. Since intermittent punishment is not effective in eliminating behaviors, each instance of the behavior needs to be detected. If all instances of the behavior are not detected, punishment will probably not be very effective. Furthermore, the person delivering the punisher must never do so in anger, but always calmly, and this person should also supply positive reinforcers for desired alternate behaviors.

The use of punishment uniformly across personnel reduces the chance that those presenting the punishers become conditioned punishers. A conditioned punisher is anything that is associated with the punisher and becomes, through association, a punisher itself. If the person applying the punisher is perceived as a conditioned punisher, that person's ability to provide reinforcement for desirable alternative behavior is reduced. This is important to TRSs trying to create an enjoyable atmosphere conducive for learning skills. If the TRS administers punishment, participants may develop a negative image of that person. A location may have a similar impact on a participant. If punishments are consistently given in a certain location, participants may associate that location with negative events and therefore be less likely to go there.

Another disadvantage of punishment is that when an individual is punished, that person often attempts to escape or avoid the place where punishment occurred or the person who applied the punisher. If the person is unable to escape or avoid a punishment, aggression may surface. Therefore, an intervention designed to decrease an inappropriate behavior may actually increase inappropriate behaviors. Another problem with punishment is the likelihood that, with continued use, a punisher may lose its effectiveness and punished behavior may return to its original rate. This is especially true of punishers that are not very intense. In addition, since punishment often results in a relatively rapid decrease in the target behavior, it is possible that it may be used too readily when another procedure might be more appropriate.

Because of the aforementioned disadvantages in using punishment, this consequence should only be used when the behavior endangers the person or others, the behavior results in significant property damage, or when alternative methods have been tried and proved unsuccessful.

	Add Something	Remove Something
Behavior Increases	**Positive Reinforcement** • add something • the something is desireable • behavior increases	**Negative Reinforcement** • remove something • the something is adversive • behavior increases
Behavior Decreases	**Punishment** • add something • the something is adversive • behavior decreases	**Extinction** • remove something • the something is positive • behavior decreases

Consequences can be used individually or all together

Figure 2.2   A Summary of Consequences

Conclusion

Because TRSs attempt to change the behaviors of the people so that these individuals can experience leisure, it is important to consider that whenever one person (e.g., a therapeutic recreation specialist) is trying to change the behavior of another (e.g., person with a disability) there is an inherent imbalance of power that may result in oppression (Weiss, 1999). However, according to Corrigan (1997), effective application of behavior modification strategies can empower people. Therefore, this chapter is designed to increase understanding of aspects of behavior modification so that therapeutic recreation specialists can more effectively observe, monitor, and improve behaviors of people whom they serve. For a more comprehensive presentation refer to the text by Dattilo and Murphy (1987).

Reading Comprehension Questions

1. Name and briefly describe four common observational strategies.
2. What is positive reinforcement? Provide an example.
3. When may the use of external awards actually be harmful?
4. What is negative reinforcement? How does it differ from punishment?
5. Should negative reinforcement be used by TRSs?
6. Illustrate the use of extinction with tantrums.
7. Do you agree with Dattilo and Wolfe that behavior modification can empower people? Defend your answer.

References

Anderson, S. R. and Romanczyk, R. G. (1999). Early intervention for young children with autism: Continuum-based behavioral models. *Journal of the Association for Persons with Severe Handicaps, 24*(3), 162–173.

Burgio, L. D., Burgio, K. L., Engel, B. T., and Tice, L. M. (1986). Increasing distance and independence of ambulation in elderly nursing home residents. *Journal of Applied Behavior Analysis, 19*(4), 357–366.

Collins, B. C., Hall, M., and Branson, T. A. (1997). Teaching leisure skills to adolescents with moderate disabilities. *Exceptional Children, 63*(4), 499–512.

Cook, B. G., Tankersley, M., Cook, L., and Landrum, T. J. (2000). Teachers' attitudes toward their included students with disabilities. *The Council for Exceptional Children, 67*(1), 115–135.

Corrigan, P. W. (1997). Behavior therapy empowers persons with severe mental illness. *Behavior Modification, 21*(1), 45–61.

Dattilo, J. and Murphy, W. (1987). *Behavior modification in therapeutic recreation.* State College, PA: Venture Publishing, Inc.

Filla, A., Wolery, M., and Anthony, L. (1999). Promoting children's conversations during play with adult prompts. *Journal of Early Intervention, 22*(2), 93–108.

Fisher, W. W., Piazza, C. C., Bowman, L. G., and Amari, A. (1996). Integrating caregiver report with a systematic choice assessment to enhance reinforcer identification. *American Journal on Mental Retardation, 101*(1), 15–25.

Green, C. W. and Reid, D. H. (1999). Reducing indices of unhappiness among individuals with profound multiple disabilities during therapeutic exercise routines. *Journal of Applied Behavior Analysis, 32*(2), 137–147.

Kahng, S. W. and Iwata, B. A. (1998). Play versus alone conditions as controls during functional analysis of self-injurious escape behavior. *Journal of Applied Behavior Analysis, 31*(4), 669–672.

Kee, M., Hill, S. M., and Weist, M. D. (1999). School-based behavior management of cursing, hitting, and spitting in a girl with profound retardation. *Education and Treatment of Children, 22*(2), 171–178.

Koegel, L. K., Koegel, R. L., Harrower, J. K., and Carter, C. M. (1999). Pivotal response intervention I: Overview of approach. *Journal of the Association for Persons with Severe Handicaps, 24*(3), 174–168.

Lerman, D. C., Iwata, B. A., Shore, B. A., and DeLeon, I. G. (1997). Effects of intermittent punishment on self-injurious behavior: An evaluation of schedule thinning. *Journal of Applied Behavior Analysis, 30*(2), 187–201.

Maag, J. W. (1999). *Behavior management: From theoretical implications to practical implications.* San Diego, CA: Singular Publishing Group.

Piazza, C. C., Fisher, W. W., Hagopian, L. P., Bowman, L. G., and Toole, L. (1996). Using a choice assessment to predict reinforcer effectiveness. *Journal of Applied Behavior Analysis, 29*(1), 1–9.

Richman, D. M., Wacker, D. P., Asmus, J. M., and Casey, S. D. (1998). Functional analysis and extinction of different behavior problems exhibited by the same individual. *Journal of Applied Behavior Analysis, 31*(3), 475–478.

Roane, H. S., Vollmer, T. R., Ringdahl, J. E., and Marcus, B. A. (1998). Evaluation of a brief stimulus preference assessment. *Journal of Applied Behavior Analysis, 31*(4), 605–620.

Weiss, N. (1999). It may be non-aversive, but is it coercive?: The ethics of behavior change. *The Association for Persons with Severe Handicaps Newsletter, 11*(25), 21–23.

Chapter 3

Social Support in Therapeutic Recreation

Bryan P. McCormick, Ph.D., CTRS

The construct of social support has received considerable research attention over the past three decades (Rhodes & Lakey, 1999). In fact, over 16,000 articles can be found in the Medline database between the years 1970 and 2000 under the term *social support*. Although this may seem to be a recent explosion in interest in social support, interest in social functioning and well-being has a relatively long history in the social sciences. Just prior to the turn of the twentieth century, Emile Durkheim (1897/1951) published what was arguably the first scientific study to examine the relationship of social integration to well-being. Based on suicide rates in different regions of Europe, Durkheim argued that people who were most integrated into society were also the least likely to commit suicide. Thus began a search in social science to identify how social relationships were conducive to well-being. The construct of social support is one avenue that social scientists have followed to examine how social relationships contribute to well-being.

Defining Social Support

Among the earliest foundations of social support were concepts of support generated by reviews published in the 1970s that examined the role of social ties in well-being. For example, Caplan (1974) characterized [social] support systems as "an enduring pattern of continuous or intermittent ties that play a significant part in maintaining the psychological and physical integrity of the individual over time" (p. 7). In addition Caplan noted that these ties could be located in a variety of domains of life including work, home, church and recreational sites. Cobb (1976) further specified the nature or content of such ties indicating that social support was information supplied by others that lead people to believe that they were (a) cared for and loved,

(b) esteemed and valued, and/or (c) "belonged to a network of communication and mutual obligation" (p. 300). Thus, social support was not just the presence of a social tie, but also had to consider the nature of information shared in a social relationship. Kahn (1979) added to the developing concept of social support by suggesting that the giving and receiving of social support was the basis of relationships in one's social convoy. The idea of a *social convoy* is that people have a network of supportive people who travel with them over their life course. Kahn argued that social support was the glue that held this group together. In addition, Kahn also added to earlier conceptualizations of social support by arguing that in addition to *information* that led people to believe they were cared for and esteemed, the giving and receiving of *material aid* was also a form of social support. Thus, social support included such acts of assistance as help with household chores, providing transportation and financial assistance. Overall, social support is considered to be *the provision of material, emotional, or informational resources through social relationships that aid an individual in functioning.*

A number of review articles on social support, such as those mentioned here, provided a watershed from which a large number of subsequent studies were launched in the early 1980s (Rhodes & Lakey, 1999). As can be seen in Figure 3.1, the growth in the number of published studies on social support has grown dramatically since the 1970s.

Construct of Social Support

From these beginnings a very large body of scientific and theoretical knowledge has developed on the topic of social support. To make sense of this body of literature, the remainder of this section will present three underlying concepts that comprise the construct of social support. First, the networks in which support is provided and received have been explored. Second, a number of studies have attempted to identify the nature of supportive acts. In these studies, the nature of what is being provided in supportive relationships is examined. Finally, the perceptions of those giving and receiving social support is considered. This concept recognizes that the adequacy of support may lie in the eye of the beholder.

Support Networks

This first element of social support represents a structural component (Wills & Fegan, 2001). In this sense, social support can be examined as the linkages

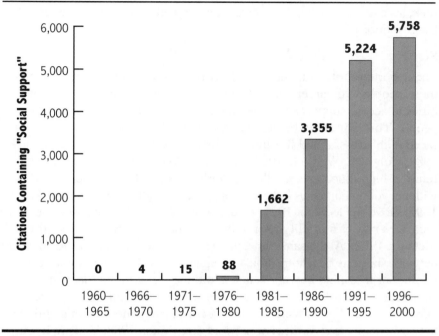

Figure 3.1   Social Support Citations in Medline 1960–2000

among a set of individuals which comprise a network. Often times this aspect of social support is considered to be an indicator of social integration (Vaux, 1988). In addition, networks are considered to be important since they influence access to resources available to people (Berkman & Glass, 2000). Vaux characterized the social support network as a subset of one's larger social network "to which a person routinely turns or could turn for assistance in managing demands and achieving goals" (p. 28). As well, it appears that there are multiple support networks that provide specific kinds of support, including emotional assistance, practical aid, financial support, advice, or guidance. Further, these networks are assumed to be stable in size and composition but are most likely to change during times of developmental transition such as school graduation or marriage, or nonnormative life changes such as illness (Lyons, Sullivan & Rivto, 1995), work layoff, or divorce. Networks are related to social support since, as noted by Gottlieb (1981) "differences in size, density, composition, and stability of people's 'personal communities' have implications for the quality, diversity, and reliability of the support available to them" (p. 28). Thus, support networks represent an opportunity structure through which support is available. Finally, social networks also represent a structure through which individuals seek, access, and participate in health and human services (Gourash, 1978; Pescosolido, 1996).

Size

The opportunity structure nature of network size is readily apparent in that those people with larger networks may have a greater number of opportunities to access support since they are in contact with a greater number of people. This appears to be particularly relevant in situations where one is faced with stressful and life-threatening events (Cassileth, Walsh & Lusk, 1988; Hobfoll & Walfisch, 1984; Lackne & Goldenberg, 1994). Overall, the relationship is such that smaller network sizes and less frequent contact with network members is indicative of poorer overall functioning (Berkman, 1995; Gove & Geerken, 1977; House, Landis & Umberson, 1988) and increased risk of mortality (Berkman & Syme, 1979; House, Robbins & Metzner, 1982). At the same time, there has been some debate as to whether network size may be a "threshold" variable, in which there is some critical number or threshold beyond which additional network members do not significantly contribute to well-being, or whether network size may be a "gradient" variable, in which there is a consistent benefit from additional network members regardless of network size (Vaux, 1988; Wills & Fegan, 2001). In studies of numbers of social contacts (an indicator of network size) and mortality, both threshold effects (House, Robbins & Metzner, 1982) and gradient effects (Berkman & Syme, 1979; Kaplan et al., 1988) have been found. Overall, Wills and Fegan (2001) noted that the bulk of studies on network size suggest that "the protective effect of social network does not occur just for a small group of socially isolated persons" (p. 215). Thus although some threshold effects have been found, there is a consistent gradient effect of network size.

Network size also appears to be related to the experience of illness and disability. In general, smaller social networks have been found to be related to such persistent illnesses as rheumatoid arthritis (Berkanovic & Hurwicz, 1990; Fitzpatrick, Newman, Lamb & Shipley, 1988), coronary heart disease (Reed, McGee, Yano & Feinleib, 1983; Vogt, Mullooly, Ernst, Pope & Hollis, 1992), multiple sclerosis (Lyons, Sullivan & Ritvo, 1995), and serious and persistent mental illness (SPMI) (Albert, Becker, McCrone & Thornicroft, 1998; Biegel, Tracy & Song, 1995; Pattison & Pattison, 1981; Sokolovsky, Cohen, Berger & Geiger, 1978). Thus the bulk of research has found that the experience of chronic or persistent illness and disability does appear to be related to reductions in social network size; however, some studies have not confirmed this pattern (e.g., Pennix et al., 1999).

Density

Another characteristic of social networks that has been examined in relationship to social support and well-being is network density. *Network density* refers to the degree to which members of a person's network know and interact with one another. Those networks in which most members know one another are considered higher in density than those networks in which few members know one another. This is an important consideration because it indicates the degree to which an individual's social network can be considered a *system* of support (Hirsch, 1981).

Research on the role of network density and social support has largely taken place in relationship to coping with stressful events. In addition, the relationship of network density to support and well-being appears to be dependent on the nature of the stressor. For example, network density appears to be *negatively* related to availability of support and mental health for those experiencing divorce and widowhood (Hirsch, 1980; Wilcox, 1981). In contrast, network density has been found to be *positively* related to avoiding rehospitalization among people with mental illness (Cohen & Sokolovsky, 1978) as well as establishing contact with treatment facilities among men in treatment for alcoholism (Strug & Hyman, 1981). In general, dense networks appear to be most effective in providing support needed for everyday functioning, whereas they are poorly suited to providing support needed in times of role change.

Composition

Another aspect of social support networks has to do with the characteristics of the people in those networks. Network members are typically characterized according to their relationship to the supported individual. For example, network members may be kin (i.e., family), nonkin (i.e., friends/acquaintances), or professionals (e.g., clergy, counselors/therapists, parole officers). There has been some evidence to suggest that the composition of networks is indicative of well-being. For example, Arling (1976) found that networks in which family members made up the largest proportion of network members were associated with low morale; however, Phillips (1981) found this characteristic to be only true for men.

Much of the research on the role of network composition in social support has been conducted in situations where support recipients are facing a potentially difficult life circumstance. For example, a number of studies have been conducted to examine the characteristics of support networks among the elderly (Gallo, 1984; Litwin, 1997; Wenger, 1984), new parents (cf., Belsky & Rovine, 1984; Levitt, Weber & Clark, 1986; Titjen &

Bradley, 1985), and people who have experienced coronary heart disease (Reed et al., 1983; Vogt et al., 1992). In general, findings have been that people experiencing such challenging life situations rely more heavily on family for support, thus a larger proportion of family members in the social network has been found to be related to better functioning and adaptation in such circumstances (Litwin & Landau, 2000).

✳ ✳ ✳ ✳ ✳

Overall, social networks are an important component of social support as they represent the structure through which social support can be accessed. In addition, social networks represent the structure through which individuals experiencing illness or disability access care. At the same time, while one's social network influences social support, it is at best only an indicator of support. This is due to the fact that social networks only provide opportunities for social support (Wills & Fegan, 2001) and are incomplete without considering the nature of support (both available and provided) as well as people's perceptions of such support.

Support Provisions

Although networks of supporters are important, there remains the question: "What is being provided by such relationships?" For example, what is happening in social relationships that:

- Reduces the risk of death? (Bloom, 1990; House, Landis & Umberson, 1988)
- Improves recovery in physical illness? (Farmer & Meyer, 1996; Kulik & Mahler, 1989; Molassiotis & van den Akker, 1997), or
- Mediates the impact of loss of steady employment on health? (Gore, 1978)

One of the first attempts to categorize what was occurring in social relationships was offered by Weiss (1974). Although Weiss did not specifically use the term social support, he did identify six types of benefits provided through social relationships. A number of others followed Weiss in categorizing the nature of support that occurred through social relationships (Table 3.1). When the wide variety of typologies is examined, it would appear that there are three general categories of support available through social relationships: social contact, feedback, and assistance.

Social Contact

First, many researchers have recognized that social contact itself is an important provision of social relationships. For example, Weiss (1974) noted that

Table 3.1 Social Support Provisions

Reference	Social Contact		Feedback				Assistance		
Weiss (1974)		Social integration	Attachment	Nurturance	Reassurance of worth	Alliance		Guidance	
Gottlieb (1978)			Emotional sustenance				Problem solving	Indirect influence	Environmental action
Kahn and Antonucci (1980)				Affect	Affirmation			Aid	
Barrera (1981)	Intimate interaction	Social participation			Feedback		Guidance	Physical assistance	Material aid
Barrera and Ainlay (1983)	Intimate interaction	Positive social interaction			Feedback		Guidance	Behavioral assistance	
Cohen and Hoberman (1983)			Belonging	Self-esteem	Appraisal				Tangible support
Wills (1985)		Social companionship	Motivational	Status	Esteem		Information	Instrumental	
House and Kahn (1985)			Emotional		Appraisal		Informational	Instrumental	
Cohen and Wills (1985)	Social companionship				Esteem		Informational	Instrumental	
Vaux, Stewart, and Riedel (1987)		Socializing	Emotional				Practical assistance	Advice/Guidance	Financial assistance
Cauce, Reid, Landesman, and Gonzales (1990)		Companionship	Emotional				Informational	Instrumental	

one of the provisions of social relationships was social integration. Through such relationships people are afforded opportunities for companionship (Cauce, Reid, Landesman & Gonzales, 1990; Cohen & Wills, 1985; Wills, 1985), social participation (Barerra, 1981), positive social interaction (Barerra & Ainlay, 1983), socializing (Vaux, Stewart & Reidel, 1987) and intimate interaction (Barerra, 1981; Barerra & Ainlay, 1983). Interestingly, many of the conceptualizations of social contact specifically mention recreation and leisure activities. For example, Wills (1985) characterized social companionship as "enjoyable social activities such as social visiting, dinners, parties, films and concerts, excursions and outdoor activities, or informal athletics" (p. 72). In addition, Weiss (1974) noted that companionship "offers a base for social events and happenings, for social engagement and social activity" (p. 23). However, how such contact is supportive has not been as well-defined. According to Weiss (1974) social contact protects one from social isolation. Another approach is offered by Vaux (1988) who stated that:

> At the extreme, one might argue that a large component of social support goes on in close relationships. What constitutes support in these relationships may be embedded in the private language that characterizes communication in close relationships—special gestures, private jokes, obscure allusions, private meanings, and shared associations. (p. 16)

Thus, it appears that companionship that occurs through social contact does contribute to well-being (Rook, 1987).

Feedback

Another function of social support is the feedback provided by other people to the supported person. One of the earliest attempts at defining social support characterized it as information leading one to believe that he or she was cared for, esteemed, and valued by others (Cobb, 1976). Later efforts to categorize social support have identified a number of functions that could be characterized as feedback. For example, Barrera and Ainlay (1983) identified that one function of social support was to provide individuals with "feedback about their behavior, thoughts or feelings" (p. 136). Others have cited supportive functions reflecting feedback in the form of *esteem support* (Cohen & Hoberman, 1983; Cohen & Wills, 1985; Wills, 1985). Esteem support reflects the notion that one way social relationships are supportive is through the provision of information that helps an individual to see himself or herself as a worthwhile human being. Others have offered similar forms of support as feedback in the concepts of *affirmation support* (Antonucci, 1990; Kahn & Antonucci, 1980) and *appraisal support* (House & Kahn, 1985). Affirmation support reflects feedback in the form of information that supports one's thoughts, views and actions as being accurate or correct. Finally, feedback has also been characterized as *emotional support* (Cauce, Reid, Landesman & Gonzales, 1990; Gottlieb, 1978; House & Kahn, 1985; Vaux, Stewart & Riedel, 1987). The emotionally supportive function of feedback is seen through the provision of actions that reassure and encourage one in times of both positive and negative emotional experience. In essence, this is the "shoulder to cry on." The characteristic common to all of these feedback functions of social support is that support is provided through provision of actions that affirm one's feelings, views, actions, and identity.

Assistance

The final functional aspect of social support is probably one of the most easily measured and understood. Often times, this is one of the first notions of social support that comes to mind when people try to identify people in their support network; that is, "Who helps me in times of need?" Assistance forms of support have included material aid (Barrera, 1981), environmental action (Gottlieb, 1978), tangible support (Cohen & Hoberman, 1983), practical and financial assistance (Vaux, Stewart & Riedel, 1987), informational support (Cauce, Reid, Landesman & Gonzales, 1990; Cohen & Wills, 1985; House & Kahn, 1985) and instrumental support (Cauce, Reid, Landesman & Gonzales, 1990; Cohen & Wills, 1985; House & Kahn, 1985). Wills (1985) characterized this function as:

> ...assistance with household chores, taking care of children, lending or donating money, running errands, providing transportation, helping with practical tasks, looking after a household when the owner is away, and providing material goods such as furniture, tools or books. (p. 71)

Thus, one way that support is provided through social relationships is in the form of direct assistance to aid one in managing the demands of everyday life.

Perceptions of Support

Although networks and support provisions are important components of the construct of social support, they do not completely capture social support. In addition to the objective characteristics of one's support network and the support functions available, subjective perceptions are also an important component of the construct. The perceptions of social support represent the qualitative dimension of social support. Although one's social support network and the kinds of support available are related to health and well-being, the quality of social support has been consistently found to be a better indicator of both physical and mental health (Sarason, Sarason & Pierce, 1990; Vandervoort, 1999). Sarason and colleagues theorized that the strength of this relationship is due to the fact that "support emanates from not so much what is done, but from what that indicates to the recipient about the relationship" (p. 17).

In addition, Vaux (1988) noted that the perception of one's social support is the principal indicator of how well support functions are being met for the supported individual. For example, Lyons, Perrotta and Hancher-Kvam (1988) compared perceptions of social support across a sample of college students, people with diabetes, and people with persistent mental illness. They found that the sample with persistent mental illness perceived the lowest levels of support from both family and friends.

Perceived social support is hypothesized to be related to health and well-being through two mechanisms. First, perceptions of support may reflect a sense of belonging (Sarason et al., 1990). This feeling of connection to a primary group of other people protects the individual from feelings of normlessness and loneliness. Through this mechanism, individuals are protected from what Durkheim (1897/1951) termed *anomie*. The second mechanism argues that the perception that support is available if needed aids people in perceiving stressors as less stressful (Wills & Fegan, 2001). As a result of this perception of available support, stressors have less impact on the individual both physically and mentally.

Social Support, Health, and Well-Being

Although the construct of social support may hold intrinsic theoretical interest, much of the research on social support has been explicitly or implicitly related to health and well-being. For example, Durkheim's (1897/1951) classic study of suicide sought to identify a social cause for a particular condition of ill health (Berkman & Glass, 2000). The relationship of social support to health has been examined in terms of both the onset of disease and recovery from disease or illness (Wills & Fegan, 2001).

Social Support and Onset of Disease

Two principal lines of research have developed in the examination of social support and its role in the onset of illness and disease, or conversely in the maintenance of health and well-being (see Figure 3.2). One line has attempted to identify how social support may mediate the impact of stress on health and well-being. This line of study has been typically characterized as a *stress-buffering model* (Cohen & Wills, 1985). The second line of study has sought to examine the contributions of social support to health and well-being regardless of the level of one's stress. This second line of inquiry is typically referred to as a *main effects model*.

Stress-Buffering Model

The stress-buffering model argues that social support affects health by minimizing (buffering) the impact of significant stressors on health. This effect is seen in studies that find that the relationship of social support to well-being is strong among people experiencing a great deal of life stress. At the same time the relationship of social support to well-being is weak or nonexistent among people experiencing little life stress. For example, Rosengren, Orth-Gomer, Wedel, and Wilhelmsen (1993) found that men with high stress and low emotional support and had a relative risk of mortality that was 15.1, whereas the relative risk for men with high stress and high emotional support was 1.2. Thus, among men experiencing high stress, available social support buffered the risk of mortality.

The stress-buffering model developed as an outgrowth of research on life stress and social networks (Rhodes & Lakey, 1999). In addition, Rhodes and Lakey noted that much of the early research in social support was

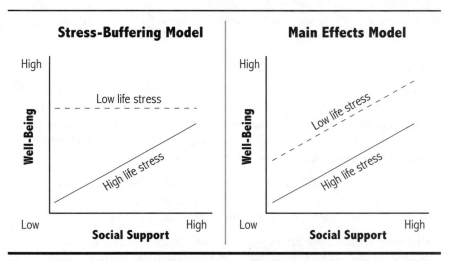

Figure 3.2   Illustration of the Stress-Buffering and Main Effects Models of Social Support

conducted by community psychologists whose interests lay in preventing psychological disorder in communities particularly as it related to coping with stressful life events. As a result, the stress-buffering model has gained considerable attention in social support research.

Main Effects Model

The main effects model assumes that social support contributes to health and well-being regardless of level of stress experienced. Thoits (1985), for example, hypothesized the relationship was such that social support contributed directly to well-being through the provision of information that enhanced one's sense of identity, belonging, esteem, and mastery. The provision of such information is assumed to bolster well-being regardless of whether one is facing stressful events or not. Although the notion of stress does appear in early conceptualizations of main effects models, it is conceptualized more broadly as a lack of information that one's actions are leading to desired or anticipated outcomes (Rhodes & Lakey, 1999). To contrast this with the stress-buffering model, the main effects model assumes that stress is a factor that results from social disorganization as opposed to a discrete factor that results from "negative life events."

The role of the main effects model in the onset of disease can be seen in mortality studies. As noted above, there has been consistent research support to indicate that social support is negatively related to mortality over time (Berkman, 1985; Bloom, 1990). House and associates (1988) argued that social support prevented mortality through "fostering a sense of meaning or coherence that promotes health or by facilitating health promoting behaviors" (p. 543).

Social Support and Disability

In addition to research on the relationship of social support to health generally, a number of studies have examined the role of social support in the course of disability. These studies have examined the role of support in both recovery from illness as well as adjustment to long-term disability. Bloom (1990) characterized the relationship such that:

> Integration with the social network and the ability to draw resources from this network can maintain health and, in the event of illness, facilitate physical recovery. (p. 635)

Social support has been found to play a role in facilitating recovery from illness in studies of people with coronary artery disease (Berkman, Leo-Summers & Horowitz, 1992; Helgeson, 1991; King Reis, Porter & Norsen, 1993; Kulik & Mahler, 1989), people in treatment for cancer (Hegelson &

Cohen, 1996; Zemore & Shepel, 1989), as well as people with arthritis, diabetes and HIV infection (Wills & Fegan, 2001). In addition, social support has been found to be related to the course and recovery from mental illnesses (Brugha, 1995), including schizophrenia (Buchanan, 1995).

The Role of Recreation and Leisure in Social Support

Iso-Ahola and colleagues (Coleman & Iso-Ahola, 1993; Iso-Ahola & Park, 1996) have examined the role of leisure in social support processes. Specifically, they have taken a stress-buffering approach in the examination of leisure activity and its function in the generation of social support arguing that leisure-based social support acts to mediate the negative influence of stress on health. They elaborated, stating that:

> Leisure impacts health by providing buffering mechanisms
> that come into play when life presents significant problems.
> On the other hand when life stress is relatively low, leisure's
> contribution to health is expected to be less substantial on
> the short-term basis. (Iso-Ahola & Park, 1996, p. 113)

Iso-Ahola and Park found that when leisure-based social support was conceptualized as friendship and companionship, there was support for both main effects and buffering effects. The relationship was such that leisure companionship buffered the effects of stress on mental health, whereas leisure friendship was found to buffer the effects of stress on physical health. In addition, leisure friendship was found to demonstrate a main effect on mental health, but leisure companionship was unrelated to physical health. However, other studies have failed to find significant relationships between leisure-based social support and well-being (e.g., Coleman, 1993).

More recently, Iwasaki and colleagues (Iwasaki, 1997; Iwasaki & Mannell, 2000; Iwasaki & Zuzanek, 2001) proposed a stress-coping model of leisure. In this model Iwasaki argued that one of the ways that leisure provides a context for stress coping is through the generation of leisure-generated *dispositional* social support and leisure generated *situation-specific* social support. Dispositional social support reflects the capacity of leisure involvement to generate social support network members as well as the perception that one is supported. In contrast, situation-specific social support refers to receiving specific acts of support, as well as nonspecific companionship gained from coparticipants in leisure activities. Iwasaki's model is predicated on a stress-buffering approach, yet it differs from the approach offered by Iso-Ahola. The principal difference between the two models can be seen in the way that stress is conceptualized. In Iso-Ahola's model, stress is conceptualized in terms of "negative life events," such as the death of a loved one, the loss of employment, and crime victimization. Although these events undoubtedly represent stressful experiences, they are also infrequently experienced by most people. In contrast, Iwasaki's model has conceptualized stress as a more common occurrence, considering stress both as daily "hassles" as well as "negative life events."

Social Support in Therapeutic Recreation

Although there have been no published studies that have examined therapeutic recreation interventions specifically targeted toward social support, there do appear to be possibilities for therapeutic recreation specialists to improve social support available to their clients.

Assessment

For meaningful interventions to take place, a clear understanding of client need is required. Through the process of assessment, the therapeutic recreation specialist can identify areas of need. Given that the construct of social support is multidimensional, the assessment process should consider the different dimensions of social support. At its most basic, the construct of social support has a structural dimension (i.e., social support network), a functional dimension (i.e., support provisions) and an evaluative component (i.e., perceived support). Thus the therapeutic recreation specialist must consider the aspects of social support he or she will target. McColl (1997) reviews a number of existing social support instruments that are useful assessment tools in practice settings.

Intervention

Lyons (1999) stated that the effect of illness on social relationships is such that it tends to reduce network size, to constrict the range of functions of relationships, and to decrease the availability of valued relationships. One of the main avenues through which therapeutic recreation professionals may be able to impact social support is through the enhancement of social networks, and ultimately social relationships. Leisure and recreation activity have long been recognized as social in nature, and the shared engagement "builds multifaceted relationships that may gain the attributes of sustained sharing that we call friendship" (Kelly & Godbey, 1992, p. 152). Such meaningful social relationships can be the foundation for social support. It is interesting to note that some intervention studies have used recreation activity groups as a means to foster improved social networks and social relationships (e.g., Dalgard, Anstorp, Benum & Sorensen, 1995; Walsh, 1994). Arguably, many community integration interventions are implicitly based on the assumption that community presence and participation results in improved quality of life through the creation and maintenance of meaningful relationships.

If therapeutic recreation specialists are to effectively use interventions to improve social support networks, then at least two areas of additional research should be considered. First, since social support is provided through relationships, a greater understanding of the nature of relationships in general (cf., Duck, 1994), as well as the impact of disability on relation-ships (cf., Lyons et al., 1995), is needed. Second, interventions that seek to enhance social relationships should keep in mind that relationships carry implications of rank and status (Gilbert, 1995). The provision and recep-tion of supportive acts that flow in social relationships imply something about the status of both givers and receivers. Gilbert noted that:

> The degree to which gaining and giving social support is
> seen to raise or reduce rank/status and the degree to which
> it is seen as reciprocal (i.e., is part of social exchange and
> equity) have important effects. (p. 123)

He went on to note that some people may not seek social support, even when available, because to do so may further reduce their status. The impli-cation is that if relationships are to be truly supportive, therapeutic recre-ation specialists must work to ensure that their clients are as likely to be able to provide support as to receive it. To place clients in social situations in which they are only the *recipients* of support may reinforce a dependent status and ultimately have a negative impact on their quality of life.

Evaluation

Finally, as part of any intervention, the therapeutic recreation specialist needs to evaluate the results of care. To identify the effectiveness of services, a clear knowledge of desired outcomes must guide all aspects of care in-cluding the evaluation of care (Lee, McCormick & Perkins, 2000). Thus the evaluation of interventions must be consistent with assessed need and intervention provided.

Summary

This chapter provided a brief overview of the concept of social support. The body of literature on the subject has grown rapidly since the mid-1970s, growing out of interest in the role of interpersonal relationships in health and well-being. Generally, social support is considered to be the provision of material, emotional, or informational resources through social relationships that aid an individual in functioning. In addition, the construct of social support can be examined in terms of its structure as indicated by the social support network, its functions as indicated by support provisions, and its evaluation as indicated by perceived support. The role of social support in the maintenance of health and well-being, and its role in recovery from illness and disability is widely recognized. The social nature of recreation and leisure activity makes social support a natural target for therapeutic recreation intervention.

Reading Comprehension Questions

1. Define *social support*. What are the three characteristic components?

2. Identify an example of each type of social support provision.

3. How does the main effects model differ from the stress-buffering model of social support?

4. What is the role of leisure or recreation in social support?

5. Give some examples of therapeutic recreation interventions where enhancing social support may be involved.

References

Albert, M., Becker, T. McCrone, P., and Thornicroft, G. (1998). Social networks and mental health service utilisation: A literature review. *International Journal of Social Psychiatry, 44*, 248–267.

Antonucci, T. C. (1990). Social supports and social relationships. In R. H. Binstock and L. K. George (Eds.), *Handbook of aging and the social sciences* (3rd ed., pp. 205–226). New York, NY: Academic Press.

Arling, G. (1976). The elderly widow and her family, neighbors, and friends. *Journal of Marriage and the Family, 38*, 757–768.

Barrera, M. Jr. (1981). Social support in the adjustment of pregnant adolescents: Assessment issues. In B. H. Gottlieb (Ed.), *Social networks and social support* (pp. 69–96). Newbury Park, CA: Sage Publications.

Barrera, M. Jr. and Ainlay, S. L. (1983). The structure of social support: A conceptual and empirical analysis. *Journal of Community Psychology, 11*, 133–143.

Belsky, J. and Rovine, M. (1984). Social network contact, family support, and the transition to parenthood. *Journal of Marriage and the Family, 46*, 455–462.

Berkanovic, E. and Hurwicz, M. (1990). Rheumatoid arthritis and comorbidity. *Journal of Rheumatology, 17*, 888–892.

Berkman, L. F. (1995). The role of social relations in health promotion. *Psychosocial Medicine, 57*, 245–254.

Berkman, L. F. (1985). The relationship of social networks and social support to morbidity and mortality. In S. Cohen, and S. L. Syme (Eds.), *Social support and health* (pp. 241–262). Orlando, FL: Academic Press.

Berkman, L. F. and Glass, T. (2000). Social integration, social networks, social support, and health. In L. F. Berkman and I. O. Kawachi (Eds.), *Social epidemiology* (pp. 137–173). New York, NY: Oxford University Press.

Berkman, L. F., Leo-Summers, L., and Horowitz, R. I. (1992). Emotional support and survival after myocardial infarction: A prospective, population-based study of the elderly. *Annals of Internal Medicine, 117*, 1003–1009.

Berkman, L. F. and Syme, S. L. (1979). Social networks, host resistance, and mortality: A nine-year follow-up of Alameda County residents. *American Journal of Epidemiology, 109*, 186–204.

Biegel, D. E., Tracy, E. M., and Song, L. (1995). Barriers to social network interventions with persons with severe and persistent mental illness: A survey of case managers. *Community Mental Health Journal, 31*, 335–349.

Bloom, J. R. (1990). The relationship of social support and health. *Social Science & Medicine, 30*, 635–637.

Brugha, T. S. (1995). Social support and psychiatric disorder: Overview of the evidence. In T. S. Brugha (Ed.), *Social support and psychiatric disorder:*

Research findings and guidelines for clinical practice (pp. 1–38). New York, NY: Cambridge University Press.

Buchanan, J. (1995). Social support and schizophrenia: A review of the literature. *Archives of Psychiatric Nursing, 9*, 68–76.

Caplan, G. (1974). *Support systems and community mental health.* New York, NY: Behavioral Publications.

Cassileth, B. R., Walsh, W. P., and Lusk, E. J. (1988). Psychosocial correlates of cancer survival: A subsequent report 3 to 8 years after cancer diagnosis. *Journal of Clinical Oncology, 6*, 1753–1759.

Cauce, A. M., Reid, M., Landesman, S., and Gonzales, N. (1990). Social support in young children: Measurement, structure and behavioral impact. In B. R. Sarason, I. G. Sarason, and G. R. Pierce (Eds.), *Social support: An interactional view* (pp. 64–94). New York, NY: John Wiley & Sons.

Cobb, S. (1976). Social support as a moderator of life stress. *Psychosomatic Medicine, 38*, 300–314.

Cohen, S. and Hoberman, H. M. (1983). Positive events and social support as buffers of life change stress. *Journal of Applied Social Psychology, 13*, 99–125.

Cohen, S. I. and Sokolovsky, J. (1978). Schizophrenia and social networks: Ex-patients in the inner city. *Schizophrenia Bulletin, 4*, 546–560.

Cohen, S. and Wills, T. A. (1985). Stress, social support and the buffering hypothesis. *Psychological Bulletin, 98*, 310–357.

Coleman, D. (1993). Leisure-based social support, leisure dispositions and health. *Journal of Leisure Research, 25*, 350–361.

Coleman, D. and Iso-Ahola, S. E. (1993). Leisure and health: The role of social support and self-determination. *Journal of Leisure Research, 25*, 111–128.

Dalgard, O. S., Anstorp, T., Benum, K., and Sorensen, T. (1995). Social network and mental health: An intervention study. In T. S. Brugha (Ed.), *Social support and psychiatric disorder: Research findings and guidelines for clinical practice* (pp. 197–212). New York, NY: Cambridge University Press.

Duck, S. (1994). *Meaningful relationships.* Newbury Park, CA: Sage Publications.

Durkheim, E. D. (1951). *Suicide: A study in sociology.* (J. A. Spaulding and G. Simpson, trans.). Glencoe, IL: Free Press. (Original work published 1897)

Farmer, I. P. and Meyer, P. S. (1996). Higher levels of social support predict greater survival following acute myocardial infarction: The Corpus Christi heart project. *Behavioral Medicine, 22*(2), 59–67.

Fitzpatrick, R., Newman, S., Lamb, R., and Shipley, M. (1988). Social relationships and psychological well-being in rheumatoid arthritis. *Social Science and Medicine, 27*, 399–403.

Gallo, F. (1984). Social support networks and the health of elderly persons. *Social Work Research and Abstracts, 20*, 13–19.

Gilbert, P. (1995). Attachment, cooperation and rank: The evolution of the need for status and social support. In T. S. Brugha (Ed.), *Social support and psychiatric disorder: Research findings and guidelines for clinical practice* (pp. 117–141). New York, NY: Cambridge University Press.

Gore, S. (1978). The effect of social support in moderating the health consequences of unemployment. *Journal of Health and Social Behavior, 19*, 157–165.

Gottlieb, B. H. (1981). Social networks and social support in community mental health. In B. H. Gottlieb (Ed.), *Social networks and social support* (pp. 11–42. Newbury Park, CA: Sage Publications.

Gottlieb, B. H. (1978). The development and application of a classification scheme of informal helping behaviours. *Canadian Journal of Behavioural Science, 10*, 105–115.

Gourash, N. (1978). Help seeking: A review of the literature. *American Journal of Community Psychology, 6*, 499–517.

Gove, W. and Geerken, M. (1977). The effect of children and employment on the mental health of married men and women. *Social Forces, 56*, 66–76.

Hegelson, V. S. (1991). The effect of masculinity and social support on recovery from myocardial infarction. *Psychosomatic Medicine, 53*, 621–633.

Hegelson, V. S. and Cohen, S. (1996). Social support and adjustment to cancer: Reconciling descriptive, correlational, and intervention research. *Health Psychology, 15*, 135–148.

Hirsch, B. J. (1981). Social networks and the coping process: Creating personal communities. In B. H. Gottlieb, (Ed.), *Social networks and social support* (pp. 149–170). Newbury Park, CA: Sage Publications.

Hirsch, B. (1980). Natural support systems and coping with major life changes. *American Journal of Community Psychology, 8*, 159–172.

Hobfoll, S. E. and Walfisch, S. (1984). Coping with a threat to life: A longitudinal study of self-concept, social support, and psychological distress. *American Journal of Community Psychology, 12*, 87–100.

House, J. S. and Kahn, R. L. (1985). Measures and concepts of social support. In S. Cohen and S. L. Syme (Eds.), *Social support and health* (pp. 83–108). Orlando, FL: Academic Press.

House, J. S., Landis, K. R., and Umberson, D. (1988). Social relationships and health. *Science, 241*, 540–545.

House, J. S., Robbins, C., and Metzner, H. L. (1982). The association of social relationships and activities with mortality. *American Journal of Epidemiology, 116*, 123–140.

Iso-Ahola, S. E. and Park, C. J. (1996). Leisure-related social support and self-determination as buffers of stress-illness relationship. *Journal of Leisure Research, 28*, 169–187.

Iwasaki, Y. (1997). A reconceptualization of leisure stress-coping dimensions. Paper presented at the 5th Annual Graduate Leisure Research Symposium, Waterloo, Ontario.

Iwasaki, Y. and Mannell, R. C. (2000). Hierarchical dimensions of leisure stress coping. *Leisure Sciences, 22,* 163–181.

Iwasaki, Y. and Zuzanek, J. (2001). The mediating effects of social support, self-esteem and sense of mastery on relationships among physically active leisure, stress, and health. *Research Quarterly for Exercise and Sport, 72,* A36–A36.

Kahn, R. L. (1979). Aging and social support. In M. W. Riley (Ed.), *Aging from birth to death* (pp. 77–91). Boulder, CO: Westview Press.

Kahn, R. and Antonucci, T. (1980). Attachment, roles and social support. In P. Baltes and O. Brim, *Life-span development and behavior* (pp. 253–286). New York, NY: Academic Press.

Kaplan, G. A., Salonen, J. T., Cohen, R. D., Brand, R. J., Syme, S. L., and Puska, P. (1988). Social connections and mortality: Prospective evidence from Finland. *American Journal of Epidemiology, 128,* 370–380.

Kelly, J. R. and Godbey, G. (1992). *The sociology of leisure.* State College, PA: Venture Publishing, Inc.

King, K. B., Reis, H. T., Porter, L. A., and Norsen, L. H. (1993). Social support and long-term recovery from coronary artery surgery: Effects on patients and spouses. *Health Psychology, 12,* 56–63.

Kulik, J. A. and Mahler, H. I. (1989). Social support and recovery from surgery. *Health Psychology, 8,* 221–238.

Lackne, S. and Goldenberg, S. (1994). The contingency of social support. *Qualitative Health Research, 4,* 224–244.

Lee, Y., McCormick, B. P., and Perkins, S. (2000, May). Are you an outcome engineer? *Parks & Recreation, 35,* 64–68.

Levitt, M. J., Weber, R. A., and Clark, M. C. (1986). Social network relationships as sources of maternal support and well-being. *Developmental Psychology, 22,* 310–316.

Litwin, H. (1997). Support network type and health service utilization. *Research on Aging, 19,* 274–299.

Litwin, H. and Landau, R. (2000). Social network type and social support among the old-old. *Journal of Aging Studies, 14,* 213–229.

Lyons, J. S., Perrotta, P., and Hancher-Kvam, S. (1988). Perceived social support from family and friends: Measurement across disparate samples. *Journal of Personality Assessment, 52,* 42–47.

Lyons, R. (1999). Personal relationships, illness and disability. *Leisurability, 26*(3), 22–32.

Lyons, R. F., Sullivan, M. J. L., and Ritvo, P. G. (1995). *Relationships in chronic illness and disability.* Newbury Park, CA: Sage Publications.

McColl, M. A. (1997). Social support and occupational therapy. In C. H. Christiansen and C. M. Baum (Eds.), *Occupational therapy: Enabling function and well-being* (2nd ed., pp. 411–425). Thorofare, NJ: Slack.

Molassiotis, A. and van den Akker, O. B. A. (1997). Perceived social support, family environment and psychosocial recovery in bone marrow transplant long-term survivors. *Social Science & Medicine, 44*, 317–326.

Pattison, E. M. and Pattison, M. L. (1981). Analysis of a schizophrenic psychosocial network. *Schizophrenia Bulletin, 7*, 135–143.

Pennix, B. W. J. H., van Tilburg, T., Kriegsman, D. M. W., Boeke, A. J. P., Deeg, D. J. H., and Van Eijk, J. T. M. (1999). Social network, social support, and loneliness in older persons with different chronic diseases. *Journal of Aging & Health, 11*, 151–169.

Pescosolido, B. A. (1996). Bringing the community into utilization models: How social networks link individuals to changing systems of care. *Research in the Sociology of Health Care, 13A*, 171–197.

Phillips, S. L. (1981). Network characteristics related to the well-being of normals: A comparative base. *Schizophrenia Bulletin, 7*, 117–123.

Reed, D., McGee, D., Yano, K., and Feinleib, M. (1983). Social networks and coronary heart disease among Japanese men in Hawaii. *American Journal of Epidemiology, 117*, 384–396.

Rhodes, G. L. and Lakey, B. (1999). Social support and psychological disorder: Insights from social psychology. In R. M. Kowalski and M. R. Leary (Eds.), *The social psychology of emotional and behavioral problems* (pp. 281–309). Washington, DC: APA.

Rook, K. S. (1987). Social support versus companionship: Effects on life stress, loneliness, and evaluations by others. *Journal of Personality and Social Psychology, 6,* 1132–1147.

Rosengren, A. Orth-Gomer, K., Wedel, H., and Wilhelmsen, L. (1993). Stressful life events, social support, and mortality in men born in 1933. *British Medical Journal, 307,* 102–105.

Sarason, B. R., Sarason, I. G., and Pierce, G. R. (1990). Traditional views of social support and their impact on assessment. In B. R. Sarason, I. G. Sarason, and G. R. Pierce (Eds.), *Social support: An interactional view* (pp. 9–25). New York, NY: John Wiley & Sons.

Sokolovsky, J. Cohen, C., Berger, D., and Geiger, J. (1978). Personal networks of ex-mental patients in a Manhattan SRO hotel. *Human Organization, 37*(1), 5–15.

Strug, D. L. and Hyman, M. M. (1981). Social networks of alcoholics. *Journal of Studies on Alcohol, 42,* 855–884.

Thoits, P. A. (1985). Social support and psychological well-being: Theoretical possibilities. In B. R. Sarason and I. G. Sarason (Eds.), *Social support: Theory, research and applications* (pp. 51–72). Dordrecht, Netherlands: Martinus Nijhoff.

Titjen, A. M. and Bradley, C. F. (1985). Social support and maternal psychosocial adjustment during the transition to parenthood. *Canadian Journal of Behavioral Science, 17,* 109–121.

Vandervoort, D. (1999). Quality of social support in mental and physical health. *Current Psychology, 18,* 205–223.

Vaux, A. (1988). *Social support: Theory, research and intervention.* New York, NY: Prager.

Vaux, A., Stewart, D., and Riedel, S. (1987). Modes of social support: The Social Support Behaviors (SSB) Scale. *American Journal of Community Psychology, 15,* 209–237.

Vogt, T. M., Mullooly, J. P., Ernst, D., Pope, C. R., and Hollis, J. F. (1992). Social networks as predictors of ischemic heart disease, cancer, stroke and hypertension: Incidence, survival and mortality. *Journal of Clinical Epidemiology, 45,* 659–666.

Walsh, J. (1994). Social support resource outcomes for the clients of two community treatment teams. *Research on Social Work Practice, 4,* 448–463.

Weiss, R. S. (1974). The provisions of social relations. In Z. Rubin (Ed.), *Doing unto others* (pp. 17–26). Englewood Cliffs, NJ: Prentice Hall.

Wenger, G. C. (1984). *The supportive network: Coping with old age.* London, UK: Allen and Unwin.

Wilcox, B. L. (1981). Social support in adapting to marital disruption. In B. H. Gottlieb (Ed.), *Social networks and social support* (pp. 97–115). Newbury Park, CA: Sage Publications.

Wills, T. A. (1985). Supportive functions of interpersonal relationships. In S. Cohen and S. L. Syme (Eds.), *Social support and health* (pp. 61–82). Orlando, FL: Academic Press.

Wills, T. A. and Fegan, M. F. (2001). Social networks and social support. In A. Baum, T. A. Revenson, and J. E. Singer (Eds.), *Handbook of health psychology* (pp. 209–234). Mahwah, NJ: Lawrence Erlbaum.

Zemore, R. and Shepel, L. F. (1989). Effects of breast cancer and mastectomy on emotional support and adjustment. *Social Science and Medicine, 28,* 19–27.

Chapter 4

Self-Determination and Enjoyment in Therapeutic Recreation

John Dattilo, Ph.D., FALS
Douglas Kleiber, Ph.D., FALS

Self-determination involves people having the degree of control over their lives that they desire in those areas they value and over which they wish to exercise control; therefore, people who are self-determined exert control over what happens to them, when and where it occurs, and with whom it takes place (Stancliffe, Abery, Springborg & Elkin, 2000). Generally, people who perceive themselves as capable and self-determining are able to deal effectively with the challenges of day-to-day life and may avoid such undesirable outcomes as depression, distress, substance abuse, and physical illness.

One challenge for therapeutic recreation specialists is to enable all citizens to be as self-determined as possible (Wehmeyer, 1998). After analyzing almost 200 studies involving close to 1,400 participants with disabilities, Hughes and colleagues (1997) concluded that there is an increasing trend to involve people with disabilities as active participants by targeting outcomes related to self-determination, autonomy, and choice. In addition, after analysis of information on the quality of life and self-determination of 50 adults with cognitive disabilities, Wehmeyer and Schwartz (1998) concluded that self-determination contributes to a more positive quality of life. Therefore, by considering another person's choices, preferences, and aspirations, therapeutic recreation specialists can not only promote a sense of self-determination, but also communicate a sense of respect (Hughes & Agran, 1998).

This chapter describes the nature of self-determination and enjoyment, and aspects of therapeutic recreation designed to support participants in achieving goals of self-determination and enjoyment and ultimately functional improvement. Strategies facilitating self-determination, intrinsic motivation, perception of manageable challenge, and investment of attention, which ultimately contribute to enjoyment and functional improvement, are described. Because self-determination involves a lifelong interplay between the individual and his or her environment, a supportive, responsive context is important when trying to encourage people to become more self-determined. Optimum environments are those in which individuals have the opportunity to express and further develop self-determination (Wehmeyer & Bolding, 1999).

Creating conditions that help concentration, effort, and a sense of control and competence while promoting freedom of choice and expression of preference is the "engineering of enjoyment" (Dattilo & Kleiber, 1993, p. 58). To do this, however, it is helpful to understand self-determination, the nature of enjoyment, and factors that interfere with each (Dattilo, Kleiber & Williams, 1998). Theories addressing self-determination and factors interfering with it provide information for developing strategies that enhance concentration, effort, and a sense of control and competence, and thus foster enjoyment.

Self-determination can be enhanced when people are encouraged and supported to become aware of themselves in leisure contexts, to make decisions and choices, to communicate their preferences, and to set goals. Intrinsic motivation is enhanced when people focus on internal standards, emphasize inherent rewards, listen to informative feedback, and become aware of their interests. Therapeutic recreation specialists can facilitate or disrupt these patterns. To increase the chance that participants consider the challenge of an activity to be manageable, they can be encouraged to assess their skills, make adaptations, make realistic appraisals of challenges, and develop activity skills. Practitioners can recognize and avoid sending messages that undermine self-direction and avoid creating conditions that are distracting. Teaching participants to make accurate attributions relative to their successes and failures encourages investment of attention and enjoyment. In turn, generating enjoyment can help facilitate functional improvements.

The American Therapeutic Recreation Association and the National Therapeutic Recreation Society (*Therapeutic Recreation*, n.d.) proposed that the purpose of therapeutic recreation is to treat "physical, social, cognitive, and emotional conditions associated with illness, injury, or chronic disability" (p. 2) through the use of a variety of interventions. While there are other agendas for therapeutic recreation specialists, teaching people, regardless of the type and degree of disability, to create environments conducive to enjoyment is consistent with that purpose. Enjoyment and the creation of environments conducive to enjoyment ultimately contribute to well-being (Massimini & Carli, 1988) and to personal growth (Csikszentmihalyi & Larson, 1984).

Self-Determination

Self-determination involves acting as a primary causal agent in one's life and making choices and decisions free from external influence or interference. Deci (1980) asserted that self-determination involves autonomy, the flexibility and ability to choose options, and the ability to adjust to situations when only one option is available.

> When autonomous, people are fully willing to do what they are doing, and they embrace the activity with a sense of interest and commitment. (Deci, 1995, p. 2)

Wehmeyer and colleagues (Sands & Wehmeyer, 1996; Wehmeyer, 1996; Wehmeyer, Agran & Hughes, 1998) have applied the theory of self-determination developed by Deci (1980, 1995) to people with disabilities.

A goal of many therapeutic recreation programs is to set the stage for people to enjoy themselves. To the extent that self-determination contributes to enjoyment, it is helpful to provide services to people with disabilities that foster self-determination. Self-determination in leisure, which includes the perception of freedom to make choices and initiation those chosen leisure activities, is essential in facilitating positive leisure experiences for people with disabilities. By creating environments that are option-rich, responsive and informative, practitioners increase the likelihood of participants becoming self-determined. In short, self-determination occurs when people take control of their freedom.

Become Aware of Self in Leisure

Sands and Doll (1996) suggested that if people are to be self-determined, they must understand their strengths, limitations, and unique learning needs, and they must know how to use these attributes to enhance their quality of life. Since awareness is "basic to all learning, growth and positive behavioral change" (Barry, 1997, p. 6), a valuable therapeutic recreation service is to assist participants to explore, discover, and develop an awareness about themselves in leisure contexts. An aspect of self-determined leisure then is engaging in self-examination (cf., Hoge, Dattilo, Schneider & Bemisderfer, 1997). More specifically, participants can be encouraged to develop an awareness of themselves in a leisure context through a processing strategy known as *debriefing*. Typically, debriefings consist of a series of questions that require participants to reflect, describe, analyze, and communicate about an activity (Brackenreg, Luckner & Pinch, 1994). People who internalize the meaning associated with the experience are in a position to apply that learning to other aspects of their lives (Knapp, 1990).

Make Leisure Decisions

After studying 54 individuals with intellectual disabilities (ages 17–30) Jenkinson (1999) noted that those people who had experiences leading to learned helplessness may require a lengthy period of supported practice in making decisions to gain greater confidence and feelings of control. In addition, Jenkinson encouraged practitioners to present manageable decisions that do not present people an abundance of information from which they must make a decision. Therefore, it would seem that therapeutic recreation specialists who want to encourage all participants to become self-determined would benefit by giving participants as many opportunities as possible to practice making manageable decisions.

As people develop an awareness of their leisure interests, Lord (1997) suggested that professionals should cultivate decision-making skills related to leisure participation. If leisure services are to foster independence, then it is imperative that participants are encouraged to make decisions (Mahon, 1994; Mahon & Bullock, 1992). Making timely and correct decisions leads to a sense of personal effectiveness and interest that subsequently promotes investment of attention and enjoyment. People who do not possess the decision-making skills needed for activity involvement are more likely to acquire these skills if they participate in recreation activities and are given considerable autonomy in doing so. Decisions about leisure involvement can be stimulated by having people identify others who could serve as resources, locate facilities that provide recreation activities, learn about participation requirements, and obtain answers to questions (Dattilo, 1999). Participants can be encouraged to evaluate their decisions, determine the effectiveness of their decisions, and given similar circumstances, decide whether they would act in a similar fashion or change.

Make Leisure Choices

One characteristic common to most discussions of self-determination is that of choice (Bambara, Cole & Koger, 1998). Bernard Wagner, President of the American Association on Mental Retardation, stated, "I have become convinced that the wave of the future will involve more and more maximum individualized choices" (1999, p. 3). However, some families and professionals make choices for people with disabilities rather than allowing participants to decide for themselves. Individuals' opportunities to express personal interests and preferences have been prevented by people who incorrectly assume that people with disabilities are incapable of making informed choices (Heller, Miller, Hsieh & Sterns, 2000).

When people are given choices they improve their engagement, interest, and enthusiasm in activities (Moes, 1998); increase their participation level (Dunlap, Kern-Dunlap, Clarke & Robbins, 1991); and reduce their challenging behaviors, such as acts of aggression (Sigafoos, 1998). To encourage self-determination, professionals promote autonomy by supporting initiation of activities (Foxx, Faw, Taylor, Davis & Fulia, 1993; Faw, Davis & Peck, 1996; Searle, Mahon, Iso-Ahola, Sdrolias & Van Dyck, 1995; Wehmeyer & Schwartz, 1997). To support these initiations, therapeutic recreation practitioners can provide participants with opportunities to express preferences, allow them to make choices regarding their leisure participation, and permit them to experience outcomes based on their choices. The strength in therapeutic recreation services may be in addressing the issue of choice (Searle, Mahon, Iso-Ahola, Sdrolias & Van Dyck, 1995), and in Deci's view, "choice is the key to self-determination" (1995, p. 10).

Communicate Leisure Preferences

Communication is important to self-determination in that effective communication facilitates involvement with others. Many people with disabilities rarely initiate conversations and frequently assume the subordinate role of respondent (Dattilo & Camarata, 1991; Dattilo & O'Keefe, 1992). One way to create a supportive environment that stimulates participants to communicate preferences and thus promote self-initiated leisure is to approach participants, attend to them, and give them adequate time to respond (Dattilo & Light, 1993).

Set Goals

Activity is conducive to enjoyment when it has clear goals (Csikszentmihalyi, 1990). In many activities the goals are implicit, and therefore, goal setting is not important. For example, when completing a painting, the main concern is to develop the skills which, when used, result in recognizing a finished product. However, one role of therapeutic recreation service providers is to encourage participants to set goals when the goals are not apparent and work toward achieving them (usually problem solving in the process) within an environment which fosters interdependence.

According to Deci,

> goals need to be individualized—they need to be suited specifically to the person who will work toward them—and they need to be set so as to represent an optimal challenge. (1995, p. 152)

Clear goals provide direction and facilitate enjoyment as these goals are achieved; however, goals that focus attention on winning (Deci & Ryan, 1985) or beating the other team (Deci, 1995) rather than doing well can be problematic since a focus on winning makes the activity an instrument for winning rather than something enjoyed for its intrinsic properties (Deci, Eghrari, Patrick & Leone, 1994).

An environment which facilitates self-determination can be established by encouraging participants to become aware of themselves in leisure, make relevant decisions, make meaningful leisure choices, communicate these choices, and consider the actions to take once choices have been made. From Deci's (1995) perspective, self-determination is reinforced in settings where interventions are being applied and individuals do activities:

> ...of their own volition, at their own initiative, so they will go on doing the activities freely in the future when [therapeutic recreation providers] are no longer there to prompt them. (p. 91)

Intrinsic Motivation

Deci and Ryan (1985) concluded that self-determination both directs and is directed by intrinsic motivation. Intrinsically motivated activity energizes behavior and results in feelings of self-determination. Interest, excitement, and relaxation provide reinforcement for activities by increasing or decreasing arousal to an optimal level. These are the experiences most often associated with leisure and recreation and are among the goals of therapeutic recreation interventions.

People who are intrinsically motivated generally seek challenges commensurate with their competencies; they will avoid those situations that are too easy or too difficult. Individuals who are intrinsically motivated in modulating arousal and seeking challenge are more likely to learn, adapt, and develop competencies that contribute to well-being. Fortunately, intrinsic motivation does not depend on a particular level of ability; therefore, interest, excitement, and relaxation can arise with anyone.

Focus on Inherent Rewards

A key question proposed by Deci that therapeutic recreation specialists can attempt to answer is "How can people create the conditions within which others will motivate themselves?" (1995, p. 10). Intrinsic motivation is reinforced to the extent that chosen behavior continues without disruption from extrinsic influences and is owned by the individual and/or is personally satisfying. According to Csikszentmihalyi,

> The most important step in emancipating oneself from social controls is the ability to find rewards in the events of each moment. (1990, p. 19)

Participants' choices can be reinforced and a concentration on participation outcomes can be minimized, thereby having participants focus on inherent rewards. If trophies, prizes, or other consequences are used to reward learning and successful participation, they can undermine intrinsic interest by changing the interpretation of the event such as "I did it for the prize" rather than "I did it for the fun of it." Mannell and Kleiber warned that:

> When people are rewarded for listening to music, playing games or volunteering, their behavior can become overjustified; that is, they may begin to attribute their participation to extrinsic motives. Research has suggested that such overjustification can be dangerous. The introduction of extrinsic rewards tends to undermine people's experience of self-determination. (1997, p. 138)

Listen to Positive Feedback

If extrinsic rewards are given, it is helpful to structure rewards so that they provide positive feedback, which either affirms a sense of competence, if competence is the issue (Koestner, Zuckerman & Koestner, 1987), or provides them with clear task feedback (Sansone, 1986). Therefore, it is useful for participants to learn to listen to positive feedback. Where rewards are informative rather than controlling, they are least likely to undermine intrinsic motivation (Deci, 1975).

> Task feedback refers to the information that conveys to people how well they are doing various aspects of the activity, or how well they are improving their activity performance, or how well they are doing by certain accepted standards. In this way the individual's performance is not compared to that of others; rather, the focus is on acquisition of the skills needed to master the activity at individually enjoyable levels. (Iso-Ahola, 1999)

Compete against Internal Standards

Although competition is a common feature of many recreation activities, when beating an opponent takes precedence over performing as well as possible, enjoyment tends to disappear.

> The real function of competition could be viewed as pro-
> viding challenge—as providing an opportunity for people
> to test themselves and to improve—and in the process have
> fun. (Deci, 1995, p. 69)

A focus on winning is often associated with direct competition, which involves pitting one person against another. Ross and Van den Haag (1957) identified that focusing on competition against internal standards is indirect competition. By focusing on indirect rather than direct competition, attention to task and associated enjoyment can be promoted, and negative emotions such as animosity, and impaired performance and aggression (Deutsch, 1969) can be avoided.

Become Aware of Interests

Intrinsic motivation must be elicited before it can be maintained. As suggested previously, intrinsic motivation is generated as a matter of interest in the environment and what one might do to feel optimally stimulated and competent. Helping participants to become aware of their interests involves some self-examination (referred to in the previous section on self-determination); however, it will likely require exposure to possibilities as well. Although observing others enjoying an activity may be one way to promote interest, direct participation is likely to be a critical way to stimulate interest.

Perception of Manageable Challenge

The word used often by participants themselves to describe the subjective experience of intense involvement or absorption is *flow* (Csikszentmihalyi, 1990). The sense of movement that this word implies is created by the merging of action and awareness around the challenges provided by an activity and the feedback that reinforces a person's ability to meet those challenges. "Flow tends to occur when a person's skills are fully involved in overcoming a challenge that is just about manageable" (Csikszentmihalyi, 1997, p. 30).

People with disabilities are often either unaware of the possibilities for challenging experiences, discouraged in the face of challenge, or prevented by others from experiencing challenges. It is important that people learn about the availability of challenging opportunities, be given the chance to engage in challenging activities, and be encouraged to overcome their fears and try. However, individuals must come to believe they can succeed if they are going to risk an uncertain outcome. Once they experience some success, they are less likely to perceive challenging situations as unmanageable.

Assess Leisure Skills

In some cases, however, the best decision-making skills, the greatest exposure, or an environment rich with feedback may fall short of bringing enjoyment if challenges are far too little or too great or are perceived to be so. To improve the likelihood of a good match between challenge and skills, participants can be encouraged to assess their skills. If an imbalance exists between the degree of challenge in an activity and participants' skills, barriers may be created to leisure participation. For instance, if a specific activity is too easy for participants, boredom and frustration often result; however, if an activity is too difficult, anxiety and frustration can occur (Ellis, Witt & Aguilar, 1983).

Make Adaptations to Recreation Activities

One way to reduce barriers created by an imbalance of skills and challenge is to make adaptations associated with recreation activities. Adaptations can change the challenge associated with an activity to meet participants' abilities. Once adaptations are made, they are continually adjusted to meet changing skills of participants. When adapting activities, materials are chosen specifically to meet the needs of the participants, or the specific cognitive, physical, or social requirements associated with an activity may be changed. Environmental adaptations, such as reducing the size of the playing area to minimize the distance traveled for people with limited mobility and endurance, may be necessary to bring about the active involvement of participants. Finally, it can be helpful to examine possible ways to modify instructional strategies to teach people with different disabling conditions about leisure.

Appraise Degree of Challenge

At times, however, even challenges that are well-matched to skills are perceived by some people with disabilities as being too great. Fear and trepidation may occur for people who have experienced limited success when attempting new activities. Helping them gain a realistic appraisal of the degree of challenge associated with an activity is important. For instance, participants can be encouraged to attempt relatively simpler activities, such as shooting free throws, before attempting relatively more difficult tasks, such as a game of basketball. While challenges that facilitate enjoyment often exceed skills slightly, assistance may be needed when participants lack confidence in the face of such challenges.

Develop Recreation Activity Skills

Development of the participant's ability to choose and successfully engage in recreation activities of sufficient scope and variety to experience enjoyment is an aspect of therapeutic recreation services. The more skills people master, the more likely it is that they will view an activity as presenting a challenge that is manageable. Therefore, participants can be encouraged to develop an array of recreation activity skills that contribute to meaningful leisure, enjoyment, and satisfaction.

As people succeed in an optimally challenging activity, they begin to feel competent, and their motivation to continue the activity increases. Ultimately, success helps people to see new challenges as attractive rather than intimidating. Having a variety of activities in which a person feels confident can enhance self-determination. Nevertheless, as Csikszentmihalyi (1990) noted, to achieve depth of enjoyment and flow, effort and concentration of attention are needed.

Investment of Attention

According to Csikszentmihalyi (1997), attention becomes ordered and fully invested when goals are clear, feedback is relevant, and challenge and skills are in balance. From the research of Csikszentmihalyi and others, it is clear that investment of attention involves concentration, effort, and a sense of control. These factors must be understood and managed by facilitators or individuals themselves if attention and depth of involvement are to occur.

Many activities can attract one's attention. However, to maintain the person's attention, activity typically must become more challenging in keeping with the individual's expanding skills. In addition, if a person's skills decrease as a result of a progressive disorder or the side effects of medications, the challenge associated with an activity must be reduced accordingly. In any case, the challenge associated with activities must be constantly evaluated and changed to meet fluctuations in people's ability to perform.

Reduce Distractions

The number and intensity of environmental elements competing with the activity for the person's attention are important to consider when providing therapeutic recreation services (Ellis, Witt & Aguilar, 1983). Ellis and colleagues suggested that therapeutic recreation specialists:

> be very sensitive to novel aspects of the environment which might detract from focusing upon the particular activity in progress. (p. 13)

Attention to a task and subsequent enjoyment can be enhanced when individuals learn to reduce distractions surrounding activities that bring them enjoyment, or when service providers reduce distractions to the extent possible. To reduce distractions, disruptive settings and people should be avoided; however, if distractions are present, participants can learn to minimize the impact of distractions by focusing attention and deemphasizing the importance of external disruptions.

Reduce Maladaptive Attributions

Among factors that undermine attention to a task are evaluation processes that direct an individual's attention on himself or herself. To the extent possible, self-evaluations should be delayed until after an event, at which time positive attributions can be encouraged. Participants can be helped to reduce maladaptive attributions for success and failure that interfere with the investment of attention and enjoyment associated with a situation. For example, participants can be helped to recognize that, in many situations, failure should be:

a. Attributed to external factors, such as task difficulty, as opposed to internal ones, such as intelligence;

b. Viewed as an unstable outcome, such as the result of effort that is not expected to occur in each situation, rather than expecting failure to be a stable outcome, such as physical structure; and

c. Attributed to specific situations, such as failure with the expert ski slope attempted last week, as opposed to generalizing failure more globally, such as failure with all sports.

In any case, however, such attribution retraining should only be done after the fact or when it is clear that maladaptive attributions have been disruptive to attention.

Enjoyment

Enjoyment is the experience derived from investing one's attention in intrinsically motivating action patterns. The activity may be so compelling in and of itself that one becomes deeply absorbed in it and loses consciousness of self and awareness of time. Enjoyment is consistent with concentration, effort, and a sense of control and competence.

Enjoyment is often used colloquially as the equivalent of "fun," simple positive affect, or pleasure; but we are using it here, as Csikszentmihalyi (1975, 1990, 1997) and others have (e.g., Massimini & Carli, 1988), to reflect a considerable degree of psychological involvement as well. An activity is assumed to be enjoyable, then, when it commands sustained attention on its own and when it brings positive feelings.

Csikszentmihalyi (1990) considered the great availability of free time "that somehow fails to be translated into enjoyment" (p. 83) to be one of the most ironic paradoxes. Enjoyment refers to Csikszentmihalyi's notion of optimal experience, or flow, as the experience of intense involvement that is willingly enacted, psychologically absorbing, and ultimately satisfying. While enjoyment and associated functional development stand well as outcomes and as indicators of self-determination, they also are a precipitating experience. Thus, enjoyment and associated functional improvements serve to reinforce experiences and lead a person on to greater challenges and to higher levels of self-determination. As enjoyment reflects control by the individual, it evokes an orientation for making the most of circumstances and can result in improved physical, social, emotional, and cognitive functioning.

While enjoyment is a worthy goal of therapeutic recreation services, improvement associated with physical, emotional, social, and cognitive functioning is important as well. When participants independently access enjoyment and create environments conducive to enjoyment, functional improvements should result. Massimini, Csikszentmihalyi, and Delle Fave (1988) concluded that enjoyment motivates people to do things that push them beyond their present ability and contribute to their functional development. Although not extensively documented, research suggests that enjoyment contributes to functional improvements (e.g., Frewen, Schomer & Dunne, 1994; Middleton & Byrd, 1996; Paxton, Browning & O'Connell, 1997).

Conclusion

Changes to one aspect of self-determination and enjoyment are likely to influence changes in another. Therefore, if a person seems to be experiencing difficulty in one area, such as investment of attention, the source of the problem may be found in another area, such as the perception of a manageable challenge. In addition, what can be done to strengthen one aspect of self-determination and enjoyment probably will have implications for another.

Although acting autonomously is an important characteristic of self-determination, people are not completely autonomous, and few would choose to meet all their daily living demands independently and without assistance and support from others. Given this need for interdependence, Pumpian (1996) asserted that being autonomous includes being interdependent with families and others with whom we interact. Therefore, Brown and colleagues (1998) encouraged professionals to acknowledge this interdependence and focus on supporting people with disabilities to become more autonomous within the context of interdependence.

Csikszentmihalyi (1997) warned that flow can be used for constructive or destructive purposes, and thus, it is not enough to have people strive for enjoyable goals; they should be guided to establish and pursue enjoyable goals which do not bring harm to themselves or the community and may even be enhancing to either or both. Enjoyment is a worthy outcome of therapeutic recreation services only if the individual or community does not experience harm as a result of the enjoyment.

Some leisure education interventions have incorporated aspects of this model (e.g., leisure awareness, choice making, decision making, resource awareness) in their approaches. Recent studies of these interventions have demonstrated positive effects on a variety of people, including people with cognitive impairments (Bedini, Bullock & Driscoll, 1993; Dattilo & Hoge, 1999; Mahon & Bullock, 1992; Williams & Dattilo, 1997) and older adults (Dunn & Wilhite, 1997; Lovell, Dattilo & Jekubovich, 1996; Searle, Mahon, Iso-Ahola, Sdrolias & Van Dyck, 1995). Nevertheless, while these interventions utilized a variety of techniques, only the impact of the overall program was determined in each study. Systematic examination of effects of interventions associated with various components of the model is still much needed.

Because self-determination involves a lifelong interplay between the individual and his or her environment, a supportive responsive context is important when trying to encourage people to become self-determined. Optimum environments are those in which individuals have the opportunity to express and further develop self-determination. To promote self-determination therapeutic recreation professionals must begin to shift from professional-directed and professional-driven instruction and programs to participant-directed approaches to service delivery (Wehmeyer, Palmer, Agran, Mithaug & Martin, 2000).

Wehmeyer, Agran, and Hughes (1998) stated that too many people with disabilities do not have the chance to learn and use self-determination skills, and they agreed with Halloran (1993) that there is a critical need to enable people with disabilities to be in control of their lives. Self-determination is made more likely when enjoyment is facilitated. This chapter and other writings (e.g., Dattilo, Kleiber & Williams, 1998) can encourage therapeutic recreation specialists to not only facilitate participants' functional improvements, but also to promote their self-determination associated with leisure participation, to create leisure environments conducive to development of intrinsic motivation, to cultivate perceptions of manageable leisure challenges, and to foster investment of attention so that optimal experience and enjoyment will be abundant in their lives.

Reading Comprehension Questions

1. Define *self-determination*.
2. How does self-awareness contribute to self-determination?
3. How can a therapeutic recreation specialist facilitate clients making choices in leisure?
4. What conditions lead to intrinsic motivation?
5. Explain the role of challenge in activities and how it relates to self-determination and intrinsic motivation.
6. Explain methods a therapeutic recreation specialist might use to facilitate investment of attention.
7. How does self-determination contribute to enjoyment in leisure activities?

References

Bambara, L. M., Cole, C. L., and Koger, F. (1998). Translating self-determination concepts into support for adults with severe disabilities. *Journal of the Association for Persons with Severe Handicaps, 23*(1), 27–37.

Barry, V. (1997). *The dog ate my homework: Personal responsibility—how to avoid it and what to do about it.* Kansas City, MO: Andrews and McMeel.

Bedini, L. A., Bullock, C. C., and Driscoll, L. (1993). The effects of leisure education on factors contributing to the successful transition of students with mental retardation from school to adult life. *Therapeutic Recreation Journal, 27,* 70–82.

Brackenreg, M., Luckner, J., and Pinch, K. (1994). Essential skills for processing adventure experiences. *Journal of Experiential Education, 17,* 45–47.

Brown, F., Gothelf, C. R., Guess, D., and Lehr, D. H. (1998). Self-determination for individuals with the most severe disabilities: Moving beyond Chimera. *Journal of the Association for Persons with Severe Handicaps, 23*(10), 17–26.

Csikszentmihalyi, M. (1997). *Finding flow: The psychology of engagement with everyday life.* New York, NY: HarperCollins.

Csikszentmihalyi, M. (1990). *Flow: The psychology of optimal experience.* New York, NY: Harper & Row.

Csikszentmihalyi, M. (1975). *Beyond boredom and anxiety: The experience of play in work and games.* San Francisco, CA: Jossey-Bass.

Csikszentmihalyi, M. and Larson, R. (1984). *Being adolescent.* New York, NY: Basic Books.

Dattilo, J. (1999). *Leisure education program planning: A systematic approach* (2nd ed.). State College, PA: Venture Publishing, Inc.

Dattilo, J. and Camarata, S. (1991). Facilitating leisure involvement through self-initiated augmentative communication training. *Journal of Applied Behavior Analysis, 24,* 369–378.

Dattilo, J. and Hoge, G. (1999). Effects of a leisure education program on youth with mental retardation. *Education and Training in Mental Retardation and Developmental Disabilities, 34*(1), 20–34.

Dattilo, J. and Kleiber, D. A. (1993). Psychological perspectives for therapeutic recreation research: The psychology of enjoyment. In M. J. Malkin and C. Z. Howe (Eds.), *Research in therapeutic recreation: Concepts and methods* (pp. 57–76). State College, PA: Venture Publishing, Inc.

Dattilo, J., Kleiber, D., and Williams, R. (1998). Self-determination and Enjoyment Enhancement: A psychologically-based service delivery model for therapeutic recreation. *Therapeutic Recreation Journal, 32,* 258–271.

Dattilo, J. and Light, J. (1993). Setting the stage for leisure: Encouraging reciprocal communication for people using augmentative and alternative communication systems through facilitator instruction. *Therapeutic Recreation Journal, 27*(3), 156–171.

Dattilo, J. and O'Keefe, B. M. (1992). Setting the stage for leisure: Encouraging adults with mental retardation who use augmentative and alternative communication systems to share conversations. *Therapeutic Recreation Journal, 26*(1), 27–37.

Deci, E. L. (1995). *Why we do what we do: Understanding self-motivation.* New York, NY: Penguin Books.

Deci, E. L. (1980). *The psychology of self-determination.* Lexington, MA: Lexington Books.

Deci, E. L. (1975). *Intrinsic motivation.* New York, NY: Academic Press.

Deci, E. L., Eghrari, H., Patrick, B. C., and Leone, D. R. (1994). Facilitating internalization: The self-determination theory perspective. *Journal of Personality, 62*(1), 119–142.

Deci, E. L. and Ryan, W. (1985). *Intrinsic motivation and self-determination in human behavior.* New York, NY: Plenum Press.

Deutsch, M. (1969). Socially relevant science: Reflections of some studies of interpersonal conflict. *American Psychologist, 24*, 1076–1092.

Dunlap, G., Kern-Dunlap, L., Clarke, S., and Robbins, F. R. (1991). Functional assessment, curricular revision, and severe behavior problems. *Journal of Applied Behavior Analysis, 24*, 287–397.

Dunn, N. J. and Wilhite, B. (1997). The effects of a leisure education program on leisure participation and psychosocial well-being of two older women who are home-centered. *Therapeutic Recreation Journal, 31*(1), 53–71.

Ellis, G. D., Witt, P. A., and Aguilar, T. (1983). Facilitating "flow" through therapeutic recreation services. *Therapeutic Recreation Journal, 17*(2), 6–15.

Faw, G. D., Davis, P. K., and Peck, C. (1996). Increasing self-determination: Teaching people with mental retardation to evaluate residential options. *Journal of Applied Behavior Analysis, 29*(2), 173–188.

Foxx, R. M., Faw, G. D., Taylor, S., Davis, P. K., and Fulia, R. (1993). Would I be able to...?: Teaching clients to assess the availability of their community living life style preferences. *American Journal on Mental Retardation, 98*(2), 235–248.

Frewen, S., Schomer, H., and Dunne, T. (1994). Health belief model interpretation of compliance factors in a weight loss and cardiac rehabilitation programme. *South African Journal of Psychology, 24*(1), 39–43.

Halloran, W. D. (1993). Transition services requirement: Issues, implications, challenges. In R. C. Eaves and P. J. McLaughlin (Eds.), *Recent advances in special education and rehabilitation* (pp. 210–224). Boston, MA: Andover Medical.

Heller, T., Miller, A. B., Hsieh, K., and Sterns, H. (2000). Later-life planning: Promoting knowledge of options and choice-making. *Mental Retardation, 38*(4), 395–406.

Hoge, G., Dattilo, J., Schneider, S., and Bemisderfer, K. (1997). Transition through recreation and integration for life. In S. Schleien, M. Ray, and F. Green (Eds.), *Community recreation and people with disabilities: Strategies for inclusion* (pp. 180–185). Baltimore, MD: Paul H. Brookes.

Hughes, C. and Agran, M. (1998). Introduction to the special section: Self-determination: Signaling a systems change? *Journal of the Association for Persons with Severe Handicaps, 23*(1), 1–4.

Hughes, C., Eisenman, L. T., Hwang, B., Kim, J., Killian, D. J., and Scott, S. V. (1997). Transition from secondary special education to adult life: A review of analysis of empirical measures. *Education and Training in Mental Retardation and Developmental Disabilities, 32*(2), 85–104.

Iso-Ahola, S. E. (1999). Motivational foundations of leisure. In E. L. Jackson and T. L. Burton (Eds.), *Leisure studies: Prospects for the twenty-first century.* State College, PA: Venture Publishing, Inc.

Jenkinson, J. (1999). Factors affecting decision-making by young adults with intellectual disabilities. *American Journal on Mental Retardation, 104*(4), 320–329.

Knapp, C. (1990). Processing the adventure experience. In J. Miles and S. Priest (Eds.), *Adventure education* (pp. 189–197). State College, PA: Venture Publishing, Inc.

Koestner, R., Zuckerman, M., and Koestner, J. (1987). Praise, involvement, and intrinsic motivation. *Journal of Personality and Social Psychology, 53*, 383–390.

Lord, M. A. (1997). Leisure's role in enhancing social competencies of individuals with developmental disabilities. *Parks & Recreation, 32*(4), 35–39.

Lovell, T., Dattilo, J., and Jekubovich, N. (1996). Effects of leisure education on individuals aging with disabilities. *Activities, Adaptations and Aging, 21*(2), 37–58.

Mahon, M. J. (1994). The use of self-control techniques to facilitate self-determination skills during leisure in adolescents and young adults with mild and moderate mental retardation. *Therapeutic Recreation Journal, 28*(2), 58–72.

Mahon, M. J. and Bullock, C. C. (1992). Teaching adolescents with mild mental retardation to make decisions in leisure through the use of self-control techniques. *Therapeutic Recreation Journal, 26*(1), 9–26.

Mannell, R. C. and Kleiber, D. A. (1997). *A social psychology of leisure.* State College, PA: Venture Publishing, Inc.

Massimini, F. and Carli, M. (1988). Flow and biocultural evolution. In M. Csik-szentmihalyi and I. Csikszentmihalyi (Eds.), *Optimal experience: Psychological studies of flow in consciousness* (pp. 266–287). Melbourne, Australia: Cambridge University Press.

Massimini, F., Csikszentmihalyi, M., and Delle Fave, A. (1988). Flow and biocultural evolution. In M. Csikszentmihalyi and I. Csikszentmihalyi (Eds.), *Optimal experience: Psychological studies of flow in consciousness* (pp. 60–81). Melbourne, Australia: Cambridge University Press.

Middleton, R. A. and Byrd, E. K. (1996). Psychosocial factors and hospital readmission status of older persons with cardiovascular disease. *Journal of Applied Rehabilitation Counseling, 27*(4), 3–10.

Moes, D. R. (1998). Integrating choice-making opportunities within teacher-assigned academic tasks to facilitate the performance of children with autism. *Journal of the Association for Persons with Severe Handicaps, 23*, 319–328.

Paxton, S. J., Browning, C. J., and O'Connell, G. (1997). Predictors of exercise program participation in older women. *Psychology and Health, 12*(4), 543–552.

Pumpian, I. (1996). Foreword. In D. J. Sands and M. L. Wehmeyer, (Eds.), *Self-determination across the life span: Independence and choice for people with disabilities*. Baltimore, MD: Paul H. Brookes.

Ross, C. D. and Van den Haag, E. (1957). *The fabric of society*. New York, NY: Harcourt Brace Jovanovich.

Sands, D. J. and Doll, B. (1996). Fostering self-determination is a developmental task. *Journal of Special Education, 30*(1), 58–76.

Sands, D. J. and Wehmeyer, M. L. (1996). *Self-determination across the life span: Independence and choice for people with disabilities*. Baltimore, MD: Paul H. Brookes.

Sansone, C. (1986). A question of competence: The effects of competence and task feedback on recreation behavior. *Journal of Leisure Research, 16*, 34–50.

Searle, M., Mahon, M., Iso-Ahola, S., Sdrolias, H., and Van Dyck, J. (1995). Enhancing a sense of independence and psychological well-being among the elderly: A field experiment. *Journal of Leisure Research, 27*(2), 107–124.

Sigafoos, J. (1998). Choice making and personal selection strategies. In J. K. Luiselli and M. J. Cameron (Eds.), *Antecedent control: Innovative approaches to behavioral support* (pp. 187–221). Baltimore, MD: Paul H. Brookes.

Stancliffe, R. J., Abery, B. H., Springborg, H., and Elkin, S. (2000). Substitute decision-making and personal control: Implications for self-determination. *Mental Retardation, 38*(4), 407–421.

Therapeutic recreation: Responding to the challenges of health care reform. (n.d.). American Therapeutic Recreation Association and National Therapeutic Recreation Society.

Wagner, B. (1999). Visions for the new millennium II: Self-determination and choice. *AAMR News & Notes, 12*(4), 3.

Wehmeyer, M. L. (1996). Self-determination as an educational-outcome: Why is it important to children, youth and adults with disabilities? In D. J. Sands and M. L. Wehmeyer (Eds.), *Self-determination across the life span: Independence and choice for people with disabilities* (pp. 15–34). Baltimore, MD: Paul H. Brookes.

Wehmeyer, M. L. (1998). Self-determination and individuals with significant disabilities: Examining meanings and misinterpretations. *Journal of the Association for Persons with Severe Handicaps, 23*(1), 5–16.

Wehmeyer, M. L., Agran, M., and Hughes, C. (1998). *Teaching self-determination to students with disabilities.* Baltimore, MD: Paul H. Brookes.

Wehmeyer, M. L. and Bolding, N. (1999). Self-determination across living and working environments: A matched-samples of adults with mental retardation. *Mental Retardation, 37*(5), 353–363.

Wehmeyer, M. L., Palmer, S. B., Agran, M., Mithaug, D. E., and Martin, J. E. (2000). Promoting causal agency: The self-determined learning model of instruction. *Exceptional Children, 66*(4), 439–453.

Wehmeyer, M. L. and Schwartz, M. (1998). The relationship between self-determination and quality of life of adults with mental retardation. *Education and Training in Mental Retardation and Developmental Disabilities, 33*(1), 3–12.

Wehmeyer, M. L. and Schwartz, M. (1997). Self-determination and positive adult outcomes: A follow-up study of youth with mental retardation or learning disabilities. *Exceptional Children, 63*(2), 245–255.

Williams, R. and Dattilo, J. (1997). Effects of a leisure education on self-determination, social interaction, and positive affect of young adults with mental retardation. *Therapeutic Recreation Journal, 31*, 244–258.

Chapter 5

Control
A Major Element in
Therapeutic Recreation

David R. Austin, Ph.D., CTRS, FALS

Control is a key component within therapeutic recreation. Austin has written extensively about the place of control in therapeutic recreation in his textbooks (e.g., Austin, 1999; Austin, 2001a). Control is also a central concept in his Health Protection/Health Promotion Model of practice (Austin, 1998). Yet, within Austin's writings, or the therapeutic recreation literature in general, the concept of control has not received the type of through examination that this chapter attempts to provide.

Recreation therapists have traditionally attempted to allow as much control as possible to remain with their clients. An underlying assumption in the delivery of therapeutic recreation services is that:

> The client plays as large a role as possible in the therapeutic recreation process. The therapeutic recreation specialist attempts to allow as much control as is reasonable to remain with the client. (Austin, 2001b, p. 46)

Characteristic of therapeutic recreation is the provision of opportunities for clients to choose the activities in which they participate and to have a meaningful role in affecting the outcomes of the activities (Austin, 2001b, p. 53). Following an examination of the major therapeutic recreation practice models (i.e., Health Protection/Health Promotion Model, Leisure Ability Model, and Therapeutic Recreation Outcome Model), Bullock and Mahon (1997) concluded that all shared the concept of decreasing the therapist's control while increasing the client's sense of freedom and self-determination.

It is clear that the provision of control is a central element in therapeutic recreation practice. This is not to say that complete control should be offered by recreation therapists to all clients at all times. A "one size fits all" approach to individual clients simply does not work.

Psychologist Martin Ford (1992) has suggested limiting client control and assuming direct control by the therapist may be called for at times when there is an urgent matter, such as preventing destructive behavior on the part of the client. Therapeutic recreation theorists Shank and Kinney (1987) have indicated that some have urged against recreation therapists taking any control from clients. Shank and Kinney have argued convincingly, however, that at times clients may not be ready to exercise control and, in fact, control for them can be detrimental, producing stress and anxiety.

Thus, while client control is a critical concept within therapeutic recreation, complete client control may not always be therapeutic. Instead, an inappropriate level of control may lead to client distress. The concept of the provision of appropriate levels of client control is discussed in more depth later in this chapter.

Control Defined

Just what does it mean to have control? Control involves the idea that we have the ability to regulate our inner environment (i.e., ourselves and our emotions) and our outer environment (i.e., the environment in which we live). Psychologist Martin Seligman had the following to say about the concept of control: "Personal control means the ability to change things by one's voluntary actions; it is the opposite of helplessness" (1990, p. 6). Psychologists Aronson, Wilson, and Akert have defined perceived control as "the belief that we can influence our environment in ways that determine whether we experience positive or negative outcomes" (1999, p. 555). Wallston, Wallston, Smith, and Dobbins defined control as "the belief that one can determine one's own internal states and behavior, influence one's environment, and/or bring about desired outcomes" (1987, p. 5). In this chapter the terms personal control and perceived control are used synonymously because personal control is derived from having a perception, or belief, of being in control.

Perceptions of control then have to do with individuals' feelings of power over what happens to them. Possessing control is the opposite of having feelings of being at the mercy of external forces. As stated by Shapiro, Schwartz, and Astin:

> There are two self-directed pathways by which individuals can gain and maintain a sense of control: controlling oneself or exerting control over the environment. (1996, p. 1219)

Another term, locus of control, is sometimes employed in the literature to describe people's perceptions of control. *Locus of control* has been defined as:

> The extent to which people perceive their lives as internally controllable by their own efforts and actions or as externally controlled by chance or outside forces. (Myers, 1996, p. 147)

In short, control is a cognitive process that involves people's beliefs about being able to determine what will occur in terms of outcomes resulting from their efforts. As we shall learn, the literature suggests that control is something that generally we human beings wish to retain.

Importance of Control in Our Lives

Psychology literature suggests that people seem to have a motive to be in control of their lives. This motive is so prevalent today that Seligman has proclaimed this "the age of personal control" (1990, p. 282). The notion that human beings strive for control over themselves and their environments is deeply rooted in our Western culture (Grzdlak, 1985). In fact, Western cultures, including the United States, strongly emphasize and value control (Weisz, Rothbaum & Blackburn, 1984). Glasser (1998), the originator of Choice Theory, has stated that we humans are "always trying to choose to behave in a way that gives us *the most effective control over our lives.*" Shapiro and Astin (1998), in their book *Control Therapy*, have written: "The human quest for control is one of the major driving forces behind all human action, behavior, and thought." They go on to state:

> In addition to the desire for control over the external environment, there is also desire for control over one's choices, thoughts, and emotions (i.e., self-determination). (p. 25)

Control theorists, such as Bandura (self-efficacy theory; 1977) and Seligman (learned helplessness; 1975), have assumed that people generally desire control and are motivated to strive toward maintaining or increasing control (Manstead & Hewstone, 1996). In his extensive book on personal control, Burger (1992) has suggested that there are individual personality differences in the desire for control with some seeking more control than others. Yet, following his discussion of personal control, Burger concluded: "Nonetheless, all things being equal, people probably prefer exercising control over, not exercising control" (p. 9).

Importance of Control in Mental and Physical Health

As a result of their exhaustive review of the control literature, Shapiro, Schwartz, and Astin concluded:

> Hundreds of studies and dozens of books have been devoted to the theory, research, and applications of a variety of personal control strategies to numerous healthcare and psychotherapeutic concerns. This body of work has demonstrated that people's ability to gain and maintain a sense of control is essential for their evolutionary survival, ...a central element in psychotherapy and mental health, ...and important to their physical health. (1996, p. 1213)

There is a great deal of literature to suggest that control plays a significant role in people's physical and mental health. As Shapiro and Astin have written:

> Research has shown the importance of control as a critical variable in physical and mental health. Studies indicate that a sense of control can positively affect our immune system and increase our resistance to the negative effects of stress, enhance psychological well-being, and even increase longevity. (1998, p. ix)

Mental well-being has typically been defined by the level of control individuals feel they have internally (i.e., over their thoughts and feelings) and externally (i.e., over their behavior). Expressions such as "I'm losing control" or "my life is out-of-control" are typical of mental health clients initially seeking professional help. Clinical areas where control is a particularly prominent issue include stress and anxiety disorders, drug and alcohol addictions, eating disorders, borderline personality disorders, and depression. A primary role of therapists is to assist these clients to become aware of those things that are affecting them and to teach them how to gain control over those things.

Psychologically "normal" individuals tend to possess a higher level of perceived control than do clinical populations. These so-called normal individuals have a tendency to overestimate the level of perceived control they have over situations. They believe they have more abilities than they actually possess and remain optimistic about meeting challenges. Because of this they tend to protect their perceptions of control by interpreting outcomes as temporary, situational, or as something that commonly happens to people.

In addition to being positively associated with mental health, a sense of control is also related to adaptation to physical disorders. Researchers have found that persons who believe they can take action to deal with their disorders make more positive psychological adaptations to their illnesses than those who do not hold such views. Less optimistic individuals, who lack a sense of control, have been found to develop feelings of anxiety and depression. Researchers have even found that a sense of control can have a moderating effect on potentially life-threatening diseases. Those with a low sense of control, with ensuing feelings of helplessness, succumbed to their illnesses and higher probability of death than those with higher perceived control (Shapiro, Schwartz & Astin, 1996).

In a now classic study, Langer and Rodin (1976) conducted an experiment involving residents of a nursing home. With one group of residents (i.e., treatment group) the researchers emphasized their responsibilities for themselves and their right to make decisions. This group was then given the opportunity to make relatively minor decisions, such as deciding on which night to view a movie or deciding if they wished to take care of a plant they were given. With the comparison group personal responsibilities and decision making were not focused on. This group got to see the movie but was given no choice as to when they would see it. They too received a plant, but were told that the nurses would take care of it. Having the small measure of control had a profound impact on the treatment group. Those in this group became more active, were happier and healthier, and actually had lower morality rates than the residents in the comparison group. Producing a heightened sense of control in these nursing home residents had significant psychological and physical benefits. Langer and Rodin's research is a dramatic example of the type of effect properly conducted recreation therapy programs, which emphasize control, can have on individuals.

Opportunities for Control in Therapeutic Recreation and Leisure

Austin (1999) wrote about the lack of control that too often accompanies clients in healthcare settings. In many healthcare environments clients experience condescending and paternalistic behaviors from staff. A sense of mystification also may be a part of the healthcare process. In short, control is frequently taken away from clients receiving healthcare. Therapeutic recreation is a means to counter this type of atmosphere.

Austin wrote about this positive aspect of therapeutic recreation:

> Therapeutic recreation represents the antithesis of the controlling environment often encountered in healthcare facilities. In recreation, clients are allowed choice and control. They work in close partnership with therapeutic recreation specialists in choosing treatment programs that will meet their needs. There is a mutual participation by clients and therapeutic recreation specialists. Through this relationship, clients learn to select recreation experiences that help them to achieve better health. (1999, pp. 158–159)

Recreation enables clients to restore health. It is the means by which mental and physical health are protected when threatened. Clients regain their equilibrium or return to what is normal for them through the restorative or re-creative power of recreation. Once health is restored through recreation, clients go beyond stabilizing themselves and move into a growth mode motivated by the tendency to become self-actualized. Leisure offers a means to achieve self-fulfillment.

Perhaps at no times in our lives do we have the personal control that is experienced during leisure. When we are in the midst of a leisure experience, we possess a profound sense of control. In fact, control is a central defining feature of leisure. This is obvious in Caldwell and Smith's definition of leisure. They wrote:

> Empirical and qualitative research suggests that activities or experiences that are pursued voluntarily (alone or with others), in which the person feels in control of the situation, in which the person's skills are appropriately matched with a challenge, and which are enjoyable, are leisure experiences. (1988, p. S45)

Shank and Kinney have likewise emphasized the critical role of control in leisure when they wrote that "leisure is directly tied to the concepts of freedom of choice and personal control" (1987, p. 67). Leading leisure scholars (e.g., Iso-Ahola, 1980; Mannell & Kleiber, 1997) have similarly identified freedom of choice and personal control as a necessary elements in the leisure experience. Of course, freedom and control are intertwined. As Rubin and McNeil have explained: "The need for control is very closely associated with the need for freedom—that is, to be free from the controls and injunctions of other people" (1983, p. 219).

It should be clear that opportunities to exercise personal control are offered through therapeutic recreation in general, and leisure experiences in particular. An assumption that underlies the entire therapeutic recreation process is that recreation therapists allow as much control as possible to remain with their clients (Austin, 2001a).

When Control Is Threatened

Anecdotal records and research have shown that a sense of uncontrollability can develop when individuals do not believe they can control adverse life situations. When individuals repeatedly attempt to cope with adversity but come up short, they may begin to believe that no matter what they do they cannot succeed and the situation is futile. At this point they may lack a sense of control and feel helpless. *Learned helplessness* is the term that has been given to this perceived lack of control over events (Seligman, 1975). As Austin has explained:

> Feelings of helplessness lead to the development of apathy, depression, and withdrawal that, in extreme cases, may ultimately end in death due to perceived uncontrollability over a stressful environment. (1999, p. 376)

Of course, individuals do not always experience helplessness when control is threatened. Instead, they may experience reactance. *Reactance* is the opposite of giving up. When threats to freedom and control occur, a person may become motivated to regain control over the situation. This motivation is termed reactance. People experiencing reactance often successfully cope with the adversity they face and even become stronger and more confident of their abilities as a result. However, if they are not successful in restoring their freedom, they may weaken their reactions. Eventually they may become frustrated, give up, become depressed, and experience learned helplessness (Austin, 1999).

Generally then it is good for most individuals to actively seek and to have a sense of control. The more control people have the better. It should be mentioned, however, that occasionally negative outcomes do result from having a sense of control. This occurs when their is a mismatch between the amount of control available to individuals in their environments and certain personality variables. For example, because of their personalities (e.g., with a low desire for control, high external locus of control, or feelings of low sense of competence or self-efficacy) some individuals do not want increased control.

A mismatch may also occur when those with a high need for control, a strong belief in their ability to gain control, or high sense of competency (i.e., high self-efficacy) do not have an opportunity to exert active control. Or it may be that exerting control can have negative consequences (Shapiro, Schwartz & Astin, 1996). Shapiro, Schwartz, and Astin have also indicated negative consequences may occur when those patients who cannot control their situations have a belief in personal control. For instance, they may feel anxiety and self-blame if their cancer returns when, in actuality, they can do nothing to fight the recurrence of the disease. Thus with some persons in particular instances active personal control is not something that is desired. As Shapiro, Schwartz, and Astin have explained:

> Active attempts at mastery are most effective when events are actually controllable. When events are beyond an individual's personal control, problems may be exacerbated by persistent efforts at control, a strong sense of self-efficacy, or a high desire for control. (1996, p. 1216)

Thus, while in most instances people wish to maintain and gain personal control, there are occasions when it may not be desirable to do so. Therapists must remain cognizant that while facilitating control in clients who have had their sense of control threatened is generally an outcome that should be pursued, for some individuals, gains in control can actually have negative consequences.

Dynamics of Demoralization

Demoralization involves a severe lack of control. Persons who are demoralized "feel powerless to change the situation or themselves, and cannot extricate themselves from their predicament" (Frank & Frank, 1991, p. 35). To be demoralized is to feel disheartened and bewildered—without hope for the future.

How many of us have not felt demoralized at one time or another over the course of our lives? There are many instances when we may have experienced demoralization. As a child, feelings of demoralization may arise from simply not being able to perform a simple task, such as learning to tie one's shoes. As a teen, demoralization may occur when he or she is not accepted by a group of peers. Young adults may become demoralized by an "impossible" college course, such as physics, chemistry, or anatomy. Adults may become demoralized when they do not get the job they desired or a promotion they worked for.

While most of us can easily relate to these instances of demoralization, these examples pale in comparison with those faced by many individuals. Those who have suffered a great psychological loss, such as the death of a loved one, or who have become permanently disabled due to an accident, know the real meaning of demoralization. These individuals often experience feelings of powerlessness with an ensuing loss of hope. Their very futures may seem dashed by an unkind act of fate.

It is at times such as these that individuals think they cannot cope with adversity. They do not believe they have the adaptive mechanisms to stand up to their ill fortune. Commonly anxiety results as these individuals experience a sense of diminished control. Unhappily, some individuals experience a history of lack of control, leaving them vulnerable to chronic anxiety and negative emotions. These are persons who have undergone a number of early exposures to uncontrollable events, exposures that have fostered the perception that things in their environments are out of their control (Chorpita & Barlow, 1998).

Frank and Frank (1991) have explained that, in general, when a person knows how to deal with a stressful situation or when the encountered stress is clearly defined and time limited (e.g., broken leg), stress can be managed. Other stressors, however, are beyond our experiences, may lack clear solutions, and often go on indefinitely. Chronic illness is a prime example of this type of stressor.

Perhaps the majority of clients seen by recreation therapists have chronic disorders, and thus, are subject to the possibility of experiencing feelings of demoralization when dealing with their chronic conditions. Of course, other clients served by recreation therapists face more acute problems, such as dealing with a psychological loss or becoming disabled. They, too, may experience demoralization due to the nature of the resulting stress. In short, demoralization is a common characteristic of clients seen by recreation therapists.

Characteristics of Demoralization

Whether acute or chronic, persons who experience demoralization often think that they are the only ones who have been faced their dilemma and, therefore, no one can truly understand them or their situation. Those with severe demoralization further may feel that they are emotionally out of control. They do not think they can control even their own feelings and emotions. Therefore they fear that they are losing control over themselves and worry they may "go crazy." Frank and Frank have described those demoralized individuals who seek psychiatric help.

> Metaphorically, the [severely] demoralized person cowers in a spatiotemporal corner. Thus, he or she clings to a small round of habitual activities, avoids novelty and challenge, and fears making long-term plans. The state of demoralization, in short, is one of hopelessness, helplessness, and isolation in which the person is preoccupied with merely trying to survive. (1991, p. 35)

When seen by therapists, such demoralized individuals may express symptoms commonly associated with demoralization, such as anxiety and depression. Anger and resentment are other symptoms that sometimes accompany demoralization. At the other extreme may be symptoms that are not caused by demoralization but may bring about feelings of demoralization, such as the cognitive deterioration experienced by individuals with Alzheimer's disease or mood swings experienced by those with bipolar disorders. Thus demoralization may be a cause or a consequence of presenting symptoms. In any case, it is important to acknowledge that people who become clients of recreation therapists and other helping professionals often do so because they cannot adequately cope with stressors, feel the situation is beyond their control, and experience a sense of demoralization as a result (Frank & Frank, 1991).

Therapeutic Approaches

There appear to be two seemingly opposite approaches to deal with a decreased sense of control. One is to yield to it. This involves giving in to the stressor and learning to cope with associated feelings of stress. The other is to strive to regain a sense of control (Shapiro, Schwartz & Astin, 1996). Of course, making the choice to yield to the stressor may be interpreted as a means to assuming control because the individual has made a conscious decision to do so.

The first strategy of yielding may work best when there are no reasonable opportunities for control. In this instance the individual may be able to understand and accept what is not within his or her personal control, to acknowledge a lack of direct control over the stressor, and to learn to accommodate to the stress. This strategy would seem to best apply to situations in which there are threats to physical health, such as when patients have to deal with pain.

Recreation therapists can assist clients to employ yielding strategies through techniques such as relaxation training, listening to music, aromatherapy, autogenic training, guided imagery, or meditation. All these techniques allow clients to obtain a sense of calmness and relaxation. Another technique is to use recreation as an distraction or diversion. As Kleiber stated, "Activities are adopted for their power to distract from either feelings of physical pain or associated psychological distress" (1999, p. 125). The use of relaxation and escape techniques in which persons avoid pain and stress may be perceived as means to meet the lower-level physiological and safety needs proposed by Maslow's hierarchy of needs (Shapiro, Schwartz & Astin, 1996).

The second approach is helping clients to strive to regain a sense of control. This approach is commonly taken with clients experiencing the feeling of demoralization discussed earlier. Psychologists (e.g., Aronson, Wilson & Akert; 1999: Frank & Frank, 1991; Horowitz & Bordens, 1995; Shapiro, Schwartz & Astin, 1996) argued that therapists may help clients to gain and maintain feelings of control through cognitive processing and direct experiences. Establishing a sense of control is seen as a key to reducing or removing the feeling of demoralization. Closely related to a sense of control are self-efficacy, social support, mood, and optimism.

Self-Efficacy

Individuals who have a sense of control believe that they can cope with threatening occurrences. Horowitz and Borders (1995) explained: "These individuals usually express feelings of *self-efficacy*—the notion that one can do what one sets out to do." They went on to state:

> People who have strong feelings of self-efficacy are likely
> to respond to stress by throwing more and more effort and
> resources into coping with threats. (p. 652)

Thus individuals' expectations of their capacities and abilities determine how willing they are to confront their problems and how much effort they will put into meeting their problems. Research has shown that individuals' levels of self-efficacy have been found to correlate with their efforts to lose weight, exercise regularly, and benefit from treatment and rehabilitation programs (Bandura, 1997). Thus it makes sense for therapists to employ the technique of assisting their clients to heighten their feelings of self-efficacy to positively affect their sense of control.

But just how do persons increase their feelings of self-efficacy? Bandura (1986) has discussed four means to increase perceived self-efficacy. The first way to build efficacy expectations is for individuals to be able to experience successful performances which they attribute to internal, stable, global, and controllable factors (Leary & Miller, 1986). This technique of providing direct experiences is the most likely one to be employed by recreation therapists with clients. By successfully participating in activities, clients experience mastery that produces a sense of personal accomplishment. Of course, recreation therapists need to provide feedback to clients that will reinforce client feelings of success. Additionally, therapists' attributional statements to clients need to emphasize that it takes skill to succeed at the activity being performed and that the clients possess the required abilities. The second means to enhance self-efficacy is through vicarious experiences. Observing others, who are like us, enjoying success may increase feelings of self-efficacy. The third means is verbal persuasion. The more confident we are in those attempting to persuade us of our capabilities, the more likely we are to believe them and increase feelings of self-efficacy. The final means to increasing self-efficacy is reducing levels of anxiety and arousal that signal fear about our abilities. Thus lowering anxiety and arousal may increase feelings of self-efficacy.

Social Support

Stressors make demands on individuals that exceed their resources. A supportive environment can serve as a resource to clients dealing with stress and striving to retain or regain a sense of control. Clients need encouragement, and socially supportive environments provide them with the perception that others are available to listen to them, to care about them, to comfort them, to offer advice and information, and, in general, to be responsive to their needs. Social support serves as a buffer against stress by protecting clients from stressful events and by enhancing coping abilities by reassuring clients that they have the support they need to handle situations they face. Social support may also produce a direct effect on client well-being by fulfilling basic social needs. Aronson and his colleagues have stated that "when we believe that we have someone to lean on, we can deal better with life's problems" (1999, p. 570). It might be said that such a belief bolsters the individual's sense of control.

Some of the strongest statements in the literature on social support, control, and health have been made by Haften, Karren, Frandsen, and Smith in their book *Mind/Body Health: The Effects of Attitudes, Emotions, and Relationships* (1996). These authors have indicated that social support protects health and well-being by producing "positive feelings and a sense of self-esteem, stability, and control over one's environment." They have gone on to state that literature exists to suggest:

> A strong social network and healthy social ties gradually lead to a greater, more generalized sense of control. An impressive array of studies has shown that a sense of control improves and protects health, whereas a feeling of little control can have serious health consequences. (1996, p. 264)

Therapists may supply "surrogate" support by replacing those who constitute the client's normal support network. Such professional support is typically unidirectional, as therapists provide support but do not expect it back in return. Therapists also help clients to build and maintain their social support networks of friends and family. Often recreation is used as a means to the end of forming and maintaining informal client support systems (Aronson, Wilson & Akert, 1999; Stewart, 1993).

Mood

Most therapeutic recreation professionals and students know from their personal experiences that recreation and leisure experiences produce positive moods. The professional literature likewise supports the notion that recreation and leisure bring about positive changes in mood (Hull, 1990). Positive mood states have been found to affect feelings of control (Hull, 1990). For example, researchers Salovery and Birnbaum (1989) found that a positive mood increased their subjects' beliefs that they could alleviate their symptoms. Perhaps the most well-known case of mood providing a sense of control over an illness has been that of the late magazine publisher Norman Cousins (1979; 1983). While hospitalized, Cousins used the laughter he enjoyed while watching humorous films to overcome the painful inflammation of his spine and joints. Two psychologists, Horowitz and Bordens (1995) have written that:

> Cousins used laughter as a metaphor, a figure of speech, for all those emotions involved in hope, faith, and determination that affect people's perception of stress and of their ability to cope.

They went on to state:

> Note that the technique Cousins used permitted him to feel he had control over his illness and could be effective in doing something about it. (p. 654)

Optimism

Horowitz and Bordens (1995) have described optimism as "the inclination to anticipate the most favorable outcomes for events" (pp. 657–58). In their book titled *Health and Optimism*, Peterson and Bossio explained:

> Optimism or pessimism refers to someone's expectation of what the future holds. The optimist expects things to work out for the best; the pessimist, just the contrary. (1991, p. 9)

When people experience uncontrollable negative events in their lives they develop a perceived lack of control, which ultimately leads them to feel helpless or experience learned helplessness (Seligman, 1990). They become depressed and pessimistic. But persons who are given choices can develop a sense of control that can lead them toward what Seligman termed *learned optimism*. A classic example of this happening was Langer and Rodin's (1976) previously cited study where one group of nursing home residents was given active choices while members of another group were treated as passive recipients of care (similar to what is perhaps too typical in nursing homes). Those residents who were given opportunities for self-determination became much more active and enjoyed significant health gains when compared to the other group. One could say that they became more optimistic in their approach to life.

Philosophy and Principles of Practice

Control is something that most of us usually desire in our lives. There are many times when those who become clients in healthcare settings encounter threats to their sense of control. The threat may come from typical health-care environments that permit little control on the part of the client, or threat to control may result from adverse life situations. Clients dealing with severe psychological stress, disabilities, or chronic health conditions are vulnerable to demoralization. There are no easy formulas to apply in assisting clients who have encountered threats to their sense of control. Yet, there are some general principles that may prove to be effective in helping clients retain or regain control.

Portray an Optimistic Attitude That Clients' Sense of Control Is Changeable

Despite clients' feelings of demoralization and helplessness, recreation therapists must focus on the fact that their clients can experience change in their sense of control. Part of the task of the recreation therapist is to help clients understand that they can overcome self-criticism and negative beliefs and feelings. Clients need to find hope within the treatment or rehabilitation setting. It is important to create an optimistic atmosphere. Recreation therapists who exude optimistic perspectives can contribute greatly to establishing such an atmosphere.

Offer the Antithesis of a Controlling Environment

Personnel who exhibit condescending and paternalistic behaviors are too often found in healthcare facilities. In such environments, where staff are regularly doing things *to* or *for* clients, clients suffer from a lack of control. In contrast, recreation therapists do things *with* clients. There is a mutual partnership that represents the therapeutic relationship between recreation therapists and their clients. A primary approach in therapeutic recreation is to support autonomy on the part of clients. Rather than remove control from clients, recreation therapists strive to leave as much control as possible with their clients by allowing them choices in recreation and leisure. Recreation therapists work in close partnership with clients to assist them in choosing programs and activities that will meet their needs. As a result of this process, clients learn to select recreation experiences that help them to reach better health. Once engaged in true leisure (i.e., intrinsically motivated), clients experience a profound sense of control. At that point there is little or no need for the assistance of a recreation therapist.

Assess the Client's Readiness for Assuming Control

While most of us desire control most of the time, there may be occasions when clients will not be ready or willing to assume control. Due to the circumstances they are in (e.g., highly stressful, anxiety creating) or disposition (e.g., those with a low desire for control), clients simply may not be ready to immediately assume control. Increasing these clients' sense of control may be a slow process. In Austin's Health Protection/Health Promotion Model, he provides for a period of "prescriptive activities" where client choice is limited. He has written:

> When illness is initially encountered, people often become self-absorbed. They withdraw from their normal life activities and experience a loss of control over their lives. (1999, p. 156)

At times such as this, clients are not ready to assume responsibility for self-directed recreation or leisure experiences. Such clients must be engaged in life by the recreation therapist in order to combat demoralization and to become energized so that they can begin to take action to restore their health. This is done by placing clients in situations in which they may begin to experience mastery and enjoyment. It is important that the recreation therapist assess each client to determine the level of control he or she is able to assume, and whether he or she needs prescriptive activities or is ready for recreation participation or leisure opportunities.

Clients May Need to Employ Yielding Strategies

There may be occasions where there are no reasonable opportunities for clients to regain a sense of control—at least not immediately. In these instances it is a step forward for clients to understand and accept what they cannot directly control. An example is pain from a physical illness or disorder. Rather than fight for control, a yielding strategy may be more helpful for clients at this time. One approach may be to escape into recreation. When engaged in a fulfilling recreation activity, clients may be able to be distracted from the pain they have been experiencing. At the same time, this escape may provide them opportunities to get away from their discomfort so that they may "regroup" in order to strive for control once more. Other techniques may produce a calming and relaxing effect when clients are under severe stress. Participation in activities, such as relaxation training, autogenic training, guided imagery, yoga or meditation, may result in calmness and relaxation. This yielding strategy may be perceived as a means to gain *secondary control*. In secondary control, clients are able to gain a type of control "by accommodating to existing realities and maximizing satisfaction or goodness of fit with things as they are" (Wallston, 2001).

Increase Feelings of Self-Efficacy through Successes in Recreation

A major approach to clients who feel demoralized is to allow them opportunities to enjoy successes during their recreation participation. When clients are able to experience mastery, they have feelings of self-accomplishment which lead them toward increases in self-efficacy. Building self-efficacy is a major means for therapeutic recreation clients to regain their sense of control. It is important that recreation therapists offer clients feedback that will build feelings of self-efficacy. Successful efforts should be reinforced with statements that emphasize the clients' successes and their level of abilities so that clients realize their successes and attribute them to their own skills. In addition to direct experiences, recreation therapists can use vicarious experiences by permitting clients to see others similar to themselves experience success. Recreation therapists can also use verbal persuasion to convince clients that they have the abilities to be successful in meeting challenges. Finally, recreation therapists can use recreation activities that have a calming effect to assist clients to reduce feelings of anxiety and arousal that signal fear of failure. While vicarious experiences, verbal persuasion, and the reduction of anxiety and arousal can increase perceived control by increasing self-efficacy, it is the provision of direct experiences for mastery and success that offers, perhaps, the most potent intervention that can be delivered by recreation therapists to help clients to regain a sense of control.

Build on Client Strengths

Seligman reminded us of the importance of building on client strengths by writing:

> We need practitioners to recognize that much of the best work they do is amplifying the strengths rather than repairing their patients' weaknesses. (1998, p. 2)

Building on client strengths is a closely related principle to that of providing client opportunities for direct experiences to enhance feelings of self-efficacy. A first step in the therapeutic recreation process is assessment. A component of assessment is to analyze strengths possessed by the client. While client skills and abilities are the strengths that may first come to mind, other indirect strengths, such as support from friends or family, should be assessed as well. Once skills and abilities are identified, the recreation therapist can use these as means for clients to achieve mastery and success experiences so they may increase self-efficacy. Support from friends and family relate to the next principle of helping clients to obtain and build social support.

Offer Opportunities to Obtain and Build Social Support

As previously discussed, social support can provide clients with comfort and relief from stress, which may assist clients to retain or regain personal control. Recreation therapists can offer direct social support to clients by serving as "professional friends." In addition, recreation therapists can construct opportunities to draw together clients' natural social support systems of family and friends. Finally, recreation therapists can help clients to expand their social support systems by developing social and recreational skills that will attract and maintain friendships that offer the potential for social support.

Provide Opportunities for Mood Enhancement

It is widely known that recreation and leisure experiences can produce positive moods. In turn, mood enhancement tends to positively affect feelings of control. Thus it naturally follows that recreation therapists need to assist clients to identify and take part in activities that hold strong potential for enjoyment and result in positive moods.

Build Optimism in Clients

Clients who experience uncontrollable negative events often develop feelings of helplessness and pessimism. In contrast, those clients who maintain their optimism may reappraise events to see them as challenging rather than threatening. Clients who have opportunities for self-determination tend to become more optimistic. Optimistic perspectives, in turn, lead to having a sense of control. Therefore, it is important for recreation therapists to provide clients with choices in a fashion similar to the choices given to Langer and Rodin's (1976) nursing home residents who became more active and more healthy as a result. This can be done by offering clients meaningful choices both within and between activities.

Conclusion

One of the strongest motives for us as humans is to have control over our lives. A basic philosophical principle of therapeutic recreation is to allow clients as much control as possible, and to assist clients in their striving to retain or regain their sense of control. It is, therefore, critical that emerging recreation therapists understand the phenomenon of personal control and the role of their profession in helping clients to maintain a sense of control.

Reading Comprehension Questions

1. What does it mean to have control?

2. Do you agree that people have a motive to be in control of their lives? Do you possess a motive to be in control of your life?

3. What impact has control, or lack of control, been found to have on mental health? physical health?

4. Describe the Langer and Rodin (1976) study done with nursing home residents.

5. Do you agree that therapeutic recreation offers the antithesis of a controlling environment? Explain.

6. Why might leisure be seen as a time of great control?

7. Describe *learned helplessness*.

8. Are there ever times when negative outcomes may result from having a sense of control? Explain.

9. What occurs during periods of demoralization? Do therapeutic recreation clients experience demoralization? Explain.

10. Describe the concept of yielding strategies when dealing with control issues.

11. Describe *self-efficacy*. Explain how self-efficacy relates to control.

12. How does each of the following relate to control: social support, mood, optimism?

13. Examine the nine general principles provided in the chapter. Which do you personally believe are the most important? Do you disagree with any?

14. After reading this chapter, do you think control is important in therapeutic recreation?

References

Aronson, E., Wilson, T. D., and Akert, R. M. (1999). *Social psychology* (3rd ed.). New York, NY: Longman.

Austin, D. R. (2001a). Introduction and overview. In D. R. Austin and M. E. Crawford (Eds.), *Therapeutic recreation: An introduction* (3rd ed., pp. 45–56). Boston, MA: Allyn & Bacon.

Austin, D. R. (2001b). The therapeutic recreation process. In D. R. Austin and M. E. Crawford (Eds.), *Therapeutic recreation: An introduction* (3rd ed., pp. 1–21). Boston, MA: Allyn & Bacon.

Austin, D. R. (1999). *Therapeutic recreation: Processes and techniques* (4th ed.). Champaign, IL: Sagamore.

Austin, D. R. (1998). The Health Protection/Health Promotion Model. *Therapeutic Recreation Journal, 32*(2), 109–117.

Bandura, A. (1997). *Self-efficacy: The exercise of control.* New York, NY: W. H. Freeman and Co.

Bandura, A. (1986). *Social foundations of thought and action: A social cognitive theory.* Englewood Cliffs, NJ: Prentice Hall.

Bandura, A. (1977). Self-efficacy: Toward a unifying theory of behavioral change. *Psychological Review, 84*, 191–215.

Bullock, C. C. and Mahon, M. J. (1997). *Introduction to recreation services for people with disabilities: A person-centered approach.* Champaign, IL: Sagamore.

Burger, J. M. (1992). *Desire for control: Personality, social, and clinical perspectives.* New York, NY: Plenum Press.

Caldwell, L. L. and Smith, E. A. (1988). Leisure: An overlooked component of health promotion. *Canadian Journal of Public Health, 79*, S44–S48.

Chorpita, B. F. and Barlow, D. H. (1998). The development of anxiety: The role of control in early development. *Psychological Bulletin, 124*(1), 3–21.

Cousins, N. (1983). *The healing heart.* New York, NY: Avon Books.

Cousins, N. (1979). *Anatomy of an illness.* New York, NY: Bantam Books.

Ford, M. E. (1992). *Motivating humans: Goals, emotions, and personal agency beliefs.* Newbury Park, CA: Sage Publications.

Frank, J. D. and Frank, J. B. (1991). *Persuasion & healing: A comparative study of psychotherapy* (3rd ed.). Baltimore, MD: Johns Hopkins University Press.

Glasser, W. (1998). *Choice theory: A new psychology of personal freedom.* New York, NY: HarperCollins.

Grzdlak, J. L. (1985). Desire for control: Cognitive, emotional and behavioral consequences. In F. L. Denmark (Ed.), *Social/ecological psychological and the psychology of women.* New York, NY: Elsevier Science Publishing.

Hafen, B. Q., Karren, K. J., Frandsen, K. J., and Smith, N. L. (1996). *Mind/body health: The effects of attitudes, emotions, and relationships.* Boston, MA: Allyn & Bacon.

Horowitz, I. A. and Bordens, K. S. (1995). *Social psychology.* Mountain View, CA: Mayfield Publishing Co.

Hull, R. B. (1990). Mood as a product of leisure: Causes and consequences. *Journal of Leisure Research, 22,* 99–111.

Iso-Ahola, S. E. (1980). *The social psychology of leisure and recreation.* Dubuque, IA: Wm. C. Brown.

Kleiber, D. A. (1999). *Leisure experience and human development.* New York, NY: Basic Books.

Langer, E. J. and Rodin, J. (1976). The effects of choice and enhanced personal responsibility for the aged: A field experiment. *Journal of Personality and Social Psychology, 34,* 191–198.

Leary, M. R. and Miller, R. S. (1986). *Social psychology and dysfunctional behavior: Origins, diagnosis, and treatment.* New York, NY: Springer-Verlag.

Mannell, R. C. and Kleiber, D. A. (1997). *A social psychology of leisure.* State College, PA: Venture Publishing, Inc.

Manstead, A. S. R. and Hewstone, M. (Eds.). (1996). *The Blackwell encyclopedia of social psychology.* Malden, MA: Blackwell Publishers.

Myers, D. G. (1996). *Social psychology* (5th ed.). New York, NY: McGraw-Hill.

Peterson, C. and Bossio, L. M. (1991). *Health and optimism.* New York, NY: Free Press.

Rubin, A. and McNeil, E. B. (1983). *The psychology of being human* (3rd ed.). New York, NY: Harper & Row.

Salovey, P. and Birnbaum, D. (1989). Influence of mood on health-relevant cognitions. *Journal of Personality and Social Psychology, 57,* 539–551.

Seligman, M. E. P. (1998). Building human strength: Psychology's forgotten mission. *Monitor, 29*(1), 2.

Seligman, M. E. P. (1990). *Learned optimism.* New York, NY: Pocket Books.

Seligman, M. E. P. (1975). *Helplessness.* San Francisco, CA: Freeman.

Shank, J. and Kinney, T. (1987). On the neglect of clinical practice. In C. Sylvester, J. L. Hemingway, R. Howe-Murphy, K. Mobily, and P. A. Shank (Eds.), *Philosophy of therapeutic recreation: Ideas and issues* (pp 65–75). Alexandria, VA: National Recreation & Park Association.

Shapiro, D. H. and Astin, J. (1998). *Control therapy: An integrated approach to psychotherapy, health, and healing.* New York, NY: John Wiley & Sons.

Shapiro, D. H., Schwartz, C. E., and Astin, J. A. (1996). Controlling ourselves, controlling our world: Psychology's role in understanding positive and negative consequences of seeking and gaining control. *American Psychologist, 51*(12), 1213–1230.

Stewart, M. J. (1993). *Integrating social support in nursing*. Newbury Park, CA: Sage Publications.

Wallston, K. A. (2001). Conceptualization and operationalization of perceived control. In A. Baum, T. A. Revenson, and J. E. Singer (Eds.), *Handbook of health psychology* (pp. 49–58). Mahwah, NJ: Lawrence Erlbaum.

Wallston, K. A., Wallston, B. S., Smith, S., and Dobbins, C. (1987). Perceived control and health. *Current Psychological Research and Reviews, 6,* 5–25.

Weisz, J. R., Rothbaum, F. M., and Blackburn, T. C. (1984). Standing out and standing in: The psychology of control in America and Japan. *American Psychologist, 39*(9), 955–969.

Chapter 6

The Therapeutic Relationship

David R. Austin, Ph.D., CTRS, FALS

Therapeutic relationships are a critical element in the success of any therapeutic enterprise. Just how important is the therapeutic relationship? Frank
and Frank (1991) have stated the therapeutic relationship "is a necessary,
and perhaps often a sufficient, condition for improvement in any kind of
psychotherapy" (p. 40). According to the American Psychiatric Association
(APA), "research has indicated that 40% of the variance in outcome in all
forms of psychotherapy can be accounted for by the strength and quality of
the therapeutic alliance" (1993, p. 41). The APA publication goes on to state:

> More of the variance in outcome can be explained through
> the therapeutic alliance than any other variable, including
> school of therapy and specific technique used. Thus, facili-
> tating the development of a strong therapeutic alliance must
> be seen as the essential work for psychotherapy. (pp. 41–42)

Of course, therapeutic relationships transcend psychotherapy. Psychologists
Mitchell and Cornmack (1998) have exclaimed:

> Caring matters. When we are unwell or not coping—or fear
> we are—we know this in our bones. This natural desire to
> help and be helped underpins all systems of care across time,
> culture, and approach. (p. vii)

The lack of a therapeutic alliance will surely signal problems warn these
authors:

> If the quality of these human encounters begins to erode, then
> things crumble…even if interventions are appropriate and
> potent. (p. vii)

A strong working relationship is required for success in any helping enterprise (Hill & O'Brien, 1999). Therapeutic relationships are meaningful foundations for the helping enterprises of all types of professionals, such as counselors, nurses, social workers, and allied health professionals—including recreation therapists.

An understanding of the helping relationship has been termed "an essential ingredient" for the therapeutic use of self by recreation therapists (Austin, 1999, p. 4). According to Austin, the relationship between the therapist and client lies at the heart of most recreation therapy interventions. This relationship allows the client to use the recreation therapist for support and assistance, and the recreation therapist to better understand client needs, feelings, and motivations. Shared knowledge of the client's experiences with his or her illness or disorder provides a "special kind of bond" between the client and therapist (Lyons, Sullivan, Ritvo & Coyne, 1995, p. 128) and creates an atmosphere of caring and trust from which the therapist can apply his or her skills to meet client needs (Mitchell & Cormack, 1998).

What the Therapeutic Relationship Is *Not*

A therapeutic relationship does not involve a helpless client who turns to the all-knowing helping professional for wisdom and advise. A true therapeutic relationship between client and helper is *not* one in which the client becomes dependent on the helper to know what to do. Within a true therapeutic relationship the helper does *not* take power and responsibility away from the client. As Friedman (1992) has indicated, a relationship that involves the dominance of one over another leads to a power struggle with the resulting negative ramifications. She goes on to say that if both the helper and client perceive the helper as having power and the client as being helpless, a true therapeutic relationship will not exist, and healing and growth will not transpire.

Defining Therapeutic Relationships

What then is a therapeutic relationship? The answer to this question has been addressed by a number of authors.

Teyber (1992), a clinical psychologist, has emphasized that therapeutic relationships certainly develop far beyond the passive client relying on the therapist to be told what to do to solve a particular dilemma. He has written that:

> To be most effective, the therapist must…respond in a way
> that helps clients gain a greater sense of their own capabilities.
> Thus, the goal is not only to resolve specific situational prob-
> lems, but also to do so in a way that leaves clients with a
> greater sense of their own competence and mastery. (p. 27)

Within therapeutic relationships, like other types of relationships, the
parties involved acknowledge an emotional connection between them. The
helper and client form a common bond, joining together in order to achieve
an outcome or outcomes important to the client. This connection between
the helper and client is evident in the writings of Arnold and Boggs (1989).

Arnold and Boggs, both nurses, have discussed that

> it is the goal-directed, helping focus that characterizes a rela-
> tionship as "therapeutic." In this type of relationship, two
> separately existing individuals come together for the sole
> purpose of helping one of them, the client, achieve maximum
> levels of self-care functioning and well-being (p. 130).

Another nurse, Blattner (1981), has explained that the therapeutic relationship "is the *medium* through which all wellness goals are achieved" (p. 70).

Hill and O'Brien, writing from a counseling perspective, have written:

> Clients often come to helpers feeling that no one listens to
> them or cares about them. Helpers try to pay full attention to
> their clients and communicate an understanding of the client's
> feelings and experiences. They are empathic and nonjudg-
> mental, accepting their clients as they are, which allows the
> clients to feel safe enough to express their hurt and pain.
> Under this influence, clients begin to feel that if their helpers
> accept them for who they are, they must be okay….The
> clients slowly begin to build self-esteem, which is the foun-
> dation for change. They also feel safe to explore thoughts
> and feelings, come to new understandings, and make changes.
> (1999, p. 34)

It would appear that Hill and O'Brien, in reflecting an empathetic and nonjudgmental approach, have been heavily influenced by the work of eminent
psychologist Carl Rogers who regularly emphasized empathetic understanding, unconditional positive regard, and genuineness in his writings.
Rogers has defined the therapeutic relationship as follows:

> By this term I mean a relationship in which at least one of the
> parties has the intent of promoting the growth, development,

maturity, improved functioning, or improved coping with life of the other. The other, in this sense, may be one individual or a group. To put it another way, a helping relationship might be defined as one in which one of the participants intends that there should come about, in one or both parties, more appreciation of, more expression of, or more functional use of the latent inner resources of the individual. (1961, pp. 39–40)

From a counseling perspective, Okun has written that:

Helping relationships begin with a helper and a helpee meeting to focus attention on the helpee's concern. Thus, a helping relationship is distinct from other relationships in this focus on one party's concerns and issues. However, it shares ingredients common to all satisfactory relationships— ingredients such as trust, empathy, genuineness, concern and caring, respect, tolerance and acceptance, honesty, commitment to the relationship, and dependability. (1992, p. 22)

Austin, a recreation therapy educator, has echoed Okun's (1992) point that therapeutic relationships differ from social relationships or friendships. In friendships there exists a norm of reciprocity in which both parties give and take. Friendships do not last if one person is always giving and never receives. In contrast, in therapeutic relationships it is the role of the therapist to give help and it is the role of the client to receive help. Austin has stated, "The fundamental reality that the relationship exists to meet the needs of the client, not the helper, is basic to maintaining a healthy helping relationship" (1999, p. 219). He further explains:

Helping is *not* resolving problems or handling crises *for* the client. Instead, in a helping relationship we *assist* clients to meet pressing needs and then help further in their preparation for the future. (p. 219)

Within the definitions of the therapeutic relationship a number of prominent elements have been revealed. These include:

a. Therapeutic relationships do not involve resolving problems *for* clients but, instead, assisting clients to assume responsibility to cope with their problems and develop competence to meet future challenges.

b. The general goal is enhanced wellness, including improved functioning and well-being.

   c. A safe environment is provided in which the client may fully express thoughts and feelings.

   d. A common bond exists between the helper and client to achieve a goal-directed outcome. Within this relationship the sole focus is always on client needs.

   e. Among basic ingredients that help characterize the therapeutic relationship are empathetic understanding, a genuine approach, and nonjudgmental acceptance of clients.

Characteristics of the Therapeutic Relationship in Recreation Therapy

It would seem appropriate to more closely examine those things that characterize therapeutic relationships. Just what are the areas important to the success of therapeutic relationships in recreation therapy? By answering this question the reader can better understand effective helping and begin to evaluate his or her potential to enter into therapeutic relationships. Several authors have described desirable traits of helpers that characterize the therapeutic relationship including Arnold and Boggs (1989), Brammer (1979), Brill (1990), Carkhuff and Berenson (1967), Kottler (1990), Okun (1992), and Sundeen and colleagues (1994). It is from these sources that the following section is primarily based, drawing on those aspects most pertinent to the therapist–client relationship in recreation therapy. Areas emphasized as important for therapeutic relationships in recreation therapy are empathy, caring, having positive regard and respect for clients, hope, genuineness, and autonomy and mutuality.

Empathy

Helpers display empathy through their ability to accurately perceive their clients' feelings and then to communicate these perceptions clearly to their clients. Empathetic understanding involves getting into the client's world and then sharing those perceptions with the client. The helper not only has a valid understanding of what the client is going through but also is able to communicate this to the client. Brammer (1979, p. 37) has used the term *emotional mirror* to describe empathy. While we may primarily envision empathetic understandings being communicated verbally, they may be communicated nonverbally as well. For instance, a hug or a pat on the arm may well communicate empathy. At a minimum level, empathy involves responding accurately to the essence and strength of a client's feelings at times, and inaccurately at other times (Sundeen, Stuart, Rankin & Cohen, 1994). A high level of empathetic response is to communicate hidden meanings of which the client is not fully aware. Because the helper is able to be objective, he or she may be able to state hidden feelings that have been unknown to the client. For example, after discussion with the client a helper might reflect to the client: "So now you're frightened that if Bobby has pneumonia and is hospitalized, he will die, too—like your brother" (Arnold & Boggs, 1989, p. 184).

Empathy cannot be achieved by the recreation therapist simply wishing to be empathetic. It takes understanding and practice to develop skills in empathetic understanding. To begin, the therapist must communicate an openness to the client. This can be accomplished by demonstrating attending behaviors while assuming an open posture when listening to the client. Paying attention involves establishing good eye contact, leaning slightly forward toward the client without getting in the client's personal space, and using gestures such as head nods to encourage the client. The use of minimum verbal responses, such as "I see" and "mm-hmm," along with animated facial expression (e.g., occasional smiles), can further create the feeling that the therapist is listening to the client (Austin, 1999). Of course, having had similar life experiences to those experienced by clients can also be helpful to developing empathy. The therapist does, however, need to be ever aware that his or her personal experiences and feelings about them may not be the same as that experienced by clients. Your past feelings may not be the client's feelings. So while you will likely rely on your own experiences, you should not force your feelings onto your client.

To comprehend the situations and feelings of clients it is important to develop a frame of reference by being a good listener who asks the right type of questions. A wise therapist will ask questions to probe the client's internal world, such as: "What are you feeling now?" "How do you view the problem?" and "What do you see from your perspective?" (Brammer, 1979, p. 37).

The emerging recreation therapist should be warned that a certain amount of detachment or objectivity must be retained to offer empathetic responses. Otherwise, the therapist can overidentify with the client and become sympathetic rather than empathetic.

Caring

Another therapist characteristic closely related to empathy is displaying warmth and caring. Caring is an interpersonal phenomenon that promotes health and fosters growth that helps clients by allowing the freedom needed for them to move toward fulfilling their potentials.

Recreation therapists tend to reflect a depth of genuine concern for their clients. This is because recreation therapists are typically, by nature, very caring persons who really care about their clients. They are truly concerned about their clients and what will happen to them. There is also often a norm of reciprocity because clients tend to like their friendly, nonthreatening, and accepting recreation therapists who bring a positive dynamic to healthcare environments too often devoid of affirming professionals. In fact, Austin (2001) has portrayed recreation therapy as being characterized as providing "a warm, caring, and nonjudgmental atmosphere." There are, of course, a number of ways to communicate caring to clients. Being genuinely warm and friendly with clients provides a good start. Just "being there" or being accessible to clients is an important part of caring. Also important is following through on expectations so clients see that you deliver on your caring—or your actions back up your caring demeanor. Finally, the expression, "a caring touch," is one that most of us have heard. When we think of demonstrating caring, physical contact is an element that comes to mind. With most people, reaching out and touching them goes a long way to say that we care. Touch has been termed a "universally understood language" (Sundeen et al., 1994, p. 181).

The concept of caring shares much with the concept of *social support*. All of us need others in our lives with whom we can share information freely (e.g., with whom we can "rant and rave") and we require individuals who will help us meet our needs by providing psychological support (e.g., giving affirming feedback to let us know that we are "okay") or other types of support (e.g., helping us to problem solve or providing us with material support). Parents, family, and friends typically constitute the support system. But within the healthcare system recreation therapists may temporarily be a part of clients' support systems. Recreation therapists may be a source of support for clients in healthcare programs while, at the same time, assisting clients to develop their support systems outside the healthcare program so that they come to rely on their natural support systems.

Having Positive Regard and Respect for Clients

Having positive regard and respect for clients leads the recreation therapist to treating each client as a unique individual who possesses intrinsic worth. The client is not a diagnosis (e.g., a diabetic, an epileptic) but is a person who happens to have been given a diagnostic label. Using person-first language in which we employ expressions such as "person with a disability" rather than "disabled person" places the emphasis where it should be—that is, on the individual, not the illness or disorder. Clients are, first and foremost, human beings who need to be made to feel that they can be themselves and that they will be respected for who they are. Within the treatment and rehabilitation community the recreation therapist is perhaps most likely to provide instances where clients can "let their hair down" and be themselves. Recreation can be a time for clients to relax and enjoy being themselves. Further, recreation therapists have traditionally looked for the positive attributes in their clients and have drawn on these strengths as means to reach treatment and rehabilitation outcomes. Finally, many recreation therapists hold a humanistic view of clients that embraces the positive notion that their clients are motivated to fulfill their potentials or self-actualize. Having such trust in the abilities of each client to overcome his or her problems and grow beyond them is emblematic of the high regard and respect for clients in therapeutic recreation.

Empathy and caring are means by which recreation therapists can express positive regard and respect for clients. Empathy and caring lead to feelings on the part of clients that they are understood and cared about by therapists. Therapists likewise show regard and respect for clients by not requiring clients to conform to their own wishes. Therapists who respect clients do not attempt to control them, but instead allow clients to exercise freedom. An essential element within recreation therapy is allowing as much control as possible to reside with the client.

> Therapeutic recreation represents the antithesis of the controlling environment often encountered in healthcare facilities. In recreation, clients are allowed choice and control. (Austin, 1999, p. 158)

Hope

Frank and Frank (1991) have used the term *demoralization* to reflect a state in which clients feel powerless to change themselves or their environments. Clients who are demoralized feel they cannot do anything to change their plight. Hope is the opposite of demoralization. Hope combats demoralization. With hope comes an expectation that things can and will change. While uncertainty still exists in the mind of the person filled with hope, there is an expectation on the part of the hopeful individual that things can change for the better (Sundeen et al., 1994).

Sundeen and her colleagues (1994) have presented Lange's continuum of hope. On one end of the continuum is the *despair syndrome* "characterized by despair, helplessness, hopelessness, doubt, depression, apathy, sadness, and grief." At the other end is the *hope syndrome* "characterized by hope, confidence, faith, inspiration, and determination" (p. 183). Within the therapeutic relationship, the recreation therapist helps clients move away from the despair syndrome toward the hope syndrome so they may begin to take charge of themselves and their situations. Therefore, a characteristic of the therapeutic relationship is that it helps to instill hope.

How is this done? One strategy is for the recreation therapist to help clients to maintain and build their social support systems or their relationships with others who are significant in their lives. Friends and family can then provide a supportive, hopeful environment in which recovery can take place. Another means to encourage hope is to enhance the level of clients' self-esteem. Clients who feel good about themselves and their abilities to achieve are less likely to possess feelings of hopelessness or helplessness. Feelings of mastery and achievement gained during recreational opportunities bolster self-esteem and lead to a hopeful, can-do feeling. Such experiences create optimism and reinforce feelings of hope. Still another strategy to induce hope is to provide new experiences for clients (e.g., adventure challenge activities). Such activities provide an approach not previously tried by clients so there is no danger that, in the past, these activities have failed to produce desirable outcomes. Such new activities, therefore, can naturally produce a feeling of hope, which is reinforced with successes gained through participation.

A final measure recreation therapists often take to instill hope is to present themselves as optimistic individuals who are likeable, easy to know, and fun to be around. With their optimism, they radiate a great deal of positive energy. They are excited and energetic about what they do. In short, the best recreation therapists tend to be positive people who have a great deal of enthusiasm for life, and for what they do as helping professionals. This positive approach and enthusiasm translates into having optimistic views of their clients in terms of seeing their clients as having abilities to regain their health and to grow toward fulfilling their potentials. The enthusiasm of recreation therapists has the additional benefit of influencing their clients since enthusiasm tends to be contagious.

Genuineness

Along with unconditional positive regard and empathy, genuineness and congruence were among the three conditions originally stipulated by Rogers (1958) as being necessary to the development of a therapeutic relationship. By genuineness and congruence Rogers meant that helping professionals need to be sincere and honest with their clients. He also meant that helpers need to be congruent or consistent with their attitudes and actions. Helpers cannot be fakes who put up a front or facade. They need to be authentic.

Being genuine is also connected to building trust. Being genuine is being honest and authentic. Honest and authentic interactions build trust over time. If recreation therapists are consistently relating genuinely with clients, a sense of trust will be apt to develop. Another element in building trust is the maintaining of confidentiality in therapeutic relationships. Maintaining confidentiality on the part of the therapist will likely be perceived by the client as a form of honesty. Keeping confidential information confidential builds an expectation that the therapist can be trusted (Sundeen et al., 1994). Sundeen and her colleagues have emphasized the critical nature of trust by stating that:

> Trust helps the client to share more openly concerns, feelings, and hopes. Without the establishment of trust, the helping relationship will not progress beyond the level of mechanical provision for tending to superficial needs. (1994, p. 173)

How do recreation therapists establish themselves as being genuine? Brill (1990) has warned that helpers must guard against "promising more than can be delivered" (p. 96). Such promises may initially please clients but lead to broken relationships when clients learn that what has been promised will not occur. Recreation therapists can demonstrate honesty and sincerity "by being open with clients, by answering questions to the best of their ability, and by admitting mistakes or lack of knowledge" (Okun, 1992, p. 36). Recreation therapists also need to protect and maintain confidentiality in client relationships. In short, they need to be honest.

Autonomy and Mutuality

Under the old medical model, patients or clients were placed in a dependent role in which they were expected to be "cooperative" by following the directives of healthcare providers. With little control over their situations, clients often felt overwhelmed in an authoritarian and seemingly uncaring system. Happily, today healthcare has changed in an effort to allow clients to assume more responsibility in their treatment and, therefore, more control over what happens to them when receiving healthcare. Clients are seen as being capable of participating in their own treatment.

At this point the concepts of autonomy and mutuality become integral in the development of therapeutic relationships. Autonomy deals with each client's ability to maintain control or to be self-directed. Mutuality concerns the partnership or cooperative working relationship that involves both the client and helping professional (Sundeen et al., 1994).

The Health Protection/Health Promotion Model of recreation therapy practice has control as a major component (Austin, 1999; also see Chapter 1). Under this conceptual model there exists a continuum which ranges from poor health at one extreme to optimal health at the other extreme. It is the ultimate goal of the recreation therapist, under Austin's model, to help the client to move toward optimal health. As the client moves nearer and nearer to optimal health, he or she assumes more and more control. At the most extreme point of optimal health the client enjoys full control. Austin has explained:

> In recreation, clients are afforded opportunities to experience control over their environments within a supportive, non-threatening atmosphere. Through participation in activities that allow mastery experiences and build a sense of accomplishment, clients learn they are able to be successful in their interactions with the world. They learn new skills, new ways of behaving, new means to approach interactions with others, new values and philosophies, and new ways to think about themselves. Positive changes in self-concepts occur as a result of clients proving to themselves that they are capable of achieving success and of learning new skills, behaviors, and ways of thinking. Their personal evaluations of their abilities, or feelings of self-efficacy, are enhanced. Bolstered efficacy expectations allow clients to have confidence in themselves and to better face difficulties so that they can persevere even in the face of frustration (Bandura, 1986; 1997). Clients increase feelings of being able to control their lives and meet adversity as they become more and more healthy. (1999, pp. 159–160)

Recreation, by its nature, allows people to be in control or to exercise self-direction. Of course, the amount of control assumed by the client depends on the client's readiness to take control. There are times when the client may want to give some level of control to the therapist, but ultimately the recreation therapist strives to help his or her clients to be as self-directed as they wish to be.

As indicated in the previous quote, recreation therapists may assist clients to feel empowered by helping clients to select activities that have the right level of challenge so that their successful participation in the activities results in heightened feelings of self-efficacy (i.e., confidence in their abilities) with resulting feelings of being in control. Or, stated another way, clients develop can-do attitudes that produce feelings of being in control.

Austin has explained the effect of heightened feelings of self-efficacy:

> Clients' expectations of themselves largely determine how they will be able to deal with their problems, how much effort they will be willing to expend, and whether they will make a perseverant effort. Those who are self-doubters are likely to express little effort and will give up quickly if their initial efforts are not productive. Those with high efficacy expectations are apt to face their difficulties with determination, to exert maximum effort, and to persevere even when frustration is encountered. (1999, p. 384)

Bandura (1986) has explained that in addition to feeling a sense of accomplishment clients can also increase feelings of self-efficacy through vicarious experiences, verbal persuasion, and physiological arousal. A vicarious experience would be one client seeing another client experience success, and feeling that he or she could be just as successful. Verbal persuasion involves the client being convinced by a credible person that he or she can succeed. Reducing feelings of anxiety or arousal may also cause heightened self-efficacy. All of these means are open to recreation therapists when helping clients gain confidence in their abilities, and leading clients to believe in themselves and experience greater feelings of control.

Within his Health Protection/Health Promotion model of recreation therapy practice, Austin (1999) has also emphasized the concept of mutuality in the therapeutic relationship between the client and recreation therapist. As indicated previously, mutuality concerns the partnership or cooperative working relationship that involves both the client and the helping professional (Sundeen et al., 1994).

When clients are in extremely poor health they often withdraw from their normal life activities, become self-absorbed, and experience a loss of control over their lives. They are not ready to experience recreation. At this point, clients must give up control to the recreation therapist who provides direction and structure through activities he or she prescribes for clients. Austin has written, however,

> Once engaged in activity, clients can begin to perceive themselves as having the capacity for successful interaction with their environment, for making improvement, and for regaining a sense of control. (1999, p. 158)

At this time clients are ready to join in a partnership with the recreation therapist to select recreation pursuits that meet their needs and hold the potential for therapeutic benefit. This partnership helps solidify the therapeutic relationship between clients and recreation therapists.

Phases in the Therapeutic Relationship

It is important to acknowledge that therapeutic relationships do not just happen. They develop over time. Many authors have offered various stage models for the therapeutic relationship. Sundeen and her colleagues (1994) portrayed four phases of therapeutic relationships: the preinteraction phase; introductory phase; working phase; and termination phase. Hill and O'Brien (1999) listed the exploration stage, insight stage, and action stage as stages that helpers and clients together encounter. For the purpose of this discussion four phases are suggested: the planning phase, the introductory phase, the action phase, and the termination phase.

Planning Phase

The initial phase deals with the therapist's planning and does not directly involve the client. Before meeting the client the recreation therapist needs to review available assessment data about the client. The recreation therapist will want to know if there are any precautions or restrictions he or she needs to be aware of, such as the client being suicidal or having a heart problem that might restrict activity. Knowing the client's diagnosis and social history can also be highly useful. While each individual is unique, diagnostic information may reveal potential areas of client needs to be explored. Knowing the background of the individual may help the therapist to be more sensitive to certain issues when meeting the client for the first time. Of course, at this stage it is important for the recreation therapist to be aware of the danger of stereotyping individuals based on preliminary information.

Another concern for the recreation therapist is to plan for the first meeting with the client. The best arrangement is one in which there is a defined period of time during which there will be no interruptions. The setting should be one in which the client will be comfortable. It is also critical that information to be covered during the first meeting be considered. For example, the first meeting is one in which the expectations of the nature of help to be given will be discussed. Therefore it is important that, prior to the meeting, the recreation therapist consider potential areas that may be helpful for the client so that he or she is prepared to discuss them.

Introductory Phase

As a therapist, in your introductory statement you should address *who* you are, *what* you do, *when* you do it, and *why* or the purpose of what you are doing (Arnold & Boggs, 1989). For example, the recreation therapist might say: "Hello. I'm Christy Dattilo, a recreation therapist. I am here at the Center every morning to lead the recreation programs. Today I wanted to meet with you to ask you some questions about your recreation preferences to find out what you like to do."

Initially covered during the introductory phase are:

a. establishing the roles and responsibilities of the therapist and client;

b. discussing the location, frequency, and length of individual or group sessions;

c. letting the client know the purpose of the relationship and what he or she should expect from the therapist;

d. informing the client about the duration of the relationship and indications for termination; and

e. reviewing how confidential material will be handled (Sundeen et al., 1994).

The introductory phase can also be conceived as one in which rapport is established and clients are encouraged to discuss their feelings and thoughts. Recreation therapists typically pose open-ended questions, reflect client feelings, and listen using techniques such as paraphrasing, clarifying, and perception checking. As a result insights are gained, client needs can be identified, and strategies are then developed to meet goals.

Action Phase

During the action phase recreation therapists and clients work together toward reaching jointly set goals. At this time it is the role of recreation therapists to encourage clients to communicate openly. Therapeutic communication skills, such as confrontation and self-disclosure, as well as those used during the introductory phase, are employed. In this phase, it is also the role of recreation therapists to motivate clients to participate and to provide feedback to clients to reinforce behaviors that facilitate progress toward goals. All the while recreation therapists encourage self-direction and control on the part of clients.

Termination Phase

Terminating a therapeutic relationship can be traumatic for both the therapist and the client. Recreation therapists must determine which termination strategy will work best for them with each particular client. Termination can be used to review accomplishments that produce feelings of achievement for both recreation therapists and clients. If the therapeutic relationship has been a particularly close one, it may be good for both parties to openly share their feelings about terminating the relationship. Emerging recreation therapists may experience feelings of anxiety during the termination phase, and this anxiety may cause them to attempt to avoid the situation because they do not know how to handle it. A good strategy to cope with such feelings is to admit them to his or her clinical supervisor and seek this professional's advise on how to approach the situation.

Conclusion

The therapeutic relationship has not been a regularly discussed topic within the therapeutic recreation literature. This is unfortunate because of the critical nature of the therapeutic alliance in the entire therapeutic enterprise. Knowing about areas that characterize therapeutic relationships is basic to forming successful therapist–client bonds. Further, knowing strategies for promoting positive relationships is critical. Finally, recreation therapists need to know dynamics involved within the phases through which healthy helping relationships pass. As a result of reading this chapter, it is hoped that therapeutic recreation professionals and students will be better prepared to enter into therapeutic relationships with their clients.

Reading Comprehension Questions

1. How important are therapeutic relationships to the therapeutic enterprise? Explain.

2. Define the term *therapeutic relationship*. Tell what a therapeutic relationship is *not*.

3. Do you agree with the six characteristics listed as important to the success of therapeutic relationships in recreation therapy? Why or why not?

4. Describe these six characteristics: empathy; caring; positive regard and respect for clients; hope; genuineness; autonomy and mutuality.

5. Provide at least one strategy to enhance each of the characteristics reflected in the therapeutic relationships of recreation therapists and their clients?

6. Do you perceive control as a central component of recreation? Why or why not? How does control relate to recreation therapy?

7. Do you concur with the proposed four-phase model for the therapeutic relationship in recreation therapy? Why or why not?

References

American Psychiatric Association. (1993). *Psychosocial treatment research in psychiatry: A task force report of the American Psychiatric Association.* Washington, DC: Author.

Arnold, E. and Boggs, K. (1989). *Interpersonal relationships: Professional communication skills for nurses.* Philadelphia, PA: W. B. Saunders Co.

Austin, D. R. (2001). The therapeutic recreation process. In D. R. Austin and M. E. Crawford (Eds.), *Therapeutic recreation: An introduction* (3rd ed.). Boston, MA: Allyn & Bacon.

Austin, D. R. (1999). *Therapeutic recreation processes and techniques* (4th ed.). Champaign, IL: Sagamore.

Bandura, A. (1997). *Self-efficacy: The exercise of control.* New York, NY: W. H. Freeman and Co.

Bandura, A. (1986). *Social foundations of thought and action: A social cognitive theory.* Englewood Cliffs, NJ: Prentice Hall.

Blattner, B. (1981). *Holistic nursing.* Englewood Cliffs, NJ: Prentice Hall.

Brammer, L. M. (1979). *The helping relationship: Process and skills.* Englewood Cliffs, NJ: Prentice Hall.

Brill, N. I. (1990). *Working with people: The helping process* (4th ed.). New York, NY: Longman.

Carkhuff, R. and Berenson, B. (1967). *Beyond counseling and therapy.* New York, NY: Holt, Rinehart & Winston.

Frank, J. D. and Frank, J. B. (1991). *Persuasion and healing: A comparative study of psychotherapy* (3rd ed.). Baltimore, MD: Johns Hopkins University Press.

Friedman, A. M. (1992). *Treating chronic pain: The healing partnership.* New York, NY: Plenum Press.

Hill, C. E. and O'Brien, K. M. (1999). *Helping skills: Facilitating exploration, insight, and action.* Washington, DC: American Psychological Association.

Kottler, J. A. (1990). *On being a therapist.* San Francisco, CA: Jossey-Bass.

Lyons, R. F., Sullivan, M. J. L., Ritvo, P. G., and Coyne, J. C. (1995). *Relationships in chronic illness and disability.* Newbury Park, CA: Sage Publications.

Mitchell, A. and Cornmack, M. (1998). *The therapeutic relationship in complementary healthcare.* New York, NY: Churchill Livingstone.

Okun, B. F. (1992). *Effective helping: Interviewing and counseling techniques* (4th ed.). Pacific Grove, CA: Brooks/Cole Publishing Co.

Rogers, C. R. (1961). *On becoming a person.* Boston, MA: Houghton Mifflin.

Rogers, C. R. (1958). Characteristics of a helping relationship. *Personnel and Guidance Journal, 37,* 6–16.

Sundeen, S. J., Stuart, G. W., Rankin, E. A. D., and Cohen, S. A. (1994). *Nurse–client interaction: Implementing the nursing process* (5th ed.). St. Louis, MO: Mosby.

Teyber, E. (1992). *Interpersonal process in psychotherapy: A guide for clinical training* (2nd ed.). Pacific Grove, CA: Brooks/Cole Publishing Co.

Chapter 7

An Overview of Therapeutic Outdoor Programming

Alan Ewert, Ph.D., FALS
Alison Voight, Ph.D.
Brady Harnishfeger, Ph.D.

This chapter explores the use of outdoor settings as a means to generate beneficial and therapeutic outcomes of various intervention modalities. While the use of outdoor environmental settings has a relatively long history, dating back to the turn of the twentieth century and earlier, the deliberate inclusion of activities and experiences that present the client with elements of risk and danger is a much newer entry in the area of therapeutic interventions. Although a number of terms have emerged that characterize specific types of interventions, including wilderness therapy and adventure therapy, the term used in this chapter to describe the general rubric of interventions is *therapeutic outdoor programming* (TOP). Accordingly, this chapter begins with a brief overview of TOP, including the history, foundations, and documented benefits. In addition, examples of TOP applications and the underlying theoretical frameworks will be discussed within the contexts of therapeutic recreation and counseling. Following these sections will be several concluding perspectives on the future use of TOP activities and experiences.

A Brief History of Therapeutic Outdoor Programming

From a historical perspective, it is difficult to separate the recreation and human development movements from the therapeutic uses of the outdoors. By the early 1900s, numerous camps and organizations were formed within a philosophical framework advocating the belief that the outdoors could produce beneficial consequences for people of any age or nationality. What made this such a powerful belief was multidimensional. First, through the Transcendental movement of the midnineteenth century, people saw the outdoor setting as spiritually and physically uplifting. Second, the emerging group of naturalists, such as John Muir (1838–1914) and John James Audubon (1785–1851), added credibility to the concept. Third, the outdoor environment offered an antithesis to industrial development and its attendant outcomes such as pollution, noise and crowding. By intuition, it was thought this antithesis must be *good* for a person, both in body and soul, as the opposite (i.e., industrial development) was viewed, increasingly, as something *bad*.

Within this context, a number of camps, organized outings, and organizations developed that either implicitly or explicitly promoted the notion that the outdoor setting was good for people and could be therapeutic for a variety of human ills and problems. A sample of these programs is depicted in Table 7.1.

Table 7.1   Sample of Outdoor Programs with Therapeutic Intent

Program	Approximate Year of Inception	Target Area
Gunnery School for Boys	1861	Youth development
Fresh Air Camps	1872	Health
Playground Areas	1892	Delinquency
Tent Therapy Programs	1901	Tuberculosis
Camp Ahmek	1929	Socialization
Outward Bound	1941	Self-reliance
Salesmanship Club	1946	Delinquency
BYU Youth Development Program	1969	Personal growth
Project Adventure	1971	Self-systems
Breckenridge Outdoor Education Center	1976	Disabilities
Wilderness Inquiry	1978	Disabilities
Outdoor Behavioral Healthcare Industry	1996	Delinquency

As can be seen in Table 7.1, there has been a continual development in the types and range of purposes for these therapeutic programs. Indeed, Table 7.1 represents only a fraction of what is now an industry comprised of hundreds of programs in North America and across the globe. Additional programs include: the Aspen Achievement Academy, Anasazi Foundation, Summit Achievement Academy, Eckard Family Youth Alternative Program, Catherine Freer Wilderness Therapy, and Bradford Woods Outdoor Education Center. Many of these programs offer outdoor activities such as rock climbing, wilderness trekking, canyoneering, whitewater boating, and survival training. For a more detailed description of the history and development of these programs see Gass (1993), Davis-Berman and Berman (1994), and Russell and Hendee (2000).

Given the wide variety of programs, purposes, and methods, it is not surprising that several different terms have evolved which describe the use of the outdoor environment in various treatment modalities (Crisp, 1998).

A Conceptual Framework for Therapeutic Outdoor Programming

To better understand the context in which the field of TOP fits together, some basic terms, types of programs and varying interventions will be defined. A partial listing of these terms is taken from Ewert, McCormick, and Voight (2001).

Basic Terminology

Adventure Therapy

Adventure therapy frequently utilizes the components of adventure (e.g., real or perceived risk, uncertainty of outcome, personal decision making) as part of its curriculum structure. Adventure therapy refers to therapeutic interventions that utilize experiential and risk-taking activities which are physically as well as emotionally challenging, and usually involve an outdoor setting. Gillis defines adventure therapy as:

> ...an active approach to psychotherapy for people seeking behavioral change...that utilizes adventure activities, be they group games and initiatives or wilderness expeditions. (1995, p. 5)

It should be noted, however, that not *all* adventure therapy programs contain significant levels of risk and danger, nor do they all take place in undeveloped outdoor settings. For example, indoor climbing walls, ropes courses, and initiative/New Games activities have become an increasingly popular venue for some adventure therapy programs. The question thus becomes: Are these adventure-based activities, or something else?

Crisp (1998) suggests that adventure therapy is effective because it employs the "disequilibrium" principle as described by Nadler and Luckner (1992). It also emulates the widely ascribed Outward Bound process, originally outlined by Walsh and Golins (1976), in which the participant is placed in novel physical and social settings, and is encouraged to develop a new set of skills and behaviors in order to master the situation. It is then hoped that these new skills and knowledge will have some carry-over value to other aspects of a person's life.

Wilderness Therapy

Friese (1996) has identified over 700 programs that currently operate in the United States and use wilderness-type settings for therapeutic purposes. He termed these types of programs *wilderness experience programs,* or WEPs. Using data extrapolated from five of the largest such programs, Russell and Hendee (1999) estimated that there are approximately 330,000 user days generating over $60 million in revenue per year.

Russell and Hendee (2000) propose that wilderness therapy programs can be categorized into four types. These program types include: (a) *Contained expeditions* in which the client and treatment team remain together on a wilderness expedition; (b) *Continuous flow* where leaders, therapists, and often clients rotate in and out of the expedition; (c) *Base-camp expeditions* where a structured camp experience is integral to the program; and (d) *Residential expeditions* which are generally of a longer duration and where outdoor therapeutic approaches serve to augment other treatment intervention strategies.

Crisp (1998) suggests that programs using a wilderness therapy orientation incorporate the concept of "adaptation," or coping with change, either in the individual's social environment or physical setting. Moreover, like adventure therapy, wilderness therapy can involve the use of residential or base-camp facilities, small group dynamics, and group psychotherapy. Given these components, program outcomes often revolve around personal change and social development.

Therapeutic Outdoor Programming

More recently, therapeutic outdoor programming has emerged as an umbrella term that encompasses the different, but related modalities of adventure and wilderness therapy. Inherent in the term TOP is the implication that this type of therapeutic modality generally utilizes an outdoor setting and direct experience, but does not mandate that these types of therapeutic interventions automatically involve adventure (i.e., the deliberate inclusion of risk or danger), or require wilderness-like environments (Ewert, McCormick & Voight, 1999). For example, activities involving experiential opportunities typically associated with outdoor education, such as going on a nature walk, can precipitate a variety of beneficial outcomes without involving a high degree of risk or using a wilderness-like environment. Within this context, *therapeutic outdoor programming* is defined in the following way:

> A type of programming which utilizes an outdoor setting, or emulated outdoor setting, for the purposes of rehabilitation, growth, development, and enhancement of an individual's physical, social and psychological well-being through the application of structured activities involving direct experience.

For the purposes of this chapter, the term therapeutic outdoor programming will be used. TOP will encompass the terms adventure therapy and wilderness therapy.

Depth of Intervention

Whether or not the TOP interventions predominately depend on a wilderness-type location or facility, such as a camp, Gass (1993) suggests that there are differences in the depth or intent of the intervention. He lists a number of factors that help determine this depth, including the following:

a. Specific needs of the client;

b. The complexity of the client's therapeutic issue(s);

c. The expertise, training, and background of the outdoor therapist or instructor;

d. The type of program being used (e.g., setting, time, activities); and

e. Extent of follow-up interventions or treatment.

Within the context of intervention depth, Gass (1993) presents a model consisting of four program types: recreation, enrichment, adjunctive therapy, and primary therapy. This model is depicted in Figure 7.1.

In the case of *recreation* types of programs, the intervention is typically focused on personal satisfaction, enjoyment, and learning a new skill. *Enrichment* programs intensify the intervention by providing experiences

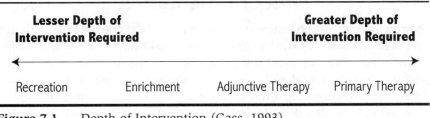

Figure 7.1   Depth of Intervention (Gass, 1993)

and activities that can have some carry-over value to other aspects of a person's life, such as enhanced self-concept and communication skills, and the ability to work with others. TOP features an *adjunctive therapy* approach that can be characterized by outdoor activities and interventions that are part of a larger treatment plan for the individual. As Gass (1993) points out, TOP interventions and activities are "blended" with other strategies and processes. Programs in which the TOP component is the *primary therapy* approach provide an alternative intervention process to more "traditional" forms of therapy. In these programs, the TOP intervention is often the only therapeutic approach utilized. As such, the activities and interventions tend to be more complex and involved than the other three approaches previously mentioned. Gass (1993) posits a number of characteristics that serve to distinguish primary types of programs from recreation, enrichment, or adjunctive. These characteristics include the following:

- The goal is to make a lasting change using the TOP experience.
- Extensive precourse assessment is often done in accordance with the assessment phase and client needs. There is substantial, and often complex, precourse framing such as goal-setting activities.
- Sequencing, progression, metaphor-building, and processing are used to create change within the client.
- Much of the therapy takes place during the activity rather than before or after.

Thus, therapeutic outdoor programs can be classified along the dimensions of program type, location, specific activities, and depth of intervention. A critical question, however, is whether this type of therapeutic approach actually works. The next section discusses some of the findings relative to TOP experiences.

Benefits Associated with Therapeutic Outdoor Programming

A growing body of literature suggests that TOP experiences and activities can exert a beneficial influence on the individual from three major domains: sociological, psychological and physiological. The following section provides a closer look at these three domains in relationship to participation in TOP. See Ewert, McCormick, and Voight (2001) for a more in-depth discussion regarding these benefits.

Sociological Outcomes

An important component of many TOP activities is the *group process* (Gillis, 1998; Schleien, McAvoy, Lais & Rynders, 1993). TOP experiences will often utilize a small group setting as part of the therapeutic intervention to enhance learning of specific social skills. It is within the group process that therapeutic interventions may enhance social skills, refine either participant-identified or externally defined personality issues, and demand expository thinking to solve group problems. In some specific instances, the group process may also be used to redirect socially inappropriate behaviors and expose group members to certain consequences based on a sequential decision-making process. A number of TOP activities have been specifically designed for this population (Davis-Berman & Berman, 1994; Kimball, 1980; Schleien, McAvoy, Lais & Rynders, 1993).

One important social benefit derived from the group process commonly used in TOP is the opportunity for positive leadership roles to emerge. For many adolescents, particularly girls, perceptions of a leadership role are often ambiguous and untried. TOP activities, especially those in a small group leadership context, can have a positive impact on self-esteem and self-confidence, especially for females (Levitt, 1994; Humberstone & Lynch, 1991).

The group process presents unique social challenges for participants. Group adventure or challenge activities (e.g., initiative tasks, trust activities) allow the opportunity for participants to establish relationships and earn the respect of fellow group members since many activities cannot be accomplished without cooperation from everyone in the group.

Psychological Outcomes

A number of studies have addressed how effective TOP interventions are within the psychological domain. A sampling of these findings is included in the following discussion.

Positive Impacts for Mental Health

Therapeutic outdoor programming activities can often challenge previously held self-perceptions about one's personality. Participants are often faced with evaluating discrepancies between their "real self" and "ideal self." Positive changes affecting self-esteem, self-confidence, self-determination and increased self-efficacy may occur as a result of group accomplishments, and reflection upon personal efforts and contributions to the group's success (Schleien, McAvoy, Lais & Rynders, 1993; Tate & Ellis, 1997). Other studies have indicated increased levels of self-actualization and perceptions of personal positive changes as a result of exposure to TOP-related activities (Davis-Berman & Berman, 1994; Gass, 1993; Itin, 1998).

Shifting Locus of Control

Internal versus external locus of control refers to the predisposition of an individual to have or *not* have control over the events that transpire in his or her life (Iso-Ahola, 1980). Internal locus of control (or stable attributions) refers to a person's belief that he or she controls the events that occur in life, whether good or bad. Persons with an external locus of control (or unstable attributions) believe the events in their lives occur due to luck, fate or chance, regardless of good or bad outcomes. Many TOP activities utilize specific therapeutic interventions (i.e., group decision-making, cognitive retraining, evaluative reflection, leisure education) to help redirect external, unstable attributions toward more stable, internal attributions (Dieser & Voight, 1998).

Increased Awareness/Appreciation for the Natural Environment

When challenge activities take place in a natural environment, the opportunity to develop an individual relationship with the outdoor world often transpires. The outdoors can allow for personal reflection without the distraction of modern technologies. Activities in a natural setting can foster a first-time bonding with the environment that, heretofore, would not have taken place in a familiar, more traditional therapeutic atmosphere. The opportunity to feel a sense of belonging to an outdoor or natural setting is often very difficult to achieve in our constantly changing and extremely fast-paced world (Kaplan & Kaplan, 1989). Kaplan and Kaplan also describe two constructs that help explain how these TOP experiences might work: (a) Being Away and (b) Soft Fascination. In other words, simply being away from those things in an individual's life that create mental fatigue can be rejuvenating. Moreover, attributes of the outdoors, such as beautiful scenery (i.e., Soft Fascination), engage an individual's involuntary attention but does not demand a high level of concentration. Cumulatively, both constructs, often present in TOP settings, serve to provide mental relief and relaxation. Finally, for those who have never had the opportunity to be in an environment that can't be readily changed or manipulated, the outdoor setting may help to recapture a sense of being a part of nature (Ralston, 1991).

Physiological Outcomes

Personal involvement in TOP activities can lead to an overall improvement in physical health. Leisure-related studies have researched the positive benefits associated with physical participation in recreation and leisure activities, such as cardiovascular improvement, reduced glucose levels, reduced fat in body mass, and increased bone and muscle mass (Paffenbarger, Hyde & Dow, 1991). Inherent in many TOP activities is the increased demand for physical involvement resulting from confrontations with specific tasks and challenges that can often contribute to increased, overall physical fitness. Moreover, Ulrich, Dimberg, and Driver (1991) suggest that involvement in outdoor activities, such as challenge activities, may have positive impacts on physical health and reduce stress, but:

> There is a need for research that investigates longer term psychophysiological influences of leisure, including challenge programs. (p. 87)

✻   ✻   ✻   ✻   ✻

Given the structure and components usually present in TOP, a broad spectrum of physical, social, and psychological benefits can be realized. This efficacy has been examined from the perspective of individual studies, and in aggregate, through a variety of meta-analyses (Cason & Gillis, 1994; Hattie, Marsh, Neill & Richards, 1997; Neill & Richards, 1999; Wilson & Lipsey, 2000). In recognition of these potential benefits, a growing number of more traditional treatment programs are including TOP activities as part of their intervention protocol. Some of these programs include cancer patients and their families; people with brain injuries; severe physical disabilities, and mental disabilities; and victims of rape (Asher, Huffaker & McNally, 1994; Bluebond-Langer, Perkel, Goertzel, Nelson & McGeary, 1990; Herbert, 2000; Nichols & Fines, 1995; Sahler & Carpenter, 1989; Witman & Preskenis, 1996).

In conclusion, the accumulated research suggests that well-planned programs that incorporate structured therapeutic components have proven to be effective means of achieving beneficial outcomes (Datillo & Murphy, 1987; McAvoy, 1987; Wilson & Lipsey, 2000). The following sections discuss how TOP activities and experiences can be incorporated into therapeutic recreation programs.

TOP and Therapeutic Recreation

One of the models commonly used in therapeutic recreation, the Health Protection/Promotion Model (Austin, 1998; 1991), is congruent with many of the practices and goals of TOP. Within this context, the model has "prescriptive activities" and "recreation" components. Prescriptive activities can serve as motivating agents for clients in a state of illness or disability. TOP activities and experiences can be useful in helping the client address issues such as learned helplessness, depression, or other issues related to the self-system.

The recreation component of Austin's model posits that the recreational aspects of an activity, such as TOP, can be re-creative to the individual. Austin suggests this in his statement "clients begin to regain their equilibrium disrupted by stressors so that they may once again resume their quest for actualization" (1998, p. 113). Not surprisingly, the re-creative aspect of the recreational experience is similar to the restorative phenomenon of natural settings previously discussed by Kaplan and Kaplan (1989).

Thus, the Health Protection/Promotion Model provides a point of congruence between the therapeutic recreation profession and TOP. Moreover, within the therapeutic recreation setting, TOP activities are often used as either an adjunctive or primary therapy to improve clients' social, personal, and physical well-being.

For example, TOP-related interventions have been successfully applied in both inpatient and outpatient settings and with a variety of populations, including elementary-age students, adolescents, single mothers, married couples, depressed or chemically dependent adults, and families. TOP intervention experiences range from brief team-building, or "energizer" activities, to 7–31 day wilderness expeditions.

TOP and the New Psychology

A recent article by Seligman and Csikszentmihalyi (2000) called for a shift in emphasis in psychology from a focus on illness and pathology to the study of positive subjective experience. Scholars of this "positive psychology" identify and study individuals' inherent strengths and virtues, and practitioners support and encourage their clients' efforts to help themselves by tapping into their own strengths. Practice in the therapeutic recreation field has espoused a similar perspective for many years (Austin, 1991; Stumbo & Peterson, 1998). Treatment has focused on the holistic recovery of a client, as opposed to merely treating one specific limitation or area, and encouraged the client to draw upon inner resources, as well as positive attributes, to progress and aid in overall wellness (Austin, 1998; Compton, 1997).

One intervention stemming from a "positive psychology" perspective is *solution-focused therapy* (e.g., deShazer, 1988). This approach assumes that clients already possess many of the skills they need to improve their situation, but may require help to identify and maximize their use. Clients are encouraged to identify "exceptions" or times when the present complaint did not exist or was less severe. This allows the counselor to focus the conversation on what the client did during that time which seemed to help. Primary emphasis in therapy then becomes identifying what the client did differently during the exceptional period, and supporting the client's increased involvement in those activities. Ultimately, clients begin to reframe their expectations of treatment—from expecting failure to that of expecting success.

TOP-based interventions seem especially reflective of this new treatment philosophy, as they help participants' identify their strengths and build confidence in their ability to help themselves. Unlike traditional counseling, which often involves one-to-one therapy focusing on problems and weaknesses and/or an abstract discussion to acquire new ideas and beliefs, TOP-based counseling interventions focus on identifying and developing personal strengths and supporting an individuals' successful involvement in structured experiences. These positive experiences are then related to the development of new ideas and beliefs about oneself and the world. Guided reflection on the personal relevance of the experience encourages participants to see how this experience was different (in a positive way) from previous experiences and offers them hope for positive change. Austin's Health Protection/Health Promotion Model also ascribes, in his recreation component, the importance of designing activities that enhance social and personal behaviors, as well as facilitate a sense of overall well-being, and ultimately a greater sense of actualization. According to Austin, "clients begin to regain their equilibrium, disrupted by stressors, so that they may once again resume their quest for actualization" (1998, p. 113). A fictitious clinical example is offered to help demonstrate the strengths implicit in TOP-based interventions.

An Intervention Example

> Mary and John are experiencing problems in their marriage and seek the counsel of a therapist. As an adjunct to therapy, the therapist encourages the couple to attend a weekend retreat for couples who wish to improve their relationship. One outdoor activity involves John leading Mary on a *trust walk* wherein John is responsible for leading Mary blindfolded down a bumpy and curvy wilderness path strewn with rocks,

sticks, and low-lying branches. Under the guidance of the activity leader, John is coached in how to communicate to Mary what obstructions he sees and what she needs to do to navigate the path safely. Mary is supported to take the risk of trusting that John can guide her safely to the path's end. Both complete the task with newfound appreciation for each other.

Opportunities for reflection are also built in to the TOP process at various stages. For example, prior to the trust walk activity, John and Mary might have been encouraged to view the approaching activity as a way of demonstrating the value of communication and trust (frontloading). Then, following the activity, they might have been asked to consider how the challenge and success of their experience with this activity could act as a metaphor for the work they need to do together to improve their relationship. Mary's experience with John's open and careful communication, and of his careful consideration for her welfare, could be explored along with John's experience of being trusted by Mary to take care of her.

The essence of the experiential methodology underlying TOP is that learning occurs more readily and at deeper levels of understanding when it is experienced directly, and when that experience is framed in such a way as to have personal meaning to that individual. Much of the therapeutic power of experiential methodology is that it sets the stage for experiencing success firsthand by providing individuals with a novel environment (which temporarily heightens anxiety), and then by maximizing the chances for success through careful development of the experience and effective therapeutic support and encouragement.

In addition, the outdoor setting used in many TOP interventions offers its own unique therapeutic value. For example, many people feel that the outdoors offers a naturally relaxing setting in which they may augment the integration of new attitudes, beliefs and corresponding behaviors. This catharsis often occurs as a result of an individual being able, at least temporarily, to escape modern technology and the many pressures of everyday life. New learning may be further enhanced by the multisensory nature of the outdoors, thus, heightening the potential for learning and enhancing physical experiences. Finally, the outdoor setting may put at ease those persons who might feel uncomfortable addressing sensitive and personal issues in the sometimes "threatening" environment of a clinical setting.

Concluding Comments

A number of questions and issues remain that should be fully addressed by those using TOP techniques. These issues are both structural (e.g., how programs are managed) and efficacy-based (e.g., how effective the programs are).

Structural Issues

Questions and issues that are structural in nature include the following:

1. What types and levels of training should CTRSs possess before engaging in TOP activities? If organizations expect therapists to have both outdoor and therapeutic skills, is there a viable pool of people available? Would the salaries be commensurate with these skill levels?

2. Traditionally, TOP activities are often viewed as "stand alone" experiences, often somewhat separated from other therapeutic interventions and processes. What strategies can a CTRS put into place that will ensure a higher level of continuity among the various intervention approaches?

3. What types of clients are inappropriate for TOP types of experiences? Would there be a systematic bias against certain groups that may collide with federal or state laws against discrimination? Would certain groups be excluded based mainly on anecdotal knowledge rather than scientific data? Who would make these decisions?

Efficacy Issues

Some questions related to the efficacy of TOP as a modality include the following:

1. What is the longitudinal effect of TOP activities and experiences? Is this effect significantly different from more traditional therapeutic programs, both in terms of effect and "durability?" Are these effects important enough to warrant exposing the client to the risks and challenges concomitant with TOP?

2. What is the dose-response effect? That is, does program length matter, or is there a length of time after which the beneficial effects decrease or are even eliminated?

3. Are primary therapy programs more or less effective, than adjunctive programs? Wilson and Lipsey (2000) suggest that for

delinquent youth, having the TOP experience as a part of a larger treatment may be less effective than the TOP experience as stand-alone, singular event. Currently, the research base is nondeclarative in this case.

4. What sequence or progression of activities and experiences are the most effective in creating which changes?

In conclusion, as the TOP modality matures and becomes more theory-based, answers to many of these and other questions will be forthcoming. While not a panacea, TOP can be effective and useful within therapeutic recreation settings as an adjunct or stand-alone treatment. Along with this effectiveness, however, comes the need for staff that have a different mix of training and background. This training and background includes both therapeutic and outdoor skills, coupled with an agency or organization that is philosophically grounded in providing therapeutic outdoor opportunities to its clients.

Reading Comprehension Questions

1. Briefly trace the historical development of TOP including the evolution of wilderness and adventure therapies. What elements are common to both?

2. What distinguishing characteristics differentiate TOP activities from traditional therapeutic recreation programs? Are all client populations suitable for TOP activities? Why or why not?

3. The benefits gleaned from participation in therapeutic outdoor programs have steadily increased their popularity as an intervention tool. Design a mini program of activities that would draw upon the therapeutic benefits in the psychological, sociological and physiological domains. Include goals and objectives for each activity and its corresponding domain.

4. What are some ways that TOP experiences can be particularly effective in a therapeutic recreation setting?

5. What recent developments in psychology promise to bring the fields of TOP and psychology closer together? Which therapeutic approach from psychology seems to fit especially well within the framework and philosophy of TOP?

6. What are the current efficacy issues with regards to TOP? What role will risk management play in designing future therapeutic outdoor programs?

References

Asher, S., Huffaker, G., and McNally, M. (1994). Therapeutic considerations of wilderness experiences for incest and rape victims. *Women and Therapy, 15* (3–4), 161–174.

Austin, D. R. (1998). The Health Protection/Health Promotion Model. *Therapeutic Recreation Journal, 32,* 109–117.

Austin, D. R. (1991). Introduction and overview. In D. R. Austin and M. E. Crawford (Eds.), *Therapeutic recreation: An introduction* (pp. 1–29). Englewood Cliffs, NJ: Prentice Hall.

Bluebond-Langer, M., Perkel, D., Goertzel, T., Nelson, K., and McGeary, J. (1990). Children's knowledge of cancer and its treatment: Impact of an oncology camp experience. *Journal of Pediatrics, 116,* 207–213.

Cason, D. and Gillis, H. (1994). A meta-analysis of outdoor adventure programming with adolescents. *Journal of Experiential Education, 17*(1), 40–47.

Crisp, S. (1998). International models of best practice in wilderness and adventure therapy. In C. M. Itin (Ed.), *Exploring the boundaries of adventure therapy: International perspectives* (pp. 56–74). Boulder, CO: Association of Experiential Education.

Compton, D. M. (Ed.). (1997). *Issues in therapeutic recreation: Toward the new millennium* (2nd ed.). Champaign, IL: Sagamore.

Datillo, J. and Murphy, W. D. (1987). Facilitating the challenge in adventure recreation for persons with disabilities. *Therapeutic Recreation Journal, 21*(3), 14–21.

Davis-Berman, J. and Berman, D. (1994). *Wilderness therapy: Foundations, theory, and research.* Dubuque, IA: Kendall/Hunt.

deShazer, S. (1988). *Clues: Investigating solutions in brief therapy.* New York, NY: W. W. Norton & Co.

Dieser, R. and Voight, A. (1998) Therapeutic recreation and relapse prevention intervention. *Parks & Recreation, 33*(5), 78–83.

Ewert, A., McCormick, B., and Voight, A. (2001). Outdoor experiential therapies: Implications for TR practice. *Therapeutic Recreation Journal, 35*(2), 107–122.

Ewert, A., McCormick, B., and Voight, A. (1999, April). *Outdoor experiential therapy: Introduction and overview.* Paper presented at the 28th Annual Midwest Symposium on Therapeutic Recreation, St. Louis, MO.

Friese, G. T. (1996). *Inventory and classification of wilderness experience programs.* Unpublished masters thesis, University of Idaho, Moscow, ID.

Gass, M. (1993). Programming applications of adventure therapy. In M. Gass (Ed.), *Adventure therapy: Therapeutic applications of adventure programming* (pp. 73–81). Dubuque, IA: Kendall/Hunt.

Gillis, H. L. (1998). The journey in OZ: From activity-based psychotherapy to adventure therapy. In C. Itin (Ed.), *Exploring the boundaries of adventure therapy: International perspectives* (pp. 9–20). Boulder, CO: Association of Experiential Education.

Gillis, H. L. (1995). If I conduct pursuits with clinical populations, am I an adventure therapist? *Journal of Leisurability, 22*(2), 5–15.

Gillis, L. and Thomsen, D. (1996, January). *A research update (1992–1995) of adventure therapy: Challenge activities and ropes courses, wilderness expeditions, and residential camping programs.* Paper presented at the Coalition for Education in the Outdoors Symposium, Bradford Woods, Indiana University, Martinsville, IN.

Hattie, J., Marsh, H., Neill, J., and Richards, G. (1997). Adventure education and Outward Bound: Out-of-class experiences that make a lasting difference. *Review of Educational Research, 67*(1), 43–87.

Herbert, J. (2000). Director and staff reviews on including persons with severe disabilities in therapeutic adventure. *Therapeutic Recreation Journal, 34*(1), 16–32.

Humberstone, B. and Lynch, P. (1991). Girls' concepts of themselves and their experience in outdoor education programmes. *Journal of Adventure Education and Outdoor Leadership, 8,* 27–31.

Iso-Ahola, S. (1980). *The social psychology of leisure and recreation.* Dubuque, IA: Wm. C. Brown.

Itin, C. (Ed.). (1998). *Exploring the boundaries of adventure therapy: International perspectives.* Boulder, CO: Association of Experiential Education.

Kaplan, R. and Kaplan, S. (1989). *The experience of nature: A psychological perspective.* New York, NY: Cambridge University Press.

Kimball, R. (1980). *Wilderness/adventure programs for juvenile offenders.* Chicago, IL: University of Chicago, School of Social Service Administration.

Levitt, L. (1994). What is the therapeutic value of camping for emotionally disturbed girls? Copublished simultaneously in *Women and Therapy, 15*(3/4), 129–137 and by Hawthorn Press.

McAvoy, L. H. (1987). Education for outdoor leadership. In J. F. Meyer, T. W. Morash, and G. E. Welton (Eds.), *High adventure outdoor pursuits* (pp. 459–476). Columbus, OH: Publishing Horizons.

Nadler, R. S. and Luckner, J. L. (1992). *Processing the adventure experience: Theory and practice.* Dubuque, IA: Kendall/Hunt.

Neill, J. T. and Richards, G. E. (1999). Does outdoor education really work? A summary of recent meta-analyses. *Australian Journal of Outdoor Education, 3*(1), 2–9.

Nichols, D. and Fines, L. (1995, Spring). Self-concept, attitude and satisfaction benefits of outdoor adventure activities: The case for recreational kayaking. *Journal of Leisurability*, 38–44.

Paffenbarger, R. S., Hyde, R. T. Jr., and Dow, A. (1991). Health benefits of physical activity. In B. L. Driver, P. J. Brown, and G. L. Peterson (Eds.), *Benefits of leisure* (pp. 49–57). State College, PA: Venture Publishing, Inc.

Ralston, H. III. (1991). Creation and recreation: Environmental benefits and human leisure. In B. L. Driver, P. J. Brown, and G. L. Peterson (Eds.), *Benefits of leisure* (pp. 393–403). State College, PA: Venture Publishing, Inc.

Russell, K. C. and Hendee, J. C. (2000). *Outdoor behavioral healthcare: Definitions, common practice, expected outcomes, and a nationwide survey of programs.* (Technical Report No. 26, 87 pp.). Moscow, ID: Idaho Forest, Wildlife and Range Experiment Station.

Russell, K. C. and Hendee, J. C. (1999). Wilderness therapy as an intervention and treatment for adolescents with behavioral problems. In A. E. Watson, G. Aplet, and J. C. Hendee (Eds.), *World congress proceedings on research management and allocation (Vol. II).* Ogden, UT: USDA Forest Service, Rocky Mountain Research Station.

Sahler, O. and Carpenter, P. (1989, June). Evaluation of a camp program for siblings of children with cancer. *American Journal of Disease of Children, 143,* 690–696.

Schleien, S., McAvoy, L. H., Lais, G., and Rynders, J. (1993). *Integrated outdoor education and adventure programs.* Champaign, IL: Sagamore.

Seligman, M. and Csikszentmihalyi, M. (2000). Positive psychology: An introduction. *American Psychologist, 55*(1), 5–14.

Stumbo, N. J. and Peterson, C. J. (1998) The Leisure Ability Model. *Therapeutic Recreation Journal, 32,* 82–86.

Tate, D. and Ellis, G. (1997). Effects of facilitation techniques on challenge initiative related outcomes among adolescents receiving mental health services. *Therapeutic Recreation Journal, 31,* 92–107.

Ulrich, R., Dimberg, U., and Driver, B. L. (1991). Psychophysiological indicators of leisure benefits. In B. L. Driver, P. J. Brown, and G. L. Peterson (Eds.), *Benefits of leisure* (pp. 73–87). State College, PA: Venture Publishing, Inc.

Walsh, V. and G. Golins. (1976). *The exploration of the Outward Bound process.* (Mimeograph). Denver, CO: Colorado Outward Bound School.

Wilson, S. J. and Lipsey, M. W. (2000). Wilderness challenge programs for delinquent youth: A meta-analysis of outcome evaluation. *Evaluation and Program Planning, 23,* 1–12.

Witman, J. and Preskenis, K. (1996). Adventure programming with an individual who has multiple personality disorder: A case history. *Therapeutic Recreation Journal, 30,* 289–296.

Chapter 8

Increasing Cultural Competence in Therapeutic Recreation

Deb Getz, Re.D., CTRS

As the people of the United Stated age and become more culturally diverse, it is increasingly important for therapeutic recreation professionals to increase their awareness of the impact of culture. According to the U.S. Census Bureau (2000), the Hispanic race has seen the largest increase in the last ten years (58%). This large increase reveals that there are more people who self-identify to be Latino than people who self-identify as African American. The number of people 65 and over increased by 12% between 1990 and 2000. In addition, different regions of the country have also seen significant growth in other races and age groups. These demographic shifts compel therapeutic recreation providers to look at their services in a different way.

As the demographics of the country change it is important to understand that there is an "increased demand for culturally sensitive services for diverse populations" (Peregoy, Schliebner & Deiser, 1997, p. 275). Austin (1999) notes, "It is vitally important that therapeutic recreation specialists educate themselves so that they are competent to serve clients with different ethnic and cultural backgrounds" (p. 239). He states:

> It has been suggested within the counseling literature that it is unethical for helping professionals to not be competent in the provision of services to clients from culturally diverse populations. (p. 238)

Knowledge of diversity issues is crucial when working with others.

Cultural Diversity and Therapeutic Recreation

The therapeutic recreation process has long been the standard for therapeutic recreation professionals (Austin, 1999; Reynolds & O'Morrow, 1985).

This process includes four steps: assessment, planning, implementation, and evaluation. Knowledge of the patient's cultural background can increase the effectiveness of each of these steps, and can ultimately increase the overall success of the treatment process.

During the *assessment* phase of the process, the client's problems, concerns, or strengths are determined (Austin, 1999). Ethically, this is where the primary questions about diversity should be addressed. The sooner the therapist gains this basic information, the sooner he or she will be able to understand the patient. Both of the accrediting bodies commonly involved with therapeutic recreation, the Joint Commission on Accreditation of Healthcare Organizations (JCAHO) and the Rehabilitation Accreditation Commission (CARF) acknowledge the need for including diversity as a key component of treatment and are increasing their focus on these issues as they complete the accreditation review process (CARF, 2001; JCAHO, 2001).

Efforts to gain knowledge of the client's culture at this phase can provide considerable insight into the patient's life. Each bit of information can increase the therapist's understanding of the client's culture and can be crucial to the therapeutic relationship. This includes understanding the client's communication style, race, religion, sexual preference, socioeconomic status, family responsibilities, and many other components. After this information is ascertained, the therapist then can work with the client to develop the treatment plan.

The next step of the therapeutic recreation process is *planning*; plans are created to meet the identified needs of the patient (Austin, 1999). During the planning phase it is important to consider the patient's interests, values, family structure, religion, and the many other aspects of culture. Success during the planning stage can be limited if cultural considerations are not included as part of the process.

During the *implementation* phase of the therapeutic recreation process, the therapist and the patient carry out the plan. Special considerations during this phase include transportation, socioeconomic status, employment, social relationships, and social support. It is important to consider culture with each aspect of the implementation.

Evaluation, the final step of the therapeutic recreation process, is conducted to determine how effective the intervention has been for the patient. Interventions take place throughout the treatment process as well as at the end. Cultural concerns specific to evaluation include the openness of the client, the interactions that may have taken place with the family or significant others, or the patient's openness to providing feedback.

Discussions About Diversity May Be Difficult

When initiating conversation or thought about diversity issues, it is important to understand that due to the personal nature of the discussion there will be components where individuals may not be comfortable. This lack of comfort generally results when people discuss or ponder topics with which they are unfamiliar, or if they are asked to discuss issues that they believe are not to be discussed outside the home. Understanding differences in communication styles are a key part of understanding a variety of cultural groups. Some cultures respect and honor the ability to keep their personal lives to themselves, other cultures place great respect in their elders and have difficulty sharing their lives with people who are older than they are. In other cultures, it is a sign of weakness to be ill; acknowledging illness is much like acknowledging weakness. Care should be taken to have an open mind and to work toward increasing knowledge about similarities and differences among and between groups. It should also be noted that any discomfort during this stage of the process will likely begin to disappear as more knowledge is gained, and familiarity with the group increases.

It is crucial to realize that every effort must be made to ensure that a level of emotional safety is achieved within a group prior to initiating any deep discussion related to cultural differences. This level of safety must be sought in an attempt to make participants feel comfortable with sharing their thoughts and beliefs as well as encouraging them to ask questions that they may not have felt comfortable with in previous settings. Due to cultural differences, some individuals may never feel comfortable with some discussions, and these individual differences should be respected. Alternatives to group discussion may be more appropriate in such cases.

Understanding Key Terms

Culture can be defined as "any group of people who identify or associate with one another on the basis of some common purpose, need, or similarity of background" (Axelson, 1993, p. 3). Common aspects of culture include: gender, age, race, ethnicity, socioeconomic status, sexual orientation, and disability.

Diversity is simply difference or variety. When discussing cultural diversity, it is considered a difference or variety regarding individual learned behavior. It is important to consider general definitions when discussing these terms, because as recreation therapists it is crucial to work to understand as much as possible about from as many different perspectives as possible.

Cultural competence is the lifelong pursuit of increasing personal awareness of other cultures. This is a conscious effort of working toward the goal of gaining a working knowledge of all cultures represented within one's personal and professional life.

Race is defined as a group of people who have genetically transmitted physical characteristics, which may include skin, eye and hair color, facial features, height, and/or body type (Sheldon & Datillo, 1997). During the 2000 U.S. Census individuals were asked to identify their race from the following list: White, Black or African American, American Indian or Alaska Native, Asian, Native Hawaiian or Other Pacific Islander, and Some Other Race. This was the first year that respondents were allowed to choose more than one race. In the year 2000, 97.6% reported as one race, 2.4% identified as "two or more races." The results by racial group reflected the following percentages: Alaska Native 0.9%, Asian 3.6%, Asian Pacific Islander 0.1%, Black 12%, White 75%, and Other 5% (U.S. Bureau of the Census, 2000).

Racism represents the "belief that some races are inherently superior to others" (Axelson, 1993).

Prejudice is an irrational attitude or behavior directed against an individual or a group, or their supposed characteristics. Prejudice has been identified as one of the:

> ...most serious psychological and social problems existing in the United States today. The faulty reasoning behind prejudice can lead to the grouping of diverse groups into a single category based on a single racial trait. (Axelson, 1993)

Cultural encapsulation is a practice in which other cultures are ignored. Features that are present during cultural encapsulation include:

a. Reality is defined according to one set of cultural norms and assumptions;

b. There is an insensitivity to cultural variation and an assumption that there is only one legitimate viewpoint from which to judge other people and situations; and

c. No proof is sought to justify assumptions about a particular culture (Peregoy & Dieser, 1997).

Kindred Professions and Diversity Education

The kindred professions of counseling, social work, and nursing have included diversity education as part of their educational requirements for more than twenty years (Kleinman, 1977; Leininger, 1995; Sue et al., 1982). Counseling professionals acknowledge multicultural counseling as the "preparation and practices that integrate culture-specific awareness, knowledge, and skills into counseling interactions" (Arredondo, 1999). In 1991, Sue stated:

> We can no longer rely on an ethnocentric orientation in the delivery of mental health services. This bias has been highly destructive…and we need to expand our perception of what constitutes [culturally] appropriate counseling/therapy practice. (p. 100)

Support for including culture as a part of psychotherapy was provided by Wehrle (1995) when he identified that culture pervades psychotherapy regardless of whether it is intercultural or obviously crosscultural. If the therapist does not acknowledge this connection then the client–therapist relationship will suffer.

Professional nursing literature reflects similar motivation. They utilize the term *transcultural nursing* which is defined as:

> A formal area of study and practice in nursing, focusing upon comparative holistic cultural care, health, and illness patterns of individuals and groups with respect to differences and similarities in cultural values, beliefs, and practices. The goal is to provide culturally congruent, sensitive, and competent nursing care to people of diverse cultures. (Leininger, 1995, p. 4)

Support for diversity education in social work is clear. Walters, Strom-Gottfried, and Sullivan stated that "social workers must be well prepared to work with any array of individuals from a variety of cultural perspectives" (1998, p. 354). The multicultural aspect of social work is defined as "teaching about a natural phenomenon; the recognition of human differences, and acceptance of this, forms as an integral part of the human social condition" (Mayadas, 1997, p. 231).

As a method to standardize education, each of these professions has established guidelines and/or competencies to use as a guide for increasing cultural competence among their respective students. As a profession, therapeutic recreation can learn from evaluating the various lists of competencies and then utilizing those competencies that are important as a part of therapeutic recreation practice.

In an analysis of these competencies, Getz (2000) revealed a list of competencies that were reviewed by a group of twenty individuals with expertise in therapeutic recreation and diversity education issues. The results of this study revealed 38 competencies which were then divided into three primary categories:

a. The primary level—awareness of worldview;

b. The secondary level—developing culturally appropriate intervention strategies and techniques; and

c. The advanced level—continuing education.

Throughout the primary level, therapeutic recreation students are encouraged to examine their own culture and, after significant thought and introspection, to examine the cultures of others. It has been well-documented (Axelson, 1993; Leininger, 1995; Sue et al., 1982) that one must understand his or her own culture before he or she can truly gain an understanding of other cultures. Throughout this level students are encouraged to evaluate their own worldview as well as the worldview of others. The focus is on a variety of issues including: communication styles, learning styles, the impact of racism, stereotyping, and discrimination.

After the primary level has been mastered, the second category of competencies is introduced. This includes the development of culturally appropriate intervention strategies and techniques. During this second level, the student is encouraged to increase their knowledge of, and ability to apply, interpersonal skills and intervention methods suited to particular groups. Competence specific to assessment tools, institutional barriers, and the types of games and activities participated in by specific groups become important issues within this category (Getz, 2000).

The last category identified by Getz (2000) is the advanced level—continuing education. This level is generally reached after undergraduate preparation, and requires that therapeutic recreation "student" seek out continuing education to continue to refine their cultural competence.

Understand Your Own Values and Beliefs

As you begin to evaluate your own culture, it is important that you reflect on your own values and beliefs. *Values* have been defined as an operational belief accepted by an individual. They serve as a determining factor in our lives and help to provide principles by which we live (Austin, 1999).

Values clarification is a task that can assist you in better understanding how you determine your beliefs and judgments. Common topics that are tied to values include religion, sexual preference, work ethic, family, culture, leisure, age, and education.

Examine Your Values and Beliefs

Consider the following list of individuals. For each individual write down the first thoughts that comes to your mind. From your written responses attempt to discern what components you value, and those components that you see having little or no value.

- A physician
- A homeless person
- A college student
- A homosexual male
- A Catholic priest

- A college professor
- An attorney
- A millionaire
- An elderly male
- A drug user

What was your emotional reaction to each of these individuals? Were you surprised by your responses? Did you make value judgments about these individuals based upon the minimal amount of information you had? Which group(s) do you know the most about? Which group(s) do you know the least about? What group(s) do you think would provide the most challenges for you as a therapeutic recreation provider?

When many individuals begin their experiences in a clinical setting there are always clients that provide special challenges. The first step in overcoming these challenges is understanding your own values and beliefs. As you mature as a therapeutic recreation professional, it will become clear which client cultures are more difficult for you. The challenge, then, is to discern if the difficulty lies within your own belief system.

When working in clinical practice, it is important to acknowledge that your cultural beliefs exist. Even more importantly, one must be willing to acknowledge that clients may not hold the same beliefs as you do. The challenge is trying to understand the perspective of the client, so that you can best understand his or her views and beliefs. This is not to say that you have to agree with clients' values and beliefs, simply that you must understand their views and beliefs in order to best develop interventions and treatment plans that are appropriate and effective.

Self-Evaluation Tool

The self-evaluation tool (Figure 8.1) was designed to assist students in determining their current level of knowledge about cultural issues. Simply rate the statements based on your level of agreement. After the statements are rated, add up your score and compare it to the scale at the end of the self-evaluation tool.

Seek More Information

Regardless of one's current knowledge of culture and cultural groups, there is always more to learn. Information is constantly changing and as a result one should continuously seek new sources of information. Working toward cultural competence as a recreation therapist is a ongoing process. There are a variety of ways that one can seek out more information about culture:

Continuing education specific to cultural competence is the ethical responsibility of the practitioner.

Professional conferences provide an excellent opportunity to increase knowledge as well as to interact with other professionals. Seek out a variety of conferences that bring together individuals from different professions, regions, or cultures.

Local cultural events provide a wealth of information. Ethnic fairs, religious festivals, and other events that are open to the public can offer opportunities to get a picture of other cultures.

Volunteer opportunities within the community can also provide a wealth of information. Seek out positions that work with a variety of people of different socioeconomic statuses, ethnicities, or other cultural groups with which you are less familiar.

Professional organizations provide another source of information. Both the American Therapeutic Recreation Association (ATRA) and the National Therapeutic Recreation Society (NTRS) have committees that focus on diversity issues. Each has been active in shaping the direction of key documents in the profession.

Local libraries offer books for leisure reading written by authors of different races which can provide insight into how other cultures view a variety of issues.

Knowledge of Cultural Issues Self-Evaluation

Rate the following statements based on your level of agreement. After you rate each statement, add up your score and compare your results to the scale that appears at the end.

1 — Strongly Disagree	3 — Somewhat Agree
2 — Somewhat Disagree	4 — Strongly Agree

1. I understand my own cultural beliefs, values, and patterns of caring. 1 2 3 4

2. I understand that my individual experiences influence how I interact with others. 1 2 3 4

3. I understand that cultural differences exist between individuals. 1 2 3 4

4. I am aware of how oppression, racism, discrimination, and stereotyping effect me personally. 1 2 3 4

5. I have an understanding of my own preferred communication style or patterns. 1 2 3 4

6. I have an understanding of my own preferred learning style. 1 2 3 4

7. I have an understanding of others' cultural heritage or background. 1 2 3 4

8. I understand that care and health practices vary among and between cultures. 1 2 3 4

9. I understand that there are different healing practices among and between cultures. 1 2 3 4

10. I understand the influence that culture has on verbal and nonverbal interactions. 1 2 3 4

11. I understand how culture can influence the manifestation of psychological disorders. 1 2 3 4

12. I understand that all cultural groups have a right to their cultural values. 1 2 3 4

13. I understand how culture can impact feelings of powerlessness. 1 2 3 4

14. I understand how culture can influence identify formation. 1 2 3 4

15. I have an understanding of how culture can influence an individual's definition of the term recreation. 1 2 3 4

Figure 8.1   Knowledge of Cultural Issues Self-Evaluation Tool

16. I have an understanding of how culture can influence an individual's definition of illness and disability.   1 2 3 4

17. I have an understanding of the role that culture has on specific intervention techniques.   1 2 3 4

18. I have an understanding of the role of communicating with clients in their primary language.   1 2 3 4

19. I am aware of the potential cultural bias that exists with many assessment instruments.   1 2 3 4

20. I have the knowledge and ability to apply interpersonal skills and intervention methods suited to particular cultural groups.   1 2 3 4

21. I have an understanding of the research literature pertaining specifically to therapeutic recreation and culture.   1 2 3 4

22. I have an understanding of the importance of valuing other cultures in my own personal and professional life.   1 2 3 4

Add your total score and compare to the following scale:

22–54 Minimal Knowledge: You need to take a long look at yourself and your profession to gain a better understanding of your culture and the cultures of those around you.

55–70 Moderate Knowledge: You have a great start toward understanding culture and its role in your personal and professional life. As you continue your education it is crucial that you take more time to seek out information about culture and the impact that it can have in your life.

71–88 Strong Knowledge: Your cultural understanding is strong and it is important that you continue to work to increase your knowledge. Be sure to find ways to increase your knowledge as you complete your formal education and work toward continuing education.

Figure 8.1   Knowledge of Cultural Issues Self-Evaluation Tool (continued)

Other suggestions for increasing one's understanding of individual differences are provided by Sheldon and Dattillo (1997). They recommend that individuals examine their own biases; learn about the community where they provide services; examine the language others use; think about families (both traditional and nontraditional); and learn about differences between individuals.

Summary

The interactive nature of the therapeutic recreation process requires that a therapeutic relationship be developed. For this to occur, the therapeutic recreation providers must seek out and utilize culturally specific information to interact effectively with their clients. All therapeutic recreation practitioners must meet the challenge to increase their personal and professional knowledge of culture, and to utilize this knowledge to create truly individualized treatment plans.

Reading Comprehension Questions

1. Why should therapeutic recreation professionals seek to increase their knowledge of culture?

2. Identify at least one aspect of culture that is important to ascertain for each step of the therapeutic recreation process.

3. Identify at least one kindred profession that has included cultural competence as a part of professional preparation.

4. Identify the three primary categories of diversity education identified in the chapter.

5. Define these terms: culture, race, prejudice, and cultural encapsulation.

6. Identify at least three ways you can increase your awareness of culture.

References

Arredondo, P. (1999). Multicultural counseling competencies as tools to address oppression and racism. *Journal of Counseling and Development, 77*(1), 102–108.

Austin, D. R. (1999). *Therapeutic recreation: Process and techniques* (4th ed.). Champaign, IL: Sagamore.

Axelson, J. A. (1993). *Counseling and development in a multicultural society.* Belmont, CA: Brooks/Cole.

Getz, D. A. (2000). *Identifying key competencies in multicultural education for entry-level therapeutic recreation practitioners.* Unpublished doctoral dissertation, Indiana University.

Joint Commission on Accreditation of Hospital Organizations. (2001). *Hospital Accreditation Standards.* Washington, DC: Joint Commission Resources.

Kleinman, A. (1977). Depression, somatization, and "the new cross-cultural psychiatry." *Social Science and Medicine, 11*, 3–10.

Leininger, M. (1995). *Transcultural nursing: Concepts, theories, research and practices* (2nd ed.). New York, NY: McGraw-Hill.

Mayadas, N. S. (1997). Should social work celebrate its unity or diversity? *Journal of Social Work Education, 33*, 229–234.

Peregoy, J. J., Schliebner, C. T., and Dieser, R. B. (1997). In D. M. Compton (Ed.), *Issues in therapeutic recreation: Toward the new millennium.* Champaign, IL: Sagamore.

Peregoy, J. J. and Deiser, R. B. (1997). Multicultural awareness in therapeutic recreation: Hamlet living. *Therapeutic Recreation Journal, 31*(3), 174–178.

Rehabilitation Accreditation Commission (CARF). (2001). *Behavioral health standards manual.* Tuscon, AZ: CARF.

Reynolds, R. P. and O'Morrow, G. S. (1985). *Problems, issues and concepts in therapeutic recreation.* Englewood Cliffs, NJ: Prentice Hall.

Sheldon, K. and Dattillo, J. (1997). Multiculturalism in therapeutic recreation: Terminology clarification and practical suggestions. *Therapeutic Recreation Journal, 31*(3), 148–159.

Sue, D. (1991). A model of cultural diversity training. *Journal of Counseling and Development, 70*, 99–105.

Sue, D., Bernier, J., Durran, A., Feinberg, L., Pedersen, P., Smith, E., and Vasquez-Nuttal, E. (1982). Professional forum, position paper: Cross-cultural counseling competencies. *The Counseling Psychologist, 10*, 45–52.

U.S. Bureau of the Census. (2000). *U.S. Census.* Washington, DC: Government Printing Office.

Walters, G. I., Strom-Gottfried, K., and Sullivan, M. (1998). Assembling pieces in the diversity puzzle: A field model. *Journal of Social Work Education, 34*(3), 353–363.

Wehrle, B. (1995). *Pathways to multicultural counseling competence: A developmental journey.* Pacific Grove, CA: Brooks/Cole.

Chapter 9

Toward Evidence-Based Therapeutic Recreation Practice

Youngkhill Lee, Ph.D., CTRS
Bryan P. McCormick, Ph.D., CTRS

The phrase *evidence-based practice* is a relatively new term within health and human services. Healthcare reform and the growing focus on cost-effective delivery of services have created an environment in which service providers are increasingly being held accountable for service effectiveness and quality (Stumbo, 1996). This higher standard of accountability is being applied to the development, implementation and evaluation of services. In addition to environmental pressures, interest in evidence-based practice has also been stimulated by increased access to information. The advancement in information technology, such as the World Wide Web, has improved access to research evidence. As access to information about health and human services has increased, barriers to using research findings in practice have diminished.

McCormick and Lee have discussed some of the basic conceptual issues related to evidence-based practice elsewhere (2001). In this chapter, they revisit basic concepts and offer some possible directions that therapeutic recreation practitioners can take given the profession's limited research evidence. The discussion is based on other professionals' views and experience as well as their own thoughts that might bring applications to therapeutic recreation. This chapter begins by visiting the basic concept of evidence-based practice followed by a discussion of some common myths related to evidence-based practice. Then, it presents a conceptual model that integrates research into the therapeutic recreation process. Next, it offers operational steps that help implement evidence-based practice in practical terms for therapeutic recreation. This chapter concludes with suggestions for the successful implementation of evidence-based practice.

What Is Evidence-Based Practice?

The purpose of evidence-based practice is to ensure that health and human service consumers have a greater assurance that they receive services based on the best available information (Brown, 1999). It is motivated not only by the minimization of clinical risk but also by maximizing the quality of care. Accountability is an ethical imperative in the current healthcare environment. Bloom, Fischer and Orme discussed accountability in terms of "the need to evaluate our practice and to provide evidence of the effectiveness of our work" (1995, p. 1). The evidence-based practice approach embraces the need for accountability. When differences in opinions emerge among clinicians with regard to managing client care, research evidence can provide objective guidelines as well as support for choosing one approach over another. In such situations, research evidence is "a respected rationale for care," and is "persuasive when logic, experience, and personal insight are not honored" (Brown, 1999, p. 7). Bury provided the following definition of evidence-based practice:

> Evidence-based practice is the conscientious, explicit and judicious use of current best evidence in making decisions about the care of individual patients, integrating individual clinical expertise with the best available external clinical evidence from systematic research. (1999, p. 12)

In evidence-based practice, an implicit motive is to ensure quality services based on the best available research evidence. As evidence-based practice has increasingly become an important approach in the current healthcare environment, many clinicians are still unsure about what exactly evidence-based practice implies (cf., Dubouloz, Egan, Vallerand & Zweck, 1999). The following section offers an additional explanation of evidence-based practice.

Conceptualization of Evidence-Based Practice

Terms such as *research-based practice, empirical practice, research utilization,* and *evidence-based healthcare* have been used to imply using research-generated knowledge to guide clinical practice (Brown, 1999; Perkins, Simnett & Wright, 1999; Reid, 1994). Other similar terms, including *review of literature, integrative review of research, evidence synthesis, systematic review, knowledge synthesis,* and *meta-analysis,* have also been used to characterize evidence-based practice (Stevens, 1999). When applied in clinical practice, these terms imply the use of research findings as a source of knowledge in the creation and implementation of interventions. Thus, evidence-based practice depends largely on the research that generates evidence demanded by the new healthcare environment.

In a sense, evidence-based practice is an attitude similar to research-mindedness. Instead, practitioners ask the following questions: (a) How do we know that what we do works? and (b) How can our practice be further enhanced? Asking these questions in practice can be applied to a number of different kinds of evidence from experience to statistics. It offers "a defense against practices that have become institutionalized on the basis of little or no evidence" (Perkins, Simnett & Wright, 1999, p. 4). Evidence-based practice implies that scientific evidence comes ahead of each clinician's experience and intuition in assessing clients, selecting interventions and delivering services, not vice versa (Bury, 1999). Evidence-based practice is the "conscientious, explicit, and judicious use of current best evidence in making decisions about the care of individual patients" (Sackett, Rosenberg, Gray, Haynes & Richardson, 1996, p. 1). However, it does not negate integrating individual clinical expertise, but instead uses it in conjunction with the best available external clinical evidence obtained from systematic review.

Evidence-based practice is a reflective process. Developing the ability to think on your feet, or reflect-in-action, is one of the roots of evidence-based practice. As reflective practitioners, therapists need to gather, assess, and use evidence as part of the way that they approach interventions (Perkins, Simnett & Wright, 1999). As well as thinking on your feet, to be reflective practitioners, therapists also need to think about their work afterwards—to reflect-on-action. This allows therapists to think about why they acted and felt the way they did, what was happening to others, what they didn't notice at the time that might have been helpful, and what they have learned which might help them to decide what to do in future. When therapists do this, they are drawing conclusions from what they have observed about both their own reactions and those of others. This is called *assessment of evidence.* In short, evidence-based practice is more than a technique—it's an attitude that characterizes reflective practice.

Reid (1994) identifies three facets of evidence-based practice:

a. The use of research methods in practice to facilitate assessment, to guide intervention planning, and to evaluate the results;

b. The application of interventions with demonstrated effectiveness; and

c. Knowledge building through disseminated studies carried out by practitioner-researchers.

Based on these elements, evidence-based practice can be (re)defined as *practice that is being continuously informed and guided by the systematic collection and inclusion of research and practice evidence in clinical work.* This definition suggests that many more empirical issues should be addressed and a wide array of systematic data collection and information processing activities can and should be used to inform practitioners and guide them in their practice.

Myths of Evidence-Based Practice

In addition to identifying what evidence-based practice is, it is also useful to identify what it is not. This section presents some common myths associated with evidence-based practice. In spite of its good intention, there are some myths and skepticism related to evidence-based practice.

A myth is a commonly believed but false idea. In generalized use, it is an untrue, popular tale, or half-truth. Sexton, Whiston, Blener and Waltz noted that various myths related to outcome research originated from "tensions inherent in any field of applied research, rather than the incomparability of research and practice" (1997, p. 10). The myths identified here are the result of introducing the concept of evidence-based practice in both graduate and undergraduate courses. Other professionals also share these myths regarding evidence-based practice.

Myth 1: Evidence-based practice ignores practitioners' clinical intuition and experience.

Evidence-based practice does not negate therapists' clinical experience. Instead, it implies that good therapists use both individual clinical expertise and the best available research evidence, and neither alone is enough (cf., Brown, 1999; Perkins, Simnett & Wright, 1999; Sackett et al., 1996). Sackett and colleagues pointed out that without clinical expertise:

> Practice risks becoming tyrannized by evidence, for even excellent external evidence may be inapplicable to, or inappropriate for, an individual patient. (1996, p. 1)

On the other hand, clinical experience itself is vulnerable to distortion and self-interest; it needs to be balanced by systematic research (Perkins, Simnett & Wright, 1999). In short, it is not that therapists' experience and intuition are unimportant sources of information for clinical practice, but that experience should not overrule the evidence presented in research.

Myth 2: Evidence-based practice is a "cookbook" approach.

Evidence-based practice does not take such a top-down approach like a cookbook. A cookbook approach would imply that all a practitioner needed to do was to find an intervention with research support and then apply it, without modification, to all clients with demonstrated need. Instead, evidence-based practice incorporates the best external research evidence by respecting individual clinical expertise and clients' choices and preferences associated with treatment (Bury, 1999). The incorporation of client choices and preferences into practice decisions requires that the practitioner employs research evidence flexibly. External research evidence can inform and guide the intervention, but does not fully replace individual clinical expertise. It is this expertise that "crafts" the intervention with external evidence that applies to client care. Research evidence should guide the intervention, but not to dominate all clinical decisions.

Myth 3: Evidence-based practice has primarily emerged and been implemented as a hidden cost-cutting idea in managed care.

Some clinicians fear that purchasers and managers "hijack" evidence-based practice to cut the costs of healthcare. This would not only be a misuse of evidence-based practice but also suggests a fundamental misunderstanding of its financial consequences. Evidence-based practice allows clinicians to identify and apply the most efficacious interventions to maximize the quality and quantity of life for individual clients. Therefore, an evidence-based practice approach may help to implement cost-effective intervention, although doing so is not the primary reason for its approach.

Myth 4: Without new research evidence, new interventions are impossible.

Research evidence does not necessarily come in a timely manner, and there are situations where therapists may have to move on with imperfect knowledge. Sometimes, it is not practical to wait for research evidence to definitively support an intervention before practitioners must implement it. Therefore, they need to proceed with what is available. In other words, practitioners have to learn how to work with incomplete knowledge while using the maximum amount of existing research findings. If practitioners wait for the evidence before they try anything new, there won't be any progress in practice (Perkins, Simnett & Wright, 1999). Although evidence-based practice is strongly influenced by research evidence, it is not completely dependent upon it for innovation.

Myth 5: Research evidence from nonexperimental designs should not be considered viable evidence.

It is true that well-controlled experimental studies (i.e., random control trials) are the best evidence. However, evidence-based practice is not restricted to randomized trials and meta-analyses. Practitioners can utilize the best external evidence with which to answer their clinical questions. Of course, most textbooks in research methods claim that nonexperimental designs have minimum explanatory power of cause-and-effect relationships. Thus, the most recommended approach is the randomized trial, which is the so-called "gold standard." The randomized trial is more likely to guide than to mislead when determining whether a treatment does more good than harm. However, some questions about therapy do not require randomized trials or cannot wait for the randomized control trials to be conducted. If research findings with randomized control trials are not available, the next best external evidence should guide practice.

Myth 6: Establishing and maintaining evidence-based practice demands too much time commitment.

This statement may be correct in a sense that recreation therapists have numerous pragmatic challenges in keeping abreast of all the research studies reported in journals. It takes time to keep up with evolving research findings and attend continuing education workshops and professional conferences. However, providing high-quality intervention does require a commitment by the practitioner to take the time and do what is needed to stay up-to-date (Persons, 1999). Practitioners who set aside time for locating and appraising research relevant to their practice will find that their day-to-day professional life is more interesting and satisfying (Brown, 1999). Further, integration of new ideas from research into day-to-day practice can be an intellectually and professionally fulfilling experience. Guided by research evidence, therapists provide their research rationale as they carry out a certain course of actions with clients. In short, being informed about current research provides therapists with a rich knowledge base to bring to professional conversations and consultations (Brown, 1999).

How To Do It

What does evidence-based practice mean to therapeutic recreation practice? Embracing evidence-based practice in therapeutic recreation services offers promise for improving the quality of therapeutic recreation practice. In other words, the use of evidence-based practice would increase the accountability of therapeutic recreation services. Some may argue, however, that while evidence-based care makes sense conceptually, it does not sound very practical due to the lack of research evidence in therapeutic recreation. In fact, the issue related to insufficient volume of research in therapeutic recreation is not a new one; numerous therapeutic recreation authors have raised this concern (e.g., Compton & Dieser, 1997; Lee & Yang, 2000; Witt, 1988). Does this mean that evidence-based practice is not a plausible option for therapeutic recreation practice? Although evidence-based practice is a plausible approach to therapeutic recreation practice, there are some obstacles.

Unfortunately, therapeutic recreation practitioners who wish to employ research findings in their practice have little guidance. One important deterrent to integrating evidence into practice is the lack of a conceptual model that guides evidence-based practice. Sexton and associates argued that:

> Many of the reasons for the research-practice gap are due to a lack of knowledge and awareness rather than because of any justifiable division between these two activities. (1997, p. x)

A clear conceptual model should exist to offer clear guidelines for this approach.

Conceptual Model

This conceptual model begins with the popular assessment, planning, implementation and evaluation (APIE) process model (Austin, 1999; O'Morrow & Reynolds, 1989). The APIE process "provides a systematic method of problem solving through a progression of phases" (Austin, 1999, p. 163). As Figure 9.1 (p. 172) indicates, the knowledge base of therapeutic recreation is the core of evidence-based practice in therapeutic recreation. As indicated earlier, the volume of research regarding therapeutic recreation is quite small as compared to that of physical rehabilitation or psychology, for example. This would appear to limit the ability of therapeutic recreation personnel to acquire research evidence to support practice. However, this model takes the approach that therapeutic recreation is an applied field, which uses research from a variety of areas to provide a foundation for practice. Granted, the strongest evidence to support activities in any of the APIE components would come from a clinical trial of relevant therapeutic recreation interventions. However, in the absence of such research evidence, the therapeutic recreation specialist should draw from related research evidence. The total knowledge base guides the assessment, planning, implementation and evaluation processes. Evidence-based practice addresses activities in (a) assessment of clients' need and baseline status; (b) the selection and identification of interventions; and (c) the evaluation of client progress and intervention effectiveness (Blythe, Tripodi & Briar, 1994).

Assessment

The use of valid and reliable measurement in the assessment process affords the practitioner the ability to use the assessment information as a basis for not only intervention, but also for the purposes of comparison of baseline to outcomes. Research evidence helps practitioners understand the illness experience of clients; what to ask; and what to look for. Research findings can enrich practitioners' understanding of how illness affects the lives of clients and their families. They can further direct attention to the psychosocial factors that influence health and illness behaviors and responses; and they can offer "descriptions of interpersonal approaches and actions that make the caregiving relationship more comfortable for patients" (Brown, 1999, p. 4). Research evidence also helps in selecting and using clinical assessment tools. Without proper validity and reliability information for assessment tools, a therapist is cautioned that the use of tools with unknown characteristics may produce erroneous results.

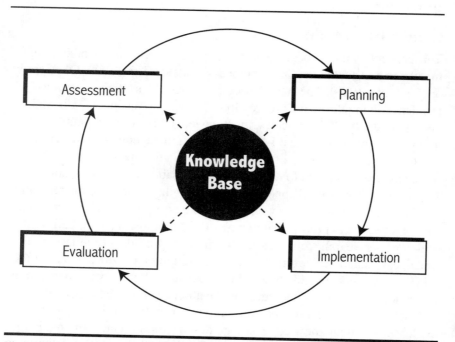

Figure 9.1   Evidence-Based Conceptual Model

Planning

Research evidence can direct the purpose and content of the intervention in terms of resultant outcomes. Research data provides an objective rationale for choosing one approach over another. Research evidence helps particularly when differences of opinion exist with regard to managing problems and making a clinical decision regarding an intervention. Research findings provide a rationale for the interventions, therapies, and strategies used by therapists. A useful starting point for identifying empirical evidence to support the planning phase is to examine reviews of research (e.g., Coyle, Kinney, Riley & Shank, 1991; Lee & Yang, 2000; McCormick & Funderburk, 2000). In addition to research evidence, Bury (1999) also suggested that both clinical expertise and client preference be included as evidence in planning. For example, what is the institutional history of success in providing a particular intervention? Is the client likely to consent to a particular intervention? What is the potential impact of the treatment on such things as health status or client satisfaction? Although these sources of evidence are not considered to be as strong as research evidence, research evidence should never entirely replace clinical judgment.

Implementation

The implementation stage of the model is the step in which the plan is put into action (Austin, 1999). In this stage, evidence guides how a plan is carried out. For example, a number of studies have found that certain types of feedback are more effective in impacting efficacy beliefs than others (Bandura, 1997; Ellis, Maughan-Pritchett & Ruddell, 1993). This evidence should be considered during the implementation of a plan of intervention aimed to improve a client's self-efficacy. Thus, evidence guides the identification of the content and process of carrying out the plan.

Evaluation

How does the knowledge base guide the evaluation of practice? One of the most important ingredients of evidence-based practice is the use of measurable data in the examination of the results of services. Evaluation in this evidence-based practice model enhances accountability through demonstration of the effectiveness of the services provided. Practitioners can demonstrate effectiveness by *systematically* tracking whether the service provided achieved its intended results. Evidence-based practice uses quantifiable data to make such determinations through the measurement between the baseline and end-point client data. In addition, the degree of attainment of treatment goals also may be used as a measurable basis for determining effectiveness (Kiresuk, Smith & Cardillo, 1994). Thus, in this phase of the model, evidence is used to guide best practices in evaluating the effectiveness of care.

The Strength of Research Evidence

Not all evidence is equally useful. There are a number of sources of evidence, and practitioners should carefully discern various types of evidence sources representing strong to weak evidence. Research evidence is derived from high-quality, systematic research. Clinical expertise is a clinician's experience with patients, established practice, experts in the field, and development of skills through continuing professional development. Related to this type of evidence are therapist's personal beliefs and values regarding their intervention based on previous experience. In addition, clients' beliefs and values also provide an important source of evidence. The inclusion of such evidence increases the client's sense of participation and control which is important to successful intervention (cf., Dattilo & Kleiber, Chapter 4).

Bury and Mead (1999) provided useful guidance in terms of the hierarchy of strength of evidence. When reviewing research evidence, the idea is to rank studies on the degree to which the observed results are likely to be attributable to the intervention being studied. It should be remembered that the hierarchy is based on high-quality studies being carried out in each category. As Table 9.1 indicates, the strongest types of evidence include research studies with well-designed randomized control trials. Designs using randomized control trials are considered the strongest form of evidence because they employ an experimental design. The research method of experimental design is the best approach to identify cause-and-effect relationships. However, Bury and Mead pointed out that one systematic review of multiple studies with this design contains stronger evidence than a single randomized control trial. It is this systematic review that differentiates the first and the second strongest evidence.

Why should systematic reviews be at the top of the list? First of all, it is important to draw a distinction between systematic reviews and other types of reviews. While many reviews summarize the results from a number of studies and draw conclusions, they have often been produced without a thorough search for all the available studies. Also, individual studies may not have been quality assessed. A systematic review, however, uses explicit methods to identify, select and critically appraise relevant research, and to collect and analyze the data from individual studies (Brown, 1999). This search for information is based on a clearly defined question.

Table 9.1	Hierarchy of Strength of Research Evidence (Bury & Mead, 1999)

Level	Type
I	Strong evidence from at least one systematic review of multiple, well-designed randomized control trials
II	Strong evidence from at least one properly designed randomized control trial of appropriate size
III	Evidence from well-designed trials without randomization, single group pre–post tests, time series, or matched-case control studies.
VI	Evidence from well-designed, nonexperimental studies
V	Opinions of respected authorities and descriptive studies or reports of expert committees

The difference between the second and third best evidence is the employment of *randomization* in research design. Randomization indicates that study participants were assigned to treatment and control groups at random, thus increasing the likelihood that the two groups are similar at the outset of the study. In addition, studies with experimental designs (Levels I–II) contain stronger evidence than those studies with nonexperimental designs (Levels III–IV). Finally, published accounts of authorities and descriptive studies provide the weakest research evidence.

Steps to Evidence-Based Practice

Rosenberg and Donald (1995) identified the following steps (Figure 9.2, p. 176) to implement evidence-based practice. These simplified steps are similar to Brown's (1999) pathway to evidence-based practice. Basically, the steps cover all necessary components for successful evidence-based practice.

Step 1: Formulate a clear clinical question from a patient's problem.
A recreation therapist can develop clinical questions when they involve any aspect of the clinical practice including causes of a problem, assessment, prognosis, treatment methods, and evaluation. If a recreation therapist is dealing with treatment methods, for example, guiding questions may be: Is intervention *x* effective? If so, what aspects of intervention *x* are helpful (e.g., the modality, structure of session, facilitation process, length and

frequency of the chosen intervention, physical and social contexts)? How can the effects of this intervention be enhanced? Further guiding questions might include: What might work with this type of client? What combination of clinical process will be most effective with this type of client?

Step 2: Search evidence for relevant clinical articles.

Journals provide important sources for evidence that are directly useful in clinical practice. Table 9.2 (pp. 179–180) provides a list of databases that recreation therapists will find useful to conduct literature searches to answer a particular question. Making clinical decisions using the research findings with similar client types is the most recommended approach. However, a recreation therapist should not eliminate or ignore research studies with different client populations. In spite of the fact that types of disability are different, practitioners can start consulting the research findings on specific problems. For example, if there are a number of strong research studies dealing with depression and stroke, practitioners

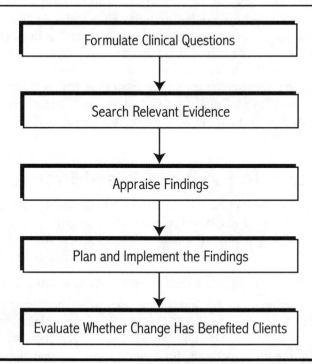

Figure 9.2   Operational Model for Evidence-Based Practice

may be able to apply the findings of this research to the similar types of physical disabilities (e.g., spinal cord injury, traumatic brain injury).

Step 3: Appraise the evidence.

The core of this step is to carefully discern good evidence from poor evidence. Readers might want to revisit the section entitled The Strength of Research Evidence and Table 9.1 (p. 175) which provide fundamental concepts for examining the hierarchy of evidence (i.e., from strong to weak evidence). While Levels I–II are the best types of evidence, a recreation therapist should not ignore findings from Levels III–V but instead interpret the findings cautiously. While most peer-reviewed research papers may utilize reliable and valid instruments to measure outcomes, a recreation therapist should make sure that the researchers report evidence related to reliability and validity of their measures.

Step 4: Implement useful findings in practice.

This step of the pathway involves actual implementation of the appraised studies. In this phase, a recreation therapist might want to consider if the treatment is consistent with clients' values, expectations, and preferences. The most efficacious treatment for Client A does not automatically mean that it is good for Client B. Therefore, a recreation therapist should not generalize findings to all clients. Related this issue is clinical judgment between study population and individual client. What similar characteristics exist between the study population and the clients? A recreation therapist should carefully apply the findings when significant differences exist between the subjects of a research study and the clientele he or she is working with.

Step 5: Evaluate the impact of change in practice.

A recreation therapist continuously monitors his or her own performance as well as evaluates the treatment applied. A guiding question may be asked: Is this intervention working for my client? Modification of treatment should occur when systematic evaluation indicates that no effect or a negative effect results for clients. The evaluation of the impact of the intervention can occur on both an individual and group basis. A recreation therapist might want to know what aspects of treatment (e.g., modality, structure of treatment, facilitation process, length and frequency of the treatment) were particularly helpful. Through evaluation, a recreation therapist becomes confident when he or she finds effectiveness and efficacy of treatment drawn from research evidence.

Conclusion and Recommendations

This chapter presented the basic concept of evidence-based practice and intended to help readers become aware of some common myths related to evidence-based practice. The conceptual model presented in this chapter also provides some possible directions that a recreation therapist can take. Further, the operational model (Figure 9.2, p. 176) might facilitate implementing evidence-based practice. In fact, there are various web-based databases (see Table 9.2) that can help recreation therapists access research evidence within healthcare and social sciences disciplines. Using these databases, recreation therapists are encouraged to apply the operational model introduced in this chapter to implement evidence-based practice.

Fortunately, the body of therapeutic recreation research continues to grow, and therapeutic recreation practitioners should be active and wise consumers of research studies by using this important form of evidence as a basis for practice. In order to successfully integrate research into practice, there are some suggestions that therapeutic recreation professional might want to consider.

First, successful implementation of evidence-based practice demands a collaborative relationship between practitioners and researchers. For the successful integration of research and practice to proceed, both practitioners and researchers need to understand the interdependent relationship between research and practice. In such a relationship, the experience of practitioners generates questions as researchers investigate those questions in a systematic manner. According to Sexton and colleagues (1997), practitioners need to be involved in both generating questions and using findings appropriately. In turn, researchers must focus on useful questions for clinical practice. The challenge is not to turn clinicians into researchers, but to help them recognize the need for partnership. An effective service to clients cannot be maximized unless practitioners and researchers forge a closer relationship.

Second, the content of continuing education in therapeutic recreation should reflect evidence-based practice. Continuing education is one important means to bridge the gap between research and practice. Grasso, Epstein, and Tripodi (1988) suggested that practice-oriented research training is effective in enhancing pro-research attitudes and facilitates the use of available information by practitioners. The new evolution of evidence-based practice demands that some continuing education programs in therapeutic recreation should address skills associated with gathering and interpreting research. As Alsop (1997) pointed out, failure to keep up with current research may lead to decay in professional knowledge and expertise, and

---

Table 9.2   Selected Online Research Databases

DATABASE   **Web Site**
Description
Time frame; Entries

CANCERLIT   **http://www.cancer.gov/cancer_information**
Comprhensive, international cancer-related research records from journal articles, governing reports, technical reports, meeting abstracts and papers, monographs, letters, and theses. Produced by the U.S. National Cancer Institute in cooperation with the National Library of Medicine.

1976–present; 4,000+ journals, 1.5 million records

THE COCHRANE LIBRARY   **http://www.cochrane.org/**
Regularly updated electronic library designed to make available the evidence needed to make informed healthcare decisions. Presents the growing body of work of the Cochrane Collaboration and others interested in evidence-based medicine. Maintains four databases: (a) the Cochrane Database of Systematic Review; (b) the Database of Abstracts of Reviews of Effectiveness; (c) the Cochrane Controlled Trials Register; and (d) the Cochrane Review Methodology Database.

CINAHL (Cumulative Index to Nursing and Allied Health Literature)   **http://www.cinahl.com/**
Literature related to nursing and the allied health disciplines; covers cardiopulmonary technology, physical therapy, emergency services, physician assistants, health education, radiological technology, medical laboratory, technology therapy, medical assistants, social service, healthcare, medical records, surgical technology, and occupational therapy; also includes alternative/complementary therapies, consumer health, biomedicine, and health science. Besides journals, selectively indexes audiovisual materials, educational software, conference proceedings, healthcare books, dissertations, and standards of practice.

1982–present; 350,000 records

EMBASE   **http://www.elsevier.com/** or **http://www.embase.com**
Covers nursing, dentistry, veterinary medicine, normal psychology, and alternative medicine; consider this database after searching MEDLINE and CINAHL.

1966–present; 4,000+ journals, 900,000 records

MEDLINE   **http://www.ncbi.nlm.nih.gov/PubMed/**
One of the most widely recognized medical sources; covers biomedical literature in allied health, information science, biological sciences, physical sciences, communication disorders, popuation biology, humanities, and reproductive biology.

1966–present; 4,500+ journals, 11 million records

National Library of Medicine (NLM) Gateway   **http://gateway.nlm.nih.gov**
Allows users to search in multiple retrival systems at the U.S. National Library of Medicine (NLM). The current Gateway searches MEDLINE/PubMed, OLDMEDLINE, LOCATORplus, MEDLINEplus, DIRLINE, AIDS meetings, Health Services Research meetings, Space Life Sciences meetings, and HSRProj.

1958–present; 15 million records

Table 9.2   Selected Online Research Databases (continued)

DATABASE	**Web Site**
Description	
Time frame; Entries	

PsycINFO   http://www.apa.org/psycinfo/

Indexes psychological research from journal articles, dissertations, reports, book chapters, books and other documents. Known for high-quality, worldwide information. Selectively indexes materials from the disciplines of business, medicine, nursing, law, and social work.

1967–present; 2 million records

SciSearch   http://www.isinet.com/isi/

Multidisciplinary database containing various research in general sciences; spans over 158 disciplines. Offers cited reference searching and traditional search by author and keyword.

1974–present; 5,300+ journals, 10 million records

Social SciSearch   http://www.isinet.com/isi/

Multidisciplinary database containing journal literature in social sciences research; spans 50 disciplines. Also includes selected items from over 3,300 of the world's leading scientific and technical journals. Offers cited reference searching and traditional search by author and keyword.

1972–present; 2,400+ journals, 2.5 million records

---

consequently to outmoded or ineffective practice. Continuing professional development encompasses both formal and informal learning.

Third, therapeutic recreation curriculum needs to be modified to accommodate evidence-based practice. Numerous articles exist about how to bridge the gap between research and practice, and many writers provide suggestions from a curricular point of view (Glisson, 1982; Reinherz, Grob & Berkman, 1983; Siegel 1984). They propose modifying the teaching of research and core professional courses. One concern has to do with the way research is presented in most therapeutic recreation curricula. As has been argued elsewhere (McCormick & Funderburk, 2000; McCormick & Lee, 2001), the conceptual separation of "research issues" from "practice issues" in most therapeutic recreation texts presents research as an add-on to practice. Research and evaluation should be just as much a part of therapeutic recreation practice as assessment or treatment planning, for example. Unless the profession strengthens research and evaluation competencies, and integrates evidence-based practice in core therapeutic recreation courses, overcoming the long-standing gap between therapeutic recreation practice and research is unlikely. Therapeutic recreation curricula should help students become active and wise consumers of research throughout their careers.

Reading Comprehension Questions

1. How would you define evidence-based practice?

2. Give examples of sources of evidence that can be used as a basis for practice. What are the advantages of each source? What are the disadvantages?

3. What is a randomized control trial? Why is it one of the strongest forms of evidence?

4. Identify a clinical question. Search for evidence related to your question. What kinds of evidence can you find? How strong is it? How clear is it?

References

Alsop, A. (1997). Evidence based practice and continuing professional development. *British Journal Occupational Therapy, 60*(11), 503–508.

Austin, D. R. (1999). *Therapeutic recreation: Processes and techniques* (4th ed.). Champaign, IL: Sagamore.

Bandura, A. (1997). *Self-efficacy: The exercise of control.* New York, NY: W. H. Freeman.

Blythe, B. J., Tripodi, T., and Briar, S. (1994). *Direct practice research in human service organizations.* New York, NY: Columbia University Press.

Bloom, M., Fischer, J., and Orme, J. G. (1995). *Evaluating practice: Guidelines for the accountable professional* (2nd ed.). Needham Heights, MA: Allyn & Bacon.

Brown, S. J. (1999). *Knowledge for health care practice: A guide to using research evidence.* Philadelphia, PA: W. B. Saunders.

Bury, T. (1999). Evidence-based healthcare explained. In T. Bury and J. Mead (Eds.), *Evidence-based healthcare: A practical guide for therapists* (pp. 3–25). Oxford, UK: Butterworth-Heinemann.

Bury, T. J. and Mead, J. M. (1999). *Evidence-based healthcare: A practical guide for therapists.* Oxford, UK: Butterworth-Heinemann.

Compton, D. M. and Dieser, R. (1997). Research initiatives in therapeutic recreation. In D. M. Compton (Ed.), *Issues in therapeutic recreation: Toward the new millennium* (pp. 299–325). Champaign, IL: Sagamore.

Coyle, C. P., Kinney, W. B., Riley, B., and Shank, J. (Eds.) (1991). *The benefits of therapeutic recreation: A consensus view.* Ravensdale, WA: Idyll Arbor.

Dubouloz, C., Egan, M., Vallerand, J., and Zweck, C. V. (1999). Occupational therapists' perceptions of evidence-based practice. *American Journal of Occupational Therapy, 53*(5), 445–453.

Ellis, G. D., Maughan-Pritchett, M., and Ruddell, E. (1993). Effects of attribution based verbal persuasion and imagery on self-efficacy of adolescents diagnosed with major depression. *Therapeutic Recreation Journal, 28*, 83–97.

Glisson, C. (1982) Research teaching in social work doctoral programs. *Social Service Review, 56*, 629–639.

Grasso, A., Epstein, I., and Tripodi, T. (1988). Agency-based research utilization in a residential childcare setting. *Administration in Social Work, 12*(4), 61–80.

Institute for Scientific Information (1998). Retrieved: http://www.isinet.com

Kiresuk, T. J., Smith, A., and Cardillo, J. E. (Eds.) (1994). *Goal attainment scaling: Applications, theory, and measurement.* Hillsdale, NJ: Erlbaum & Associates.

Lee, Y. and Yang, H. (2000). A review of therapeutic recreation outcomes in physical medicine and rehabilitation between 1991–2000. *Annual in Therapeutic Recreation, 9*, 21–33.

McCormick, B. P. and Funderburk, J. (2000) Therapeutic recreation outcomes in mental health practice. *Annual in Therapeutic Recreation, 9*, 9–19.

McCormick, B. P. and Lee, Y. (2001). Research in practice: Building knowledge through empirical practice. In N. Stumbo (Ed.), *Professional issues in therapeutic recreation* (pp. 383–400). Champaign, IL: Sagamore.

O'Morrow, G. S. and Reynolds, R. P. (1989). *Therapeutic recreation: A helping profession* (3rd ed.). Englewood Cliffs, NJ: Prentice Hall.

Perkins, E. R., Simnett, I., and Wright, L. (1999). Creative tensions in evidence-based practice. In E. R. Perkins, I. Simnett, and L. Wright (Eds.), *Evidence-based health promotion* (pp. 1–22). New York, NY: John Wiley & Sons.

Persons, J. B. (1999). How to incorporate evidence-based methods into routine clinical care. *Outcomes & Accountability Alert, 4*(7), 1–4.

Reid, W. J. (1994). The empirical practice movement. *Social Service Review, 68*, 163–184.

Reinherz, H., Grob, M., and Berkman, B. (1983). Health agencies and a school of social work: Practice and research in partnership. *Health and Social Work, 8*, 40–46.

Rosenberg, W. and Donald, A. (1995). Evidence-based medicine: An approach to clinical problem solving. *British Medical Journal, 310*, 1122–1226.

Sackett, D. L., Rosenberg, W. M. C., Gray, J. A., Haynes, R. B., and Richardson, W. S. (1996). Evidence-based medicine: What it is and what it isn't. *British Medical Journal, 312*, 71–72.

Sexton, T. L., Whiston, S. C., Blener, J. C., and Waltz, G. R. (1997). *Integrating outcome research into counseling practice and training*. Alexandria, VA: American Counseling Association.

Siegel, D. H. (1984). Defining empirically based practice. *Social Work, 29*, 325–331.

Stevens, K. R. (1999). Advancing evidence-based teaching. In K. R. Stevens and V. R. Cassidy (Eds.), *Evidence-based teaching: Current research in nursing education* (pp. 1–22). Sudbury, MA: Jones and Bartlett Publishers.

Stumbo, N. J. (1996). A proposed accountability model for therapeutic recreation services. *Therapeutic Recreation Journal, 30*, 246–259.

Witt, P. A. (1988). Therapeutic recreation research: Past, present, and future. *Therapeutic Recreation Journal, 22*(1), 14–23.

Chapter 10

Healthcare in America
An Overview

Bryan P. McCormick, Ph.D., CTRS

Although the healthcare arena is not the only area of practice for therapeutic recreation specialists, it is a principal practice arena. Riley and Connolly (1997) found that among all persons sitting for the certification exam offered by the National Council for Therapeutic Recreation Certification, 78.3% reported health-related settings as their primary service setting. In contrast, only 6.5% of those taking the certification exam listed public parks and recreation, camps, or schools as their primary place of practice. Although health-related settings are not the only practice settings of therapeutic recreation, they are the practice settings of the majority of therapeutic recreation specialists.

Arguably no other aspect of American society has changed more than healthcare during the twentieth century. The nature and structure of healthcare in 1900 bears little resemblance to the nature of care in the year 2000. At the turn of the century, most healthcare was provided by physicians either in their own office or in patients' homes (Ayres, 1996). Yet by the late 1990s, hospital services accounted for one third of all healthcare spending (Dranove & White, 1999). In addition, at the beginning of the twentieth century, payment was made directly to healthcare providers by patients instead of being paid for by a third party. At present, the majority of healthcare services are paid for by such entities as government agencies, private and not-for-profit organizations through a wide variety of payment systems. The purpose of this chapter is to provide a brief overview of the healthcare system in the United States. Particular attention will be paid to examining key themes in public policy that have affected healthcare as well as the present structure of healthcare. Finally, the implications of the healthcare system to therapeutic recreation practice are presented.

Government Involvement in Healthcare Policy

As noted previously, early healthcare involved a direct transaction by the care provider (usually a physician) and a patient. This relationship did not typically involve any other agents such as governments or insurance companies. How is it then that the U.S. federal government is the single largest purchaser of healthcare services (Gapenski, 1993) and healthcare policy occupies such a prominent place in political debates in this country (Marmor & McKissick, 2000)? Mueller (1993) stated that the government's intervention in healthcare is based on the belief that healthcare should be available to all people. Although this basic belief may underlie government involvement in healthcare, Mueller cited two principal variants on the theme.

Two Approaches to Involvement

First, the belief that healthcare should be available to all people can be interpreted to mean that all people have the right to the *same level* of healthcare. Under this variant all members of a society have access to essentially identical services either through (a) the government providing identical health insurance to all citizens (e.g., Canadian model), or (b) through the government making available identical health services to all citizens (e.g., British model). The second variant on the theme underscoring government involvement in healthcare is that all people have a right to a *minimum level* of care. In this approach, the role of government is to ensure that there is a safety net to protect the most vulnerable segments of the population. Through this approach specified members of the society have access to government supported, basic health services (e.g., U.S. model).

Because the United States has adopted this second variant, what one sees in policy are relatively narrowly written pieces of legislation that attempt to fill gaps (Mitchell, Kruger & Moody, 1991; Mueller, 1993). For example, the Social Security Act of 1965, which created both the Medicare (Title XVIII) and Medicaid (Title XIX) programs, was developed in order to provide minimum healthcare coverage for those who either had no access (e.g., retirees) or could not afford (e.g., the poor) private health insurance (Hoffman, Klees & Curtis, 2000; Vorderer, 1997). More recently, the State Child Health Insurance Program (CHIP) was enacted in 1997 to expand public health insurance coverage, through Medicaid, for children in low-income families (Hill, 2000). Again, this policy represents a stopgap measure to ensure that healthcare is available to a single vulnerable segment of the population. As a result of this pattern of piecemeal legislation, some have argued that it is difficult to characterize healthcare in the United States as a "system" (Mitchell, Kruger & Moody, 1991; Shi & Singh, 2001).

Implications of the U.S. Approach

One implication of the U.S. approach is that all government support need not be available to all people. As noted previously, the U.S. approach has sought to provide health insurance for designated segments of the population. Since most Americans obtain health insurance through employment (Fronstin, 2000), governmental policies have been based on assumptions that citizens who are employed and earning incomes above the poverty level can obtain health insurance privately. A problem with this assumption is that the cost of health insurance continues to rise faster than incomes. The assumption may be in error. Hanson (2001) cited figures that indicated that in 1996, there were 7.7 million families with children who were either without any health insurance (3.2 million) or who only had health insurance for some family members (4.5 million). This figure represents 24% of all families with children in the United States. In addition, by 1998, the estimate was that 44.3 million Americans were without health insurance, and half of these were made up of the working poor (Gemignani, 1999). The *working poor* refers to that segment of the U.S. population who are employed, but earn relatively low incomes. Often times, people in such employment settings earn near minimum wage and often do not have access to employer-sponsored health insurance programs. Gemignani noted that 25% of workers in households earning less than $25,000 per year have no health insurance.

Another implication of the American approach to government intervention in healthcare raises questions of what are necessary versus elective services. Again, the U.S. approach has been to ensure access to minimum healthcare services. Thus, the political debate has focused on which services are considered to be "medically necessary," and which services are "elective." For example, dentures, dental care, most optical and audiologic services as well as nursing home care are excluded from Medicare coverage (Vladeck, 2001). Given that the debate surrounding the issue of necessary versus elective services has been a largely political debate, it should not be surprising that there is an ever increasing need for therapeutic recreation professionals to be politically astute and assertive (Compton, 1997; Shank, 1997).

Key Themes in Health Policy

In addition to understanding the basis and characteristics of government involvement in healthcare policy in the United States, healthcare policy generally can be examined as having three dominant themes (Mueller, 1993). These three themes have principally revolved around the nature and quality of care, obtaining access to care, and containing the cost of care. Furthermore, these themes have predominated during different periods in the evolution of healthcare in the United States over the past 100 years.

Quality

At the turn of the twentieth century, healthcare was relatively risky business for patients. Care was largely provided in peoples' homes by physicians with little standardized training. Ayers (1996) characterized the practice of medicine from the time of the Revolutionary War to the first decades of the twentieth century as "marked by therapeutic adventurism and just plain foolishness" (p. 11). Although there were approximately 160 medical schools in the United States at the turn of the century (Ayers, 1996), the nature of that education was highly suspect. For example, Beeson (1980) found that only about 6% of the medical interventions found in *Cecil's Textbook of Medicine*, a standard of medical education in 1927, were considered effective interventions in 1980. The condition of medical education was such a growing problem that the fledgling American Medical Association employed Abraham Flexner to survey the state of medical education in the United States. In 1910, Flexner issued *Medical Education in the United States and Canada*, which largely condemned the training of physicians of the time. Among the problems he cited were that there was little medical science included in training, many graduates completed their training in six months or less, there were no entrance requirements (e.g., many students could neither read nor write!), and most faculty maintained a private practice. Largely as a result of Flexner's report, medical education changed to include: (a) a baccalaureate degree as an entrance criterion, (b) inclusion of medical science in training, and (c) the professionalization of clinical faculty.

In addition to changes in the training of physicians, the beginnings of the twentieth century saw increasing involvement of state governments in the regulation of healthcare. Some of the earliest government involvement in healthcare was seen in the certification of healthcare facilities. New York was the first state to enact such legislation in 1894, requiring private facilities to meet certain standards in order to be certified by the State Board of Charities (Mueller, 1993). In addition, there was increasing involvement of government in the credentialing of healthcare providers.

Although only 26 states had enacted licensure laws governing physicians by 1968 (Anderson, 1990), by 1952 twenty health professions were licensed in at least one state (Graddy, 1991).

A third process occurring in the early twentieth century that exemplifies the theme of quality is the changing nature of hospitals. Stevens (1989) characterized this change noting that "between 1870 and 1917 the American hospital was transformed from an asylum for the indigent into a modern scientific institution" (p. 17). During the early decades of the twentieth century hospitals saw such changes as the increasing use of antiseptic procedures, the use of anesthetics, and the employment of professional nurses. All of these forces changed the focus of hospital care to one of rational, scientific services.

Finally, the federal government was involved in the improvement of the quality of care through two important acts. First, in 1930 legislation was passed to create the National Institutes of Health (NIH). The NIH was established with a broad mandate to determine the causes, treatment and cures for diseases (Patel & Rushefsky, 1999). Thus, the U.S. federal government supported the scientific study of medicine through financial support of the NIH. In addition, in 1946 the Hill-Burton Act was passed that provided for federal aid to the states for the construction and expansion of hospitals (Mueller, 1993; Stevens, 1989). The act was largely targeted toward the provision of funds to support hospital services in rural areas and poorer states. Through the Hill-Burton legislation, many areas without any hospital services were now able to construct community hospitals.

Access

In addition to making funds available for the construction of modern hospitals, the Hill-Burton Act can also be interpreted as indicative of access to care (Mueller, 1993). First, this act made hospital care more accessible to people who had previously had little access to modern medicine. Another one of the provisions of the act was that hospitals had to agree to provide a certain amount of "charity care." In other words, to build or expand a hospital under the Hill-Burton funding, the hospital had to agree to provide some care for those too poor to pay for services. The inability to pay for hospital services can also be seen as the impetus for private health insurance in the form of Blue Cross.

Blue Cross began as a hospital insurance plan at Baylor University Hospital in Dallas, Texas in 1929. O'Morrow and Carter (1997) stated that the hospital began to notice that many of its delinquent bills were incurred by teachers at Baylor University. Given that this time frame was during the Depression, even those who were employed were having diffi-culty meeting their healthcare costs. Thus, the hospital created an insurance plan, offering 1,500 teachers up to 21 days of hospital care for $6 per person per month (Starr, 1982). This initial program of insurance was duplicated by other hospitals—first in Dallas and then increasingly across the nation. In addition, similar plans were created to cover the cost of physician services in the hospital. These plans were initially sponsored by state medical soci-eties, but later adopted the name "Blue Shield" (Anderson, 1991). The Depression itself generated concern on the part of hospitals nationwide that patients were increasingly unable to cover their hospital care directly. Costs for care would have to be budgeted in advance through insurance.

Private health insurance also grew during the Second World War (Anderson, 1991). During the war, Congress had enacted controls on wages. As a result, employers were not able to use high wages to attract employ-ees; however, health insurance and pensions were not considered as a part of wages. The result was that employers began to include health insurance as a fringe benefit of employment. By 1952, more than half of the U.S. population was covered by some form of health insurance.

One of the first noted attempts of the U.S. federal government to pro-vide access to care via financial support occurred in 1921 with the Mater-nity and Infancy Act (PL 67-97). This act was designed provide funding to the states in order for states to develop health services for mothers and children. However, this act was allowed to lapse in 1929 due to opposition from members of Congress and the American Medical Association as "a socialist scheme" (Anderson, 1991). Although notions of national health insurance and widening the access to healthcare were raised during the administration of President Truman in the late 1940s, it was not until the mid-1960s that the federal government became significantly involved in affording access to healthcare. As noted previously, as enrollment in private insurance through employment continued to rise through the 1950s, a growing segment of the population who were not employed could not afford healthcare. With the passage of the Social Security Act Amendments (PL 89-97), the federal government became the primary insurer of the elderly, the poor, and certain segments of the population with long-term illnesses through the creation of Medicare and Medicaid. As a result of these programs, federal and state governments are now the largest purchaser of healthcare services in the United States (Shi & Singh, 2001).

It is interesting to note that access to care in the United States has al-ways been an issue of payment. Unlike countries with more socialized forms of care (e.g., Canada, Great Britain), the U.S. system has historically been based on a fee-for-service structure. If one could come up with the fee, one could access the service. A story may help to illustrate this issue. In 1992 my wife's great aunt developed difficulties with her stomach. She was 92 years old at the time and living independently in a large city in eastern Canada. Although she had national insurance (as do all Canadian citizens), she was unable to be seen in a hospital as all the hospital beds were full in the city in which she lived. She instead went to a smaller hospital in a town 75 miles from her home where there were available beds. What's striking about this case is how it differs from an American example. The idea that a person *with the ability to pay* would be turned away (or have to be assigned to a waiting list) due to lack of available services is highly unlikely in the American healthcare system.

Cost Containment

The third principal theme in healthcare policy in the United States is that of cost containment. The issue of containing the cost of care is a relatively new concern in terms of health policy. However, it is not surprising that it has become such an issue. The cost of healthcare grew dramatically for both individuals and society as a whole in the later half of the twentieth century. As can be seen in Figure 10.1 (page 192), the spending on personal healthcare made up an ever-increasing portion of the gross domestic product from 1960 through the early 1990s.

As healthcare costs continued to rise, a number of initiatives were seen to try to reign in escalating costs. First, the Congress created Professional Standards Review Organizations (PSRO) under the Social Security Amendments in 1972. These organizations were set up to review care for Medicare and Medicaid patients in hospitals, extended care, and skilled nursing facilities (Patel & Rushefsky, 1999). The PSROs had the power to deny approval of payment for services that were deemed unnecessary. Second, with support from the Nixon administration, the Health Maintenance Organization (HMO) Act of 1973 (PL 93-222) was made into law. The purpose of PL 93-222 was to stimulate competition as a means to controlling costs, by encouraging the creation of HMOs as a cost-efficient alternative to traditional care. In addition, in 1974 Congress passed the National Health Planning and Resource Development Act (PL 93-641). The purpose of this act was to prevent unnecessary expansion of the healthcare delivery system (Mueller, 1993). This represented a cost containment strategy because it was felt that the surplus in healthcare services tended to create unnecessary use. Overall, all of the cost containment activities of the early to mid-1970s were

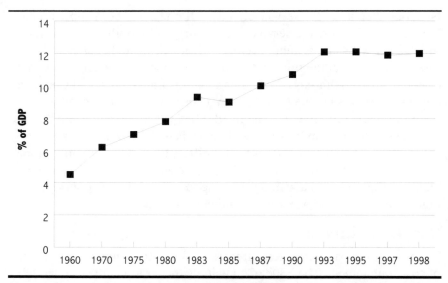

Figure 10.1 Personal Healthcare Expenditures as Percent of U.S. Gross Domestic Product 1960–1998 (Source: U.S. Department of Health and Human Services, 2001)

largely ineffective in containing costs. As a result, the federal government began looking toward more radical departures from past policies.

The more radical departure came in the form of the Tax Equity and Fiscal Responsibility Act (TEFRA) of 1982 (PL 97-248) and the Social Security Amendment Act of 1983 (PL 98-21). These two pieces of federal legislation drastically changed the way healthcare was purchased by the U.S. government. The most important changes were that healthcare was no longer paid for based on a fee-for-service structure. Instead healthcare was now to be reimbursed through a prospective payment system (PPS) on a cost-per-case basis (Skalko, 1998), and cases were to be grouped according to diagnosis-related groups (DRGs). What this implied was that the cost of care was no longer set by the healthcare providers' fees. A simplified explanation of the PPS is that a "lump sum" payment is set in advance based on the typical costs associated with treating a particular diagnosis. As a result, the incentive for healthcare providers was to provide cost-efficient care since additional services would not result in additional revenues. Although the initial PPS was implemented only in short-stay inpatient hospitals (Shi & Singh, 2001), it has since been expanded to include skilled nursing facilities (SNFs), post-acute rehabilitation facilities, and will soon include mental/behavioral health facilities.

Finally, cost containment approaches could be seen in the private sector in the growth of managed care organizations (MCO). Patel and Rushefsky (1999) defined MCOs as organizations offering health insurance plans that seek to restrain the use of health services. This is done through a variety of approaches, but principally this is done through the restriction of choice of service providers. The main impetus for the growth of MCOs appears to be the result of employers, who are one of the largest purchasers of insurance, seeking to contain costs. HMOs, for example, have grown from a nation-wide enrollment of 9.1 million in 1980 to 66.8 million in 1997. In other words, by 1997 over 25% of the U.S. population was enrolled in an HMO.

Current Focus

Each of the above themes had its period of dominance. The issue of quality was the predominant theme at the turn of the twentieth century and continued through to almost midcentury. The theme of access, while having its roots in hospital insurance programs during the Great Depression, only achieved predominance in the period following the Second World War and really reached its zenith with the creation of Medicare and Medicaid in 1965. Finally, the period of the mid-1970s until the late 1980s was dominated by efforts at containing healthcare costs. So, what is the current focus of health-care policy? It has been argued that the period beginning with the 1990s has seen a combination of the three themes (Mueller, 1993). Others have argued however that quality has been pushed aside in favor of cost containment and access (McGlynn & Brook, 2001). There may be some validity to this claim as the most recent public policy debates and actions have focused on increased access (e.g., Clinton administration national health insurance, Medicare prescription drug benefits) and cost containment (e.g., Medicare managed care, expansion of PPS into SNFs and rehabilitation settings). The inattention to quality also can be seen in the U.S. ranking in comparison to other countries. The World Health Organization (2000) recently ranked the United States 37th in overall health system performance and 72nd in population health, and at the same time, the United States ranks first among industrialized nations in healthcare expenditures (Shi & Singh, 2001). Thus, current policy does seem to principally involve issues of access and cost containment with little attention on quality.

Structure of Healthcare Delivery

The structure of healthcare delivery is relatively complex with a variety of care providers offering services through a variety of care settings (Nosse, Friberg & Kovacek, 1999; Shi & Singh, 2001). Although therapeutic recreation specialists tend to be employed in greater numbers in some areas of the system than in others, it is useful to understand the structure of the healthcare system.

Care Providers

Care in the U.S. healthcare system is provided by a variety of individuals and organizations. Healthcare providers include the those providing preventative care, primary care, and specialty care.

Preventative Care

This type of healthcare provider focuses on the prevention of illness or the enhancement of wellness, including wellness programs, health screening, education programs, and immunization programs. Often times these services are provided through public departments of health, employer-sponsored programs or hospital-affiliated centers. The key characteristic of this form of care is that it occurs *prior* to the onset of illness, injury, or disability. This component of the healthcare system has gained importance as the cost of corrective care has increased (Nosse et al., 1999). Although there seem to be obvious implications for therapeutic recreation services within preventative care (Russoniello, 1997), there is little evidence to indicate that therapeutic recreation specialists are employed in large numbers in preventative care.

Primary Care

Primary care providers are the initial point of contact with the healthcare system for most people following the onset of illness. The main provider of primary care is the general practice physician, although other care providers are increasingly offering primary care. The role of the primary care provider has grown increasingly important as managed healthcare has grown. The role of the primary care provider has expanded from the diagnosis and treatment of illness to that of gatekeeper. Given that specialty care is typically more costly than primary care, the primary care provider role has evolved in such a way that they are now tasked with making determinations about the need for more costly specialized care. Thus they are the gatekeepers for access to specialty care. Although physicians account for the vast majority of primary care, other nonphysician providers such as nurses, physical therapists and social workers provide primary care (Nosse et al., 1999). In some settings case managers act in this capacity, and it is through the case management role that therapeutic recreation specialists are most likely to provide primary care.

Specialty Care

The most costly and complex services in the healthcare system are those provided by specialty care providers. Specialty care includes those services, equipment and facilities that are not available at the primary level. One of the key distinctions between primary and specialty care is that specialty care typically involves a team approach to care in which the services of a number of specialists must be coordinated. In contrast, primary care typically involves the use of a single care provider. Within specialty care services there are secondary care and tertiary care services.

Secondary care includes such services as routine surgeries, inpatient rehabilitation, pediatric rehabilitation, and diagnostic laboratories. In addition, secondary services also include specialized mental health and substance abuse treatment, as well as geriatric services. Most hospitals constitute this form of care. Tertiary care is the most intensive and specialized (and, hence, costly) form of healthcare provision. They typically serve as regional referral centers, meaning that primary and secondary providers may refer their clients to these centers. Examples of this form of care includes trauma centers, transplant services, cardiac specialty hospitals, and burn care centers. Tertiary care providers typically have the most technologically advanced equipment for diagnosis and treatment of illness and injury. A majority of therapeutic recreation specialists working in healthcare settings are employed in settings that are characteristic of secondary and tertiary specialty care (Riley & Connolly, 1997)

Care Settings

In addition to there being a number of healthcare providers, the U.S. healthcare system involves a variety of settings. Although the beginning of the twentieth century was dominated by healthcare provided by primary care providers to patients in their own homes, at present, home care settings are a minority setting for the provision of healthcare services. In the U.S. healthcare system there are three principal settings for the delivery of healthcare (Nosse et al., 1999).

Ambulatory Settings

These are services provided in a setting that does not keep patients/clients overnight. For example, most care by general practice physicians constitutes this form of care setting. A person goes to see his or her family physician with symptoms of the flu, is seen by the physician, given a prescription and sent home. However, other forms of care are provided in ambulatory settings. Other examples include urgent and some emergency care, adult daycare, and all outpatient services including diagnostics, surgery, and rehabilitation. Day and partial hospitalization programs that may be seen in mental/behavioral health services are also examples of ambulatory care. Finally, virtually all preventative care is provided through ambulatory settings.

Inpatient Settings

Those receiving services in inpatient settings receive 24-hour care. Furthermore inpatient care can be subdivided into acute, postacute, and extended care settings. *Acute care* settings imply that the nature of the illness or disability that caused entry into the setting is relatively serious or severe. In addition, the course of treatment in acute settings is typically the shortest of all inpatient settings. By contrast, *postacute care* settings provide skilled inpatient services, but at a lower intensity or variety of care. Examples of this setting include long-term rehabilitation, surgical recovery centers, brain injury care centers, as well as hospice and respite care (Nosse et al., 1999). The final inpatient setting is that of *extended care*. In the extended care setting, the intensity and variety of services is typically less than even that of postacute care settings. In addition, extended care settings demonstrate the longest length of stay, on average, and discharge is often indefinite. Examples of extended care settings include skilled nursing facilities (SNF), specialized Alzheimer's units, residential services, as well as state hospitals for people with mental illnesses and developmental disabilities. In addition, supported living arrangements, particularly group homes, would constitute this setting of care given that clients are living in a home that is owned and operated by a healthcare provider.

Home Setting

The home care setting is self-explanatory. In this setting, care is provided by a healthcare provider in the home of the care recipient. It has been noted that this is one of the fastest growing care settings (Sensenig, Heffler & Donham, 1997). Examples of home care services include hospice care, patient and family education, as well as wound and disease management.

Healthcare Financing System

The system of financing healthcare services in the United States is highly fragmented. Payment for healthcare services is provided by public entities (i.e., local, state and federal governments), private companies (i.e., not-for-profit, stock and mutual companies) and individual healthcare consumers (see Figure 10.2). Thus the U.S. system is characterized as a *multi-payer*

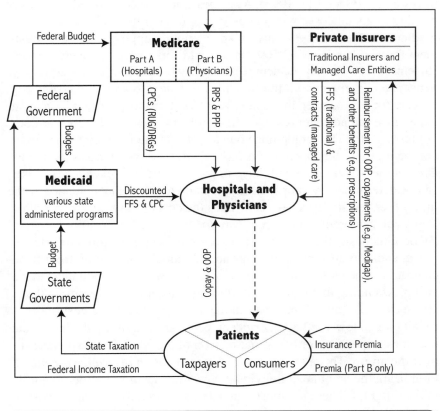

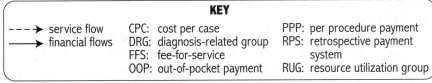

Figure 10.2   U.S. Healthcare System Financial and Service Flows (adapted from McCarthy & Minnis, 1994)

system. This is in contrast to single-payer systems in which the national government is the sole purchaser of healthcare, such as in Canada or the United Kingdom. Explaining the complexity of this system of finance and reimbursement is beyond the scope of this section. Instead, the purpose here is to provide a conceptual overview.

Insurance Basics

In general, American healthcare financing is based on the basic concepts of insurance (Gapenski, 1993). At its heart, insurance is based on ideas of pooling financial costs over a large group in order to make costs more predictable. This can be seen with an example. Suppose the cost of treatment for a broken leg is $2,500. Based on historical data, an average of ten students a year have an accident resulting in a broken leg at your university. What is the likely amount the student sitting next to you will have to pay for care for a broken leg in the next year? Well, that depends on if he or she experiences an accident resulting in a broken leg (cost = $2,500) or does not (cost = $0). The problem is you cannot accurately predict whether or not the injury will happen *to this individual*. However, what is the likely amount the student body will have to pay for care of broken legs? This can be determined by simply using the knowledge of the incidence of the injury (i.e., ten students per year) times the cost of the care (i.e., $2,500). Thus, you can predict the cost of care *for the group*, at $25,000 per year. By pooling costs, the cost of care for a group becomes more predictable.

In addition, insurance prevents an individual in the group from financial catastrophe by *transferring the financial costs* for the individual to the group. Assuming that there are 10,000 students at the university in the above example (and all take part in the insurance plan), the cost of care for all broken legs is $2.50 per student, per year. As a result, the individual becomes responsible only for that portion of the cost of care spread out over the group. This average cost is the basis for an *insurance premium*. Premia are the amount an individual pays to an insurer in order to enroll in the program. These are most typically paid monthly and since most people obtain insurance through their employer, they are paid through a payroll deduction.

A final characteristic of insurance is that it is based on costs arising from the *random occurrence* of illness and injury resulting in appropriate care (Gapenski, 1993). If illness and injury occur at random, costs are more predicable within the group. However, some people may seek healthcare services without necessity. For example, lonely people may visit an emergency room out of a need for human contact. The attention and concern paid by healthcare personnel for socially isolated people may meet a social need, but emergency room services creates costs that are inappropriate to the need. The intentional use of healthcare services and funds without medical necessity is termed *moral hazard,* and insurers have disincentives built into most plans to minimize moral hazards.

Insurers use deductibles and copayments to reduce *moral hazards.* Deductible payments are a fixed amount that the insured must pay out-of-pocket before insurance benefits will cover costs. For example, if a person has a $250 per year deductible with her health insurance plan, and she receives $750 in healthcare services, she must pay the first $250 in costs before her insurer will pay for the remaining $500. Copayments are also used to minimize moral hazards. *Copayments* are an amount, usually as a percentage, that the insured must pay for the cost of care. A standard copayment is referred to as "80/20," indicating that for all covered care the insured must pay 20% of the costs, while the insurer pays 80%.

Principal Payers

As can be seen in Figure 10.2 (p. 197), there are two payer types for healthcare in the United States. The first and single largest type is public payers (i.e., state and federal governments) who pay for healthcare principally through the Medicare and Medicaid programs. The second payer type represents the multiple private payers. In the U.S. healthcare system there are approximately 1,500 different purchasers of healthcare services (Ayers, 1996), most of them being private companies and organizations.

Public Payers

The principal form of payment for health services by the public is through the Medicare and Medicaid programs. The *Medicare* program provides payment for hospital and physician care to (a) people 65 and older, (b) people with disabilities entitled to social security benefits, and (c) people with end-stage renal disease (Hoffman, Klees & Curtis, 2000). In addition, the program is administered through two parts. Part A provides for hospital insurance, skilled nursing facility (SNF) care, home healthcare and hospice services (Shi & Singh, 2001). For the most part, Part A is free to any U.S. citizen meeting the enrollment criteria, and is financed through social security payroll taxes. Medicare Part B, provides supplemental medical insurance to those enrolled in Part A and is financed through tax revenues as well as premium payments by enrollees. Part B covers physician services as well as outpatient services, emergency department visits, and medical equipment. It is worth noting that Part B also covers outpatient physical therapy, occupational therapy and speech therapy. The Medicare program is administered by the Centers for Medicare and Medicaid Services (CMS; known prior to 2001 as the Health Care Finance Administration or HCFA) which is part of the U.S. Department of Health and Human Services.

Medicaid is the other principal public payer for health services. The Medicaid program is designed to provide access to healthcare services through funding healthcare for those who are financially unable to do so for themselves. Unlike Medicare, Medicaid is not a single payer. The reason this one program actually represents multiple payers is that the Medicaid program is set up on a state-by-state basis since the states must provide up to half of the funding for their Medicaid programs (Hoffman et al., 2000). The federal government provides the balance of the cost. Under the legislation, people are eligible for Medicaid if (a) they are receiving support from the Temporary Assistance to Needy Families (TANF) program, (b) they are receiving Supplemental Security Income (SSI), or (c) they are children or pregnant women whose income is at or below 133% of the federal poverty guidelines (Shi & Singh, 2001). In addition, most states have defined additionally eligible people, most notably those in nursing and psychiatric facilities, assuming these individuals have financial assets or incomes that classify them as "indigent" or "poor." Although services do vary by state, they all are mandated to cover hospital and physician costs, nursing facility services, home health, prenatal care, family planning services, medical services to dependent children under age 12, and nurse–midwife services.

Private Payers

A variety of companies make up the mix of private payers. One of the largest private payers is the Blue Cross/Blue Shield system. As noted previously, the origins of this system were in the provision of insurance during the Great Depression. At present, the Blue Cross/Blue Shield system is a group of independent, nonprofit membership corporations insuring hospital, medical and surgical costs for its members in limited geographical areas (Shi & Singh, 2001). Typically the corporations are organized as single or multistate corporations. In addition to the "Blues," private payers also come in the form of commercial insurers including stock and mutual companies (Gapenski, 1993). Stock companies are for-profit entities that provide health insurance in order to make a profit and provide return on investments for stockholders. In contrast, mutual companies are commercial insurers in which policyholders, mainly enrolled through group plans, elect directors to manage the health insurance funds. Although mutual companies are not in business to make a profit, they do work to manage policyholders' funds as efficiently as possible. A final form of private pay is that of the self-insured (Shi &

Singh, 2001). Self-insured does not mean self-pay. In self-pay, the care recipient pays for care directly. A self-insurer is a situation where an employer actually acts as its own insurance company. Gapenski noted that this is only feasible for very large employers, such as the automobile industry or state governments.

Healthcare Reimbursement Methods

Reimbursement methods in the U.S. healthcare system can be based on charges, costs or payments (Gapenski, 1993). Given that there are a very large number of payers in the system, each method may be employed simultaneously at a single healthcare facility since each client may have a different health plan. *Fee-based reimbursement* is one of the simplest forms of payment. This is the typical system of payment for most goods and services outside healthcare. The care provider simply provides to the insurer the "bill" or "fee" for providing services to the insured. This system is also referred to as a *fee-for service structure*. In some cases large insurers will work out a negotiated fee with the care provider so that they receive a standard discount (e.g., 10%) on all charges. *Cost-based reimbursement* is based on costs incurred by the provider to provide care (Nosse et al., 1999). Typically "allowable costs" are determined by the payer and payers will not provide any payment beyond the cost cap. Nosse and colleagues stated that this form of payment is limited although it continues to play a part in Medicare reimbursement. The third form of reimbursement is set according to *case groups*. Unlike cost-based and charge-based structures, case-based structures are not based on fees or costs but instead based on averaged costs per case. Case groups can be set according to per diem (i.e., a fixed rate per person per day), per admission (i.e., a fixed rate per person per admission), patient characteristics (e.g., diagnosis, resource utilization, functional ability), and capitation (e.g., payment is based on number of plan enrollees). Under capitation, a provider accepts preset dollar amount per plan enrollee in exchange for agreeing to provide specified services to a specified group without any further compensation.

Implications of the U.S. Healthcare System for Therapeutic Recreation

As should be clear from the preceding presentation, healthcare in America is a highly complicated mix of public policy and care providers working through a variety of structures and finances. It is not surprising that as a profession therapeutic recreation appears to be less than knowledgeable about issues of healthcare structure and finance (Skalko & Malkin, 1992). However, if therapeutic recreation is to remain viable in healthcare settings, it is time we become more astute about the environment in which we practice. Over ten years ago Reitter (1989) warned that:

> Disciplines which are most adequately prepared, anticipate changes, and take action in advance to minimize the impact of revisions in financing policy will have the best opportunity to survive in today's highly competitive health career environment. (p. 239)

The statement remains true and can be applied to healthcare policy generally, not just as it relates to finance.

Discussion Questions

1. Consider the two approaches to government involvement in healthcare. What are the advantages to the "same level of care for all?" disadvantages? What are the advantages of the "minimum level of care for all?" disadvantages?

2. Identify a recent piece of state or federal healthcare legislation. Which of the three themes does it most clearly represent: quality, access, or cost containment?

3. Think about a time when you received healthcare services. What type of provider did you see? What was the setting of care?

4. Do a search of newspaper and magazine articles about Medicare or Medicaid. What is the tone of the article? Does the article favor expansion or restriction of the program? Does it discuss costs? the uninsured? the underinsured? the quality of care?

References

Anderson, O. W. (1991). Health services in the United States: A growth enterprise for a hundred years. In T. J. Litman and L. S. Robins (Eds.), *Health politics and policy* (2nd ed., pp. 38–52). Albany, NY: Delmar.

Anderson, O. W. (1990). *Health services as a growth enterprise in the United States since 1875*. Ann Arbor, MI: Health Administration Press.

Ayres, S. M. (1996). *Health care in the United States: The facts and the choices*. Chicago, IL: American Library Association.

Beeson, P. (1980). Changes in medical therapy during the last half century. *Medicine, 59*, 79–99.

Compton, D. M. (1997). Political imperatives for therapeutic recreation. In D. M. Compton (Ed.), *Issues in therapeutic recreation: Toward the new millennium* (pp. 53–76). Champaign, IL: Sagamore.

Dranove, D. and White, W. D. (1999). *How hospitals survived*. Washington, DC: AEI Press.

Flexner, A. (1910). *Medical education in the United States and Canada*. New York, NY: Carnegie Foundation.

Fronstin, P. (2000). Sources of health insurance and characteristics of the uninsured: Analysis of the March 2000 Current Population Survey. *Employee Benefit Research Institute Issue Brief, 228*, 1–27.

Gapenski, L. C. (1993). *Understanding healthcare financial management*. Ann Arbor, MI: AUPHA Press/Health Administration Press.

Gemignani, J. (1999, November). Multiple studies paint a grim picture for the working poor. *Business & Health, 17*(11), 14–16.

Graddy, E. (1991). Interest groups and/or the public interest—Why do we regulate health occupations? *Journal of Health Politics, Policy and Law, 16*, 25–47.

Hanson, K. L. (2001, Jan-Feb). Patterns of insurance coverage within families with children. *Health Affairs, 20*(1), 240–246.

Health Maintenance Organization Act of 1973, Pub. L. No. 93-222, 87 Stat. 914 (1974).

Hill, I. (2000). Charting new courses for children's health insurance. *Policy & Practice of Public Human Services, 58*(4), 30–39.

Hoffman, E. D. Jr., Klees, B. S., and Curtis, C. A. (2000). Overview of the Medicare and Medicaid programs. *Health Care Financing Review, 22*, 175–193.

Marmor, T. R. and McKissick, G. J. (2000). Medicare's future: Fact, fiction and folly. *American Journal of Law and Medicine, 26*, 225–254,

Maternity and Infancy Act of 1921, Pub. L. No. 67-97, 42 Stat. 224 (1923).

McCarthy, T. and Minnis, J. (1994). The health care system in the United States. In U. K. Hoffmeyer and T. R. McCarthy (Eds.), *Financing health care* (Vol. II, pp. 1147–1293). Dordrecht, Netherlands: Kluwer.

McGlynn, E. A. and Brook, R. H. (2001, May-Jun). Keeping quality on the policy agenda. *Health Affairs, 20*(3), 82–90.

Mitchell, P. H., Kruger, J. C., and Moody, L. E. (1991). The crisis of the health-care nonsystem. *Nursing Outlook, 38,* 214–217.

Mueller, K. J. (1993). *Healthcare policy in the United States.* Lincoln NE: University of Nebraska Press.

National Health Planning and Resource Development Act of 1975, Pub. L. No. 93-641, 88 Stat. 2225 (1976).

Nosse, L. J., Friberg, D. G., and Kovacek, P. R. (1999). *Managerial and supervisory principles for physical therapists.* Baltimore, MD: Williams & Waverly.

O'Morrow, G. S. and Carter, M. J. (1997). *Effective management in therapeutic recreation service.* State College, PA: Venture Publishing, Inc.

Patel, K. and Rushefsky, M. E. (1999). *Healthcare politics and policy in America* (2nd ed.). Armonk, NY: M. E. Sharpe.

Reitter, M. S. (1989) Third-party payers: Are we getting our share? In D. M. Compton (Ed.), *Therapeutic recreation: A profession in transition,* (pp. 239–256). Champaign, IL: Sagamore.

Riley, B. and Connolly, P. (1997). Statistical results of the NCTRC certification exam: The first five years. *Therapeutic Recreation Journal, 31,* 38–52.

Russoniello, C. (1997). Behavioral medicine: A model for TR. In D. M. Compton (Ed.), *Issues in therapeutic recreation: Toward the new millennium* (2nd ed., pp. 461–487). Champaign, IL: Sagamore.

Sensenig, A. L., Heffler, S. K., and Donham, C. S. (1997). Hospital, employment, and price indicators for the healthcare industry: Fourth quarter 1996 and annual data for 1988–1996. *Health Care Financing Review, 18*(4), 133–149.

Shank, J. W. (1997). Engaging the legislative process: Legislative and regulatory imperatives for therapeutic recreation. In D. M. Compton (Ed.), *Issues in therapeutic recreation: Toward the new millennium* (pp. 77–102). Champaign, IL: Sagamore.

Shi, L. and Singh, D. A. (2001). *Delivering healthcare in America: A systems approach* (2nd ed.). Gaithersburg, MD: Aspen.

Skalko, T. K. (1998). Reimbursement. In F. Brasile, T. K. Skalko, and j. burlingame (Eds.), *Perspectives in recreational therapy* (pp. 447–462). Ravensdale, WA: Idyll Arbor.

Skalko, T. K. and Malkin, M. J. (1992). Current status of third party reimbursement for therapeutic recreation: Where do we go from here? *Annual in Therapeutic Recreation, 3,* 80–89.

Social Security Act of 1965, Pub. L. No. 89-97, 79 Stat. 286 (1966).

Social Security Act of 1983, Pub. L. No. 98-21, 97 Stat. 65 (1985).

Starr, P. (1982). *The social transformation of American medicine*. New York, NY: Basic Books.

Stevens, R. (1989). *In sickness and in wealth: American hospitals in the 20th century*. New York, NY: Basic Books.

Tax Equity and Fiscal Responsibility Act of 1982, Pub. L. No. 97-248, 96 Stat. 324 (1984).

U.S. Department of Health and Human Services. (2001). *Medicare and Medicaid Statistical Supplement, 2000*. (Pub. #03424). Baltimore, MD: Author

Vladeck, B. C. (2001, May). Medicare: Can its benefits be sustained as cost of coverage grows? *Geriatrics, 56*(5), 50–54.

Vorderer, L. (1997). Healthcare in America: Containing costs while expanding access. In D. M. Compton (Ed.), *Issues in therapeutic recreation: Toward the new millennium* (2nd ed., pp. 121–139). Champaign, IL: Sagamore.

World Health Organization (2000). *The world health report 2000: Health systems— Improving performance*. Geneva, Switzerland: Author.

Chapter 11

Therapeutic Recreation Education
A Call for Reform

David R. Austin, Ph.D., CTRS, FALS

An earlier version of this chapter appeared in *Issues in Therapeutic Recreation* (2nd ed.), edited by David M. Compton. Special thanks are given to Dr. Compton for permission to use portions of the previous chapter in this one.

Today issues abound related to the adequacy of therapeutic recreation curricula to prepare recreation therapists for clinical practice. Is therapeutic recreation preparation distinct enough to certify that graduates have mastered the unique knowledge and skills needed to practice as healthcare professionals? Are consumers assured of the professional competence of graduates of therapeutic recreation curricula? Should those with no more than a superficial understanding of clinical practice be making curricular decisions in universities, and setting standards for therapeutic recreation?

A starting point to seek answers to these and other questions about therapeutic recreation curricula is to identify the assumptions that form the basis for it. Underlying every set of education experiences defined as a curriculum is a set of assumptions. These assumptions need to be made clear and explicit. What assumptions underlie therapeutic recreation curricula? Have they been made explicit? The problems facing therapeutic recreation professional preparation today exist because these questions have not been resolved.

This dilemma has not occurred because of a lack of effort. Lengthy discussions by educators at Bradford Woods and Oglebay Park to resolve curricular issues took place during a series of postdoctoral institutes held by Indiana University and the University of Maryland from 1980 through 1985. Educators in therapeutic recreation debated assumptions underlying curricula with particular attention given to establishing boundaries for professional practice. Unfortunately, these efforts brought little resolution as to how to define the practice of therapeutic recreation.

In 1995, the American Therapeutic Recreation Association (ATRA) held a Curriculum Conference to examine undergraduate preparation in therapeutic recreation. Outcomes of this meeting appeared in the *Guidelines for Completing Assessment and Curriculum Planning in Therapeutic*

Recreation (Kinney & Witman, 1997). This document expressed a clinical orientation in therapeutic recreation practice. While the *Guidelines* publication has perhaps moved the profession closer to a clinical practice model, therapeutic recreation has remained very broadly defined. As a result, the field has been perceived by many as one concerned with the provision of any recreation service for people who are disabled. The assumption underlying numerous curricula is that all persons, including persons with disabilities, should have opportunities for leisure experiences and that the provision of such services shall be termed *therapeutic recreation*. Based on this assumption, it is further assumed that therapeutic recreation is a specialization within parks and recreation. Therefore it is taken for granted that a therapeutic recreation specialist is a parks and recreation professional who specializes in serving people with disabilities and, as such, needs the basic curriculum all parks and recreation students need plus some additional training and knowledge about disabilities, and perhaps some clinical skills.

Carrying these assumptions further, faculty from all aspects of parks and recreation have the core knowledge of therapeutic recreation and are experts who can dictate curriculum content for therapeutic recreation. Is this not the very situation we have now since the Council of Accreditation determines standards for therapeutic recreation? How many Council members are trained in therapeutic recreation? Some might say, "all of them" because they know parks and recreation—the assumed core of therapeutic recreation. Others might claim that few of them have expertise because they have not been trained in therapeutic recreation and know little or nothing about clinical practice. Whichever view one takes, it is clear that to the Council on Accreditation, therapeutic recreation is simply a specialization under parks and recreation like any others, such as outdoor recreation, or recreation and park management.

Is this "right?" Of course it is, once it is assumed that therapeutic recreation is simply defined as the provision of recreation services for persons with disabilities, and that its goal is "improved leisure lifestyle," as long claimed by Peterson's Leisure Ability Model (Peterson & Gunn, 1984; Peterson & Stumbo, 2000).

On the other hand, the given assumptions are not "right" if one starts with a more precise definition of therapeutic recreation rather than using the broad definition. If one were to adopt, for instance, the clinical perspective as defined by the American Therapeutic Recreation Association (ATRA), the assumptions that flow from this clinical approach would differ from those elaborated thus far. A historical perspective will help explain the differences between the broad definition of therapeutic recreation often reflected in curricula today, and the clinical approach championed by ATRA.

Historical Perspective

Historically, therapeutic recreation grew from two streams of thought. One might be termed the *recreation for all perspective*. Those with this point of view hold that recreation is inherently beneficial and should be available to all, including those in institutions and those who are disabled. This view was held by the old Hospital Recreation Section of the American Recreation Society (ARS) in the 1940s. Today it could be termed the "civil rights perspective" since no one should be excluded from the civil right of recreation participation.

The other major perspective is that of *recreation as therapy*. Recreation as therapy is seen as a means to ameliorate, improve, or correct conditions in order to protect and promote health. It is a modality that involves purposeful intervention to bring about expected outcomes. This position was held by the National Association of Recreational Therapists (NART) in the 1950s.

ARS and NART championed these two positions until the groups merged into the National Therapeutic Recreation Society (NTRS) in 1966. At that time, *therapeutic recreation* was adopted as an umbrella term to describe both recreation for persons with disabilities (the ARS position) and recreation therapy (the NART position). Since then NTRS has tried to maintain both positions by adopting a broad view of therapeutic recreation that attempts to encompass both special recreation (i.e., recreation specifically designed for persons with disabilities) and recreation therapy (i.e., recreation as a clinical intervention). A number of authors (e.g. Austin, 1986b; Carter, Van Andel & Robb, 1995; Meyer, 1980) have objected to the NTRS position after having observed that its all-encompassing approach is too broad and lacks the focus needed to direct a profession.

Partly because NTRS had not provided clear boundaries for the profession, the American Therapeutic Recreation Association (ATRA) formed. The focus of ATRA is to advance clinical practice. Since 1984, ATRA has championed the cause of using recreation as an intervention in treatment, rehabilitation, and long-term care. Unfortunately, ATRA's clinical approach has not placed enough emphasis on health promotion. Illness prevention and health promotion are major parts of the recent health movement that takes a holistic approach to health, and that looks beyond the traditional medical mainstream for solutions to health problems (Goldstein, 1992).

Were ATRA to include health promotion within its clinical approach, it would embrace the full spectrum of therapeutic recreation/recreation therapy practice. A philosophical approach that encompasses both treatment/rehabilitation and health promotion/wellness aspects of practice has been proposed as a basis for therapeutic recreation curriculum by Monroe and Connolly (1997/98).

Recently NTRS has advocated for inclusive recreation (i.e., the full acceptance and integration of persons with disabilities into the recreation mainstream) as a way to permit people with disabilities to exercise their right to community recreation opportunities (Smith, Austin & Kennedy, 2001). Perhaps the Americans with Disabilities Act (ADA) served as a motivational force to inspire NTRS toward a larger role in promoting inclusive recreation. In any case, this role fits in well with NTRS's nonclinical approach to therapeutic recreation.

Implications for Curriculum

The past broad interpretation of the profession has lead to problems in curricula development. Because of the expansive approach, the broad field termed therapeutic recreation is not seen as a profession with defined boundaries, but simply a specialty within parks and recreation.

The time has come to restructure the system of education based on a clear definition of the therapeutic recreation profession. This reform needs to rest on boundaries that distinguish special and inclusive recreation from therapeutic recreation. It may also be time to adopt the term *recreation therapy* to more clearly represent the clinical approach that uses recreation as an intervention and follows the systematic process of assessment, planning, implementation, and evaluation. If therapeutic recreation curricula do not take this step, therapeutic recreation will remain "lost in familiar places" (Dumas, 1994), and doomed to the long tradition of basing curricula on a definition lacking clear boundaries. As Dumas (1994) stated:

> Boundaries enable us to set limits, and to distinguish what
> to divide and separate. They denote the relative position of
> each entity within the organizational structure. Boundaries
> define roles, responsibilities, and prerogatives. (p. 13)

Would clear lines of demarcation between special and inclusive recreation, and therapeutic recreation (or recreation therapy) be beneficial to curricula development? A case can be made that a definitive separation of the two could enhance both.

Special and inclusive recreation could be seen clearly as part of the leisure service delivery system. The assumption would be that the core of the curriculum would be the provision of recreation and leisure services—the traditional parks and recreation curriculum. The responsibility for training personnel for the provision of services for persons with disabilities would be that of parks and recreation curricula. This position has been taken by Smith, Austin, and Kennedy (2001) in their widely used textbook about the provision of recreation opportunities for persons with disabilities.

Therapeutic recreation/recreation therapy could then be perceived as a segment of the healthcare system. The assumption would be that the core of the therapeutic recreation/recreation therapy curriculum would be healthcare and intervention strategies. At least one study (Brasile, 1992) has suggested that therapeutic recreation/recreation therapy curricula need to become more standardized in order to assure quality control over graduates to insure that they can perform in clinical settings post graduation.

The American Therapeutic Recreation Association's *Guidelines for Competency Assessment and Curriculum Planning in Therapeutic Recreation: A Tool for Self-Evaluation* (Kinney & Witman, 1997) may be perceived as an initial step toward greater standardization of therapeutic recreation/recreation therapy curricula. This document provides both guidelines for curriculum planning and recommends structural components for professional preparation programs.

Are we likely to experience revolutionary changes in therapeutic recreation professional preparation programs? Will therapeutic recreation/recreation therapy curricula redefine themselves and move from parks and recreation to some other area such as allied health?

The answer is "probably not." A very practical problem stands as a barrier to such realignment. In many university departments today, one third to two thirds of the students are in therapeutic recreation (or recreation therapy). Without these students, these park and recreation departments might dissolve. It is not likely that these departments will be willing to give up therapeutic recreation/recreation therapy under such circumstances. Assuming change is necessary, a more likely scenario would be some type of compromise to give therapeutic recreation/recreation therapy more autonomy within university park and recreation departments. Recreation therapy might be expected to remain in university park and recreation departments as a distinct curriculum. Perhaps even a distinctive degree in therapeutic recreation/recreation therapy will eventually evolve. At least five universities have already established such a degree.

At the present time, therapeutic recreation/recreation therapy curricula will probably remain in parks and recreation departments. But it is perhaps time that two areas of curricula are identified within parks and recreation—one for general parks and recreation, and a second for therapeutic recreation/recreation therapy. Such an arrangement would properly distinguish therapeutic recreation/recreation therapy from the field of parks and recreation. This will allow therapeutic recreation/recreation therapy (TR/RT) the following:

1. *To interpret TR/RT to others better.* Today therapeutic recreation is competing for its very existence within the marketplace. Providers must be able to interpret and sell themselves to healthcare administrators as professionals grounded in clinical skills, not as "good guys" who offer recreation opportunities. Clear, concise boundaries make this job much easier. In a healthcare industry faced with financial concerns, accountability and more sophisticated requirements, specialists need to be able to clearly describe to others not what they do to enhance "leisure lifestyle," but how to improve the client's level of health.

2. *To define the boundaries of the profession to facilitate the growth of a documented body of knowledge.* Recreation professionals must show in a precise manner how therapeutic recreation/recreation therapy is valuable in treatment and rehabilitation. Nearly all allied health disciplines have begun efforts to demonstrate the value and worth of their practice. Such empirical evidence can become the basis to teach students the skills and knowledge needed to deliver quality clinical services.

3. *To better prepare students and to provide them with a clear sense of professional identity.* As therapeutic recreation educators become more focused in their curriculum, students will develop a clearer sense of mission and purpose. This will allow students to take greater pride in themselves and their profession.

4. *To create sharper focus for TR/RT, which will allow those involved with special and inclusive recreation to take command of their area.* Those responsible for the delivery of recreation services (i.e., general park and recreation professionals) can regain the leadership from recreation therapists for the provision of special and inclusive recreation services. It is time that TR/RT let go of its role of parenting special and inclusive recreation and give this mission to those with whom it belongs—the providers of public parks and recreation (Austin, 1986b).

5. *To credentialize recreation therapy professionals will become more meaningful as TR/RT separates from general parks and recreation.* Members of any professional group, such as recreation therapists, must employ credentials that certify mastery of the unique knowledge and skills needed in the defined area of practice.

Consumers of services need an identifiable label that enables them to differentiate one professional from another, and offers some assurance of professional competence in the services delivered.

Recommendations for Curricular Reform

Once the clinical concerns of therapeutic recreation/recreation therapy have been made explicit and its boundaries with special and inclusive recreation are clear, what specific steps need to be taken to reform recreation therapy curricula? This is the question to which this final portion of this chapter is dedicated. The material is organized into two sections. The first lists general areas of reform; the second provides specific areas of reform.

General Areas of Reform

Retain the Baccalaureate as the Entry-Level Degree While Improving Master's Degree Programs

The bachelor's degree shall remain the professional entry-level degree. Students with bachelor's degrees will be prepared broadly to work with a variety of client groups. Specialization with client groups will occur at the master's degree level, as well as specialized preparation in such areas as leisure counseling, adventure/challenge therapy, and advanced clinical practice.

Because it is critical to have advanced practice clinicians and properly prepared managers, strong master's degree programs must be provided. While a study by Austin, Kastrinos, and Stumpt (1998) found that faculty judged the general health of therapeutic recreation graduate programs to be relatively good, surprisingly few university master's degree therapeutic recreation programs (7 of 43) were focused toward advanced clinical practice. Most (58.1%) master's programs were emphases (with some therapeutic recreation course work as a part of a master's degree). Another 34.9% of the programs were options (with a structured sequence of therapeutic recreation courses in addition to the master's core). Just two universities listed their programs as stand-alone degrees (i.e., separate curriculum in therapeutic recreation). Only one offered a separate degree (i.e., specific master's degree in therapeutic recreation). In examining their findings the researchers concluded the need for increased sophistication and greater autonomy in the therapeutic recreation master's programs. Specifically, they called for more consistency in therapeutic recreation course requirements and internships, along with a greater focus on preparing students for advanced clinical practice skills.

Insist on Liberal Education for Undergraduates

Undergraduates "have come to view general education as an irritating interruption—an annoying detour on the way to their degree" (Boyer, 1987, p. 112). This is highly unfortunate because the liberal learning dimension of professional education should deepen students' understandings of themselves and their world. It should contribute to acquaint students with the broader cultural context in which they exist personally and professionally. Liberal education provides students with an appreciation of Western thought and traditions as well as other cultures. Such a perspective enlarges the vision of students by helping them to appreciate differences between people and to build a better world.

For recreation therapists to have the depth and breadth of education needed to be contributing citizens of the world, they need to become generally educated human beings. Such a background provides a context for professional practice and allows for wider appreciation of the diversity of clients and environments that they will encounter.

General education courses that relate to recreation therapy can be selected to enable students to establish foundations for professional study. Within the biological sciences, students should study anatomy and physiology. Social science preparation should include developmental psychology, abnormal psychology, and social psychology, with a particular focus on the social psychology of leisure. Sociological concerns such as group dynamics, community organization, and family structures should form a basis for further study.

Recreation therapy curriculum developers continually need to weigh the relative importance of such core recreation courses in the philosophy and history of the recreation movement, area and facility design, recreation and park management, and professional issues in parks and recreation against the necessity for students to gain a sound general, liberal education base along with necessary professional skills for recreation therapy.

Revise Core Requirements for the Recreation Therapy Curriculum

Closely related to the previous recommendation is one to revise the core courses in recreation typically required of students in recreation therapy. If recreation therapy is truly different from general recreation, as suggested previously, it follows that recreation therapy curricula should not be simply layering recreation therapy courses on top of parks and recreation courses. Instead, the recreation therapy curriculum should reflect those competencies needed by recreation therapists to perform as clinicians.

Those in recreation therapy certainly need a background from which to understand leisure and leisure behavior. Beyond courses in the social science of leisure, however, there is much room for debate as to the value of students in recreation therapy taking some of the courses required for general park and recreation students. As with liberal education, curriculum planners need to measure the importance of requirements in the philosophy and history of the recreation movement, area and facility design, recreation and park management, professional issues in parks and recreation and similar courses, comparing them against educational experiences directly related to clinical applications of recreation therapy.

A therapeutic recreation core needs to be established. It would contain the "Basic 3" of *Introduction to Therapeutic Recreation*, *Techniques in Therapeutic Recreation*, and *Issues in Therapeutic Recreation* (or similar titles). In addition, courses in therapeutic communication and clinical interventions would be added to expand the basic therapeutic recreation core to the "Basic 5." Of course, necessary competencies for professional practice in therapeutic recreation would need to be organized under these five courses. Published lists of competencies needed for professional practice, such as those found in the ATRA *Guidelines* (Kinney & Witman, 1997), can serve as a basis for these courses. In addition to the "Basic 5," there should be a requirement of at least one full-time twelve- to fifteen-week internship to be completed under a Certified Therapeutic Recreation Specialist (CTRS). Some type of preinternship field work or practicum would precede this internship experience.

Gain Practitioner Involvement and Emphasize Agency Responsibility

Practitioners need to play a more active role in professional preparation programs. Practitioner involvement should range from advising university faculty on curriculum to assisting in classroom instruction and providing clinical supervision for students during field experiences to serve as mentors.

Agencies, likewise, need to assume a larger responsibility in the preparation of future professionals. Colleges and universities can educate students, but the actual training in the techniques of therapeutic recreation practice must be gained at agencies delivering recreation therapy services (Austin, 1974).

Agencies must gear up to provide high-quality clinical supervision for students doing practicum and internship experiences. With clinical supervision being a relatively undeveloped aspect of therapeutic recreation (Austin, 1986a), it would benefit agencies to establish formal clinical supervision programs, and universities to teach students to give and receive clinical supervision. Universities also need to prepare future agency supervisors to design and implement the overall field experience (Kunstler, 1982).

Adopt Guidelines for Self-Studies

A final general area of reform for university therapeutic recreation/recreation therapy programs involves the profession adopting guidelines for use by universities in self-studies. Included should be structural components for the number of therapeutic recreation/recreation therapy faculty; faculty qualifications; teaching resources; library resources; and providing an adequate number of approved opportunities for clinical experiences for students. Of course, in addition to the structural components, a listing of competencies to be gained from the curriculum needs to be provided in these guidelines. The *Guidelines for Competency Assessment and Curriculum Planning in Therapeutic Recreation: A Tool for Self-Evaluation* (Kinney & Witmann, 1997) might serve well as a basis for self-studies documentation.

Specific Areas of Reform

Redefine the Terms "Clinical" and "Health"

The term *clinical* needs to be redefined if it is to be used effectively to unite recreation therapists who employ purposeful interventions to strengthen individuals' coping abilities as well as to modify those parts of clients' lives and environments that negatively affect their well-being. The traditional usage of the term *clinical* connotes sickness or illness, evoking images of medical staff in white garb diagnosing and treating diseases and disorders through medication or surgery. As applied in behavioral health settings, it brings to mind psychiatrists prescribing psychotropic drugs or conducting insight-oriented psychotherapy.

Therapeutic recreation/recreation therapy clients may find that they need help that family and friends cannot give, yet they do not have to be sick or pathological to benefit from therapeutic recreation/recreation therapy. Therapeutic recreation/recreation therapy should not be narrowly conceived under a traditional medical model. Therapeutic recreation/recreation therapy can be concerned not only with health protection but illness prevention and health promotion as well. Such programs do not have to be done exclusively in hospitals and rehabilitation centers. Therapeutic recreation/recreation therapy can be practiced in schools, community psychosocial programs for elderly persons, or any setting where recreation therapists use interventions with therapeutic intent. The systematic process of assessment, planning an intervention, implementing the intervention, and evaluating outcomes with individual clients makes therapeutic recreation/recreation therapy clinical in nature.

Recreation therapists must also learn to perceive health to be much more than the mere absence of medical symptoms. Perhaps the best known definition of health is that of the World Health Organization (1947), which defined health as "a state of complete physical, mental, and social well-being, not merely the absence of disease or infirmity." Such a definition leads us toward a holistic perception of individuals and relates health to self-fulfillment and creative living. Under this definition, health can be seen as running along a continuum with "poor health" at one end and "optimal health" or "high-level wellness" at the other extreme. Our clients can receive our services at any point along that continuum.

Accentuate Knowledge of the Full Spectrum of Healthcare

To function as clinicians, it is critical that recreation therapists be well-versed in basic information related to treatment, rehabilitation, long-term care, illness prevention and health promotion. Students need to know the etiology, course, and prognosis for various diagnostic categories; disease sequelae; medical terminology; effects of major drugs; health and safety information for working with persons whose physical mobility or ability is reduced due to injury or physical conditions; effects of stress upon individuals; general principles of rehabilitation; and general understandings of wellness. Knowledge of the full range of healthcare environments and related accreditation standards should be a part of students' knowledge of healthcare.

Emphasize Skills in Promoting Healthy Lifestyles

Recreation therapists will need to know how to help clients to make wise decisions in choosing lifestyles that lead to illness prevention and health promotion (Blayney & Selker, 1992). They will need skills in leisure education and leisure counseling in order to promote healthy lifestyles on the parts of their clients (Bedini, 1990). Understandings and skills in providing community transition programs are critical in helping clients move to more independent living situations or to leave school to assume adult roles.

Maintain Clinical Practice as the Primary Focus

Clinical practice must be emphasized as the primary focus of the recreation therapy curriculum. As such, students need to be exposed to a comprehensive approach to healthcare, in contrast to only acute and episodic care. Along with treatment, rehabilitation and long-term care, students need to understand a holistic approach to healthcare including illness prevention and the promotion of high-level wellness. The time is right to train recreation therapists to prevent illness and promote wellness, as well as provide treatment, rehabilitation, and long-term care.

While recreation therapy students must understand the rights of people with disabilities and learn to become advocates for the provision of recreation opportunities for people with disabilities, inclusive and special recreation should remain the concerns of park and recreation professionals from both the public and private sectors. Therefore, inclusive and special recreation should not be a significant part of the recreation therapy curriculum.

Therapeutic recreation/recreation therapy curricula must retain clinical practice as their primary concern so students may be prepared to help clients move toward greater independent functioning and optimal health. Among the clinical competencies that should be gained by students are skills in protocol development, case conceptualization, documentation, and the motivating and teaching of clients. In addition, students need to learn to give and receive clinical supervision; to use modern technology in all phases of the therapeutic recreation process; and to practice teamwork on interdisciplinary teams.

Emphasize the Use of the Therapeutic Recreation/Recreation Therapy Process with Client Involvement

Due to the clinical orientation needed in recreation therapy, students must learn how to apply the therapeutic recreation/recreation therapy process (i.e., assessment, planning, implementation, evaluation). Competencies include doing client assessment, formulating goals and writing behavioral objectives with clients, completing plans, implementing interventions, and evaluating outcomes of interventions. Skillfully completing documentation is an important part of the evaluation phase in the therapeutic recreation/ recreation therapy process. The need to involve clients and their families in the decision-making process should be stressed as a critical element in the therapeutic recreation/recreation therapy process.

Stress Skills in Providing Activities as Clinical Interventions

Kunstler (1982) once termed activities as "the primary vehicle" for recreation therapists (p. 80). To apply activities in a therapeutic manner, it is imperative that recreation therapists have a thorough knowledge of various types of activities within fine and applied arts, social recreation, dance, music, physical fitness, sport, and games. To have the level of knowledge needed to use activities for advance treatment and rehabilitation outcomes, it is desirable for students to gain an in-depth experience with at least one specific activity area (e.g., arts and crafts, aquatics, adventure/challenge activities, strength training, drama). Obviously, the more acquainted a therapist is with a particular activity, the more likely it is that he or she may be able to use it in clinical application.

An area in which recreation therapists students today often have deficiencies is physical activity. At one time it was common for recreation therapists to have a high level of knowledge in this area. Perhaps due to the separation of recreation from physical education curricula, skills in physical activities have largely become a lost art among recreation therapists. This is highly unfortunate at a time when activities such as weight training, conditioning, running, walking, and aerobic dance are often used in stress reduction programs for illness prevention, as well as in therapy, rehabilitation and health promotion programs.

There currently exists a danger that recreation therapy students will not have the opportunity to gain required backgrounds in activities, as curricula are driven by a "recreation management model," neglecting courses in activities in favor of those with management concerns. Recreation therapy faculty and students will be remiss if they allow the omission of opportunities for students to become well-grounded in activity skills. Creative approaches to instruction in activities may take the form of permitting students to gain activity skills through general education courses and field experience, as well as through recreation therapy courses that concentrate on clinical practice.

Affirm the Importance of Self-Awareness

Possessing self-awareness, or understanding of self, is a critical part of being a therapist. Recreation therapists have to know themselves and be reasonably comfortable with themselves to be fully effective in helping relationships (Austin, 1999). Having such self-understanding permits recreation therapists to respect themselves and to respond to clients with empathy, warmth, and acceptance. Professional helping demands that the helper must remain ever cognizant that the therapeutic use of self requires the professional to keep the primary focus on the client's needs, not his or her own.

Emphasize Therapeutic Communication Skills

According to Kunstler and Austin (1982), "Training in interpersonal skills is imperative" for recreation therapists (p. 151). These researchers have found that classroom instruction, with homework assignments, can have a significant impact on the interpersonal relationship skills of recreation therapy students. Obtaining skills in attending, clarifying, reflecting, giving and receiving feedback, using silence, reinforcing, summarizing, and nonverbal communication helps assure that recreation therapists will be able to establish rapport and maintain therapeutic communications with clients. Highly developed therapeutic communication skills are at the heart of any clinical program. People possessing such skills will be likely to create an atmosphere in which empathy, genuineness, and respect may be fostered between the helper and the client.

Underscore Historical/Philosophical Foundations of TR/RT and Affirm the Importance of Theory to Practice

Students in recreation therapy need to understand and appreciate the importance of historical precedents in recreation therapy and healthcare as they influence the philosophy of practice. It is important that therapists develop a philosophical base for practice.

Closely related to philosophy is theory. Recreation therapists must base their practice on a sound foundation. Practice theories and practice models need to be embraced or developed by students so that they have a basis for their practice.

Sensitize Students to Our Racially and Culturally Diverse Society

The racial and ethnic composition of America is rapidly changing. American and other developed nations are becoming more culturally diverse. All helping professionals, including recreation therapists, will need cultural diversity training (Blayney & Selker, 1992).

Stress Knowledge of Research

Both students and practitioners need to be trained to understand the conceptualization and design of research on clinical change. Equally important as training in research methods is developing an appreciation of the necessity to complete field-based research and to utilize findings in clinical practice. Without a commitment to research on the part of practitioners few studies will be accomplished. Recreation therapists must have the desire to initiate research projects or at least cooperate with university faculty and others who wish to conduct studies in the field.

Underscore the Need for Ethical and Professional Behavior

Recreation therapy students need to become socialized into roles as healthcare professionals. They need to understand professional ethics, including the ethical need to understand their own limits in clinical competence and to keep skills current through continuing education. They need to understand the importance of remaining active in professional societies in order to advance their profession (Blayney & Selker, 1992). This understanding needs to begin to be developed while students are in school through an introduction to the trends and issues in the profession.

Summary and Conclusion

Within this chapter a case has been made that all therapeutic recreation curricula rest on a set of assumptions that need to be made clear and explicit. With the assumptions underlying recreation therapy curricula presented, an argument was put forth that recreation therapy should be clearly distinguished from the more general field of parks and recreation. Following this, positive ramifications of considering recreation therapists distinct from other areas of parks and recreation were outlined. Finally, recommendations for curriculum reform that rest on those assumptions were made.

The time has come to make explicit the identifying features that cause recreation therapists to be distinct from parks and recreation, and to call for changes in professional preparation curricula to reflect the distinctiveness of recreation therapy. Without a definition that brings recreation therapy into sharper focus, therapeutic recreation will continue to be all things to all people and lack the direction necessary for the profession to survive and prosper in the real world of the healthcare industry.

Reading Comprehension Questions

1. Do you agree that all curricula rest on a set of underlying assumptions? Why or why not?

2. Should therapeutic recreation/recreation therapy curricula be clearly distinguished from general parks and recreation curricula? Why or why not?

3. Would clearly defining *special and inclusive recreation* and *recreation therapy* as two separate areas of practice be helpful to the development of recreation therapy curricula? Why or why not?

4. Do you agree or disagree with the general areas of reform proposed? Why?

5. Do you agree or disagree with the specific areas of reform proposed? Why?

References

Austin, D. R. (1999). *Therapeutic recreation: Processes and techniques* (4th ed.). Champaign, IL: Sagamore.

Austin, D. R. (1986a). Clinical supervision in therapeutic recreation. *Journal of Expanding Horizons in Therapeutic Recreation, 1*, 7–13.

Austin, D. R. (1986b). The helping professional: You do make a difference. In A. James and F. McGuire (Eds.), *A helping profession: Selected papers from the 1985 Southeast Therapeutic Recreation Symposium* (pp. 7–32). Clemson, SC: Clemson University Extension Service.

Austin, D. R. (1974). The university can't train therapeutic recreators. *Therapeutic Recreation Journal, 8*(1), 22–24.

Austin, D. R., Kastrinos, G., and Stumpt, K. (1998). Master's programs in therapeutic recreation in the United States. In G. L. Hitzhusen and L. Thomas (Eds.), *Global therapeutic recreation V* (pp. 189–199). Columbia, MO: University of Missouri.

Bedini, L. A. (1990). The status of leisure education: Implications for instruction and practice. *Therapeutic Recreation Journal, 24*(1), 40–49.

Blayney, K. D. and Selker, L. G. (1992). *Healthy America: Practitioners for 2005: A beginning dialogue for U.S. schools of allied health: Draft.* Pew Health Professions Commission.

Brasile, F. (1992). Professional preparation: Reported needs for a profession in transition. *Annual in Therapeutic Recreation, 3*, 58–71.

Boyer, E. L. (1987). *College: The undergraduate experience in America.* New York, NY: Harper & Row.

Carter, M. J., VanAndel, G. E., and Robb, G. M. (1995). *Therapeutic recreation: A practical approach* (2nd ed.). Prospects Heights, IL: Waveland Press.

Compton, D. M. (Ed.) (1997). *Issues in therapeutic recreation: Toward the new millennium* (2nd ed.). Champaign, IL: Sagamore.

Dumas, R. G. (1994). Psychiatric nursing in an era of change. *Journal of Psychosocial Nursing, 32*(1), 11–14.

Goldstein, M. S. (1992). *The health movement: Promoting fitness in America.* New York, NY: Twayne Publishers.

Kinney T. and Witman, J. (1997). *Guidelines for competency assessment and curriculum planning in therapeutic recreation: A tool for self-evaluation.* Hattiesburg, MS: American Therapeutic Recreation Association.

Kunstler, R. (1982). Emerging special populations and how they can be helped. *Adapted Physical Activity Quarterly, 2*, 177–181.

Kunstler, R. and Austin, D. R. (1982). Instruction in interpersonal relationship skills: An evaluative research study. In L. L. Neal and C. R. Edginton (Eds.),

Extra perspectives: Concepts in therapeutic recreation (pp. 145–153). Eugene, OR: University of Oregon.

Meyer, L. (1980). Three philosophical positions of therapeutic recreation and their implications for professionalization and NTRS. *Proceedings of the First Annual Post-Doctoral Institute* (pp. 28–42). Bloomington, IN: Department of Recreation and Park Administration, Indiana University.

Monroe, J. E. and Connolly, P. (1997/98). Responsive curriculum development in therapeutic recreation: One approach to comprehensive curriculum design. *Annual in Therapeutic Recreation, 7*, 64–73.

Peterson, C. A. and Gunn, S. L. (1984). *Therapeutic recreation program design: Principles and procedures* (2nd ed.). Englewood Cliffs, NJ: Prentice Hall.

Peterson, C. A. and Stumbo, N. J. (2000). *Therapeutic recreation program design: Principles and procedures* (3rd ed.). Needham Heights, MA: Allyn & Bacon.

Smith, R. W., Austin, D. R., and Kennedy, D. W. (2001). *Inclusive and special recreation: Opportunities for persons with disabilities* (4th ed.). Boston, MA: McGraw Hill.

World Health Organization. (1947). Constitution of the World Health Organization. *Chronicles of WHO, 1*, 1, 2.

Chapter 12

A Call for Training in Physical Activity

David R. Austin, Ph.D., CTRS, FALS

When I began my career in recreation therapy in the early 1960s, few recreation therapy professionals had degrees in recreation, and fewer still had specialized in therapeutic recreation. Many who were then working as recreation therapists had been prepared in physical education. Because of our physical education backgrounds, we naturally gravitated toward providing physical activity programs including exercise, fitness, and sport.

In my first recreation therapy position, which was at a state psychiatric hospital, I conducted a Men's Fitness Club, bowling classes, softball leagues in summer, and basketball leagues in winter. A female recreation therapist, also trained in physical education, ran similar programs for women. While little research had been published in the 1960s to substantiate the value of physical activity for psychiatric patients, recreation therapists were convinced these programs held many physical and psychological benefits for their patients.

As I recall, patient reactions to engaging in physical activities were mixed. Many male patients enjoyed the opportunity to participate, especially in organized softball and basketball. However, a few were less than enthusiastic about the Men's Fitness Club—an understandable reaction to a program that emphasized routine calisthenics, such as push-ups, sit-ups, and jumping jacks.

Despite the occasional lack of patient motivation, back in the 1960s and into the 1970s a great number of opportunities existed for our clients to take part in physical activities within recreation therapy programs. However, in the decades of the 1980s and 1990s, it seems a precipitous decline occurred in the amount of recreation therapy programs and interventions that encourage physical activity.

A Decline in Physical Activity Programs

In a literature review of the leading therapeutic recreation professional publication during the 1980s and 1990s, *Therapeutic Recreation Journal (TRJ)* indicated a lack of interest in exercise, fitness, and other physical activities on the part of recreation therapists. Only a handful of articles on physical activities appeared in *TRJ* during this period. One article on "Prescriptive Exercise for the Aged" appeared (Leslie, 1980). In 1981 *TRJ* published only one article concerning physical activity, Mobily's "Attitudes of Institutionalized, Elderly Iowans toward Physical Activity." In 1986, Patrick reported on research about "The Effects of Wheelchair Competition on Self-Concept and Acceptance of Disability in Novice Athletes." In 1988, Batavia authored "Needed: Active Therapeutic Recreation for High-Level Quadriplegics."

This trend of relatively low numbers of *TRJ* articles on physical activities continued during the decade of the 1990s. In 1994, Karper and Goldfarb wrote "Effects of Exercise on Acute Upper and Lower Respiratory Tract Infections in Older Adults." In 1996 and 1997 Broach and Dattilo authored articles on the use of aquatic therapy (Broach & Dattilo, 1996; Broach, Groff & Dattilo, 1997). Finally, in 1998, Mobily, Mobily, Lane, and Semerjian published research about "Using Progressive Resistance Training as an Intervention with Older Adults."

As is evident from this quick literature review, few articles appeared on physical activity in this major therapeutic recreation journal. Further, other than Mobily's research involving exercise with older adults and Brock and Dattilo's articles on aquatic therapy, there were no authors whose articles reflected a program of inquiry.

Why the relative lack of programming and writing in the area of exercise, fitness, and physical activities during the past twenty years? At least two speculations seem to have some basis. One is that as a growing number of recreation therapists prepared in university therapeutic recreation professional preparation programs, the proportion of practitioners with physical education backgrounds in the field declined. These new recreation therapists naturally had less background and interest in exercise, fitness, and physical activities than those with a physical education preparation. A second speculation involves the changing nature of professional preparation in recreation and leisure studies curricula from the 1960s and 1970s to the period of the 1980s and beyond. Two events took place during this period. First, many recreation and leisure studies curricula that evolved from university professional preparation programs in physical education desired to separate themselves from physical education. They wanted to be independent to reflect the separate profession of recreation. As a result, they systematically removed physical education requirements from their curricula. Also during the 1980s a trend to move recreation and leisure studies curricula toward a "management model" and away from a "leadership model" took place. Training in recreation leadership gave way to much greater emphasis on management training. Therapeutic recreation students did not escape this movement, and as curricula evolved the students studying therapeutic recreation had fewer opportunities to acquire skills to lead physical activities.

A Need for Physical Activity Programs

The value of exercise, fitness, and physical activity programs has become obvious in a time when the majority of Americans are sedentary or choose to not even engage in exercise of low to moderate intensity (Centers for Disease Control and Prevention, 1991). Compounding the situation for recreation therapists is the fact that people with disabilities tend to be less physically active than people without disabilities (U.S. Department of Health and Human Services, 2000).

Inactive lifestyles, unfortunately, are linked to problems with physical health. Physical inactivity is connected to various chronic diseases including coronary heart disease (Phillips, Kiernan & King, 2001). The U.S. Department of Health and Human Services' *Healthy People 2010* states:

> The role of physical activity in preventing coronary heart disease (CHD) is of particular importance, given that this disease is the leading cause of death and disability in the United States. Physically inactive people are almost twice as likely to develop CHD as persons who engage in regular physical activity. (2000, pp. 22–23)

On average, physically inactive people do not live as long as those who are active (U.S. Department of Health and Human Services, 2000). Individuals with low levels of fitness "are more than twice as likely to die of all causes than those with moderate physical fitness" (Fowler, 1996, p. 3).

Conversely, Hays outlined the many positive impacts that exercise can have on physical health. She writes:

> Exercise not only decreases coronary heart disease risk and improves rehabilitative potential, but it also impacts coronary risk factors, including high blood pressure, cholesterol level and type, smoking, and obesity. Exercise decreases the risk of colon cancer, and results in reduced body fat (or reduced

total body mass and fat weight), lower blood pressure, and improved carbohydrate metabolism. Exercise is associated with reduced problems or delay of problems related to diabetes, assisting in the maintenance of bone density, helping insure the quality and quantity of sleep, and creating increased oxygen capacity. (1999, p. 6)

Research reviewed in the therapeutic recreation literature demonstrates that specific interventions involving physical activity can produce therapeutic outcomes. An extensive literature review by Lee and Yang (2000) reported the use of a number of intervention programs in physical medicine and rehabilitation settings. Interventions employed in these studies included warm-up and flexibility exercises, stretching, aerobic exercises, dance, tai chi, physical games, and aquatic programs. Results from these interventions included documented outcomes for clients of increased mobility, improved fitness levels, decreased depression, and improved quality of life.

An inactive lifestyle can also have adverse effects on mental health. Exercise has the potential to relieve symptoms of anxiety and depression and even reduce symptoms of schizophrenia. At least one study has found that exercise by itself was at least as effective, or more so, than psychotherapy in reducing symptoms of depression. Participation in exercise programs also provides psychiatric clients with a greater sense of accomplishment and increases feelings of social support. Finally, exercise programs for clients who are recovering from physical or sexual abuse have been found to positively affect self-esteem and body image (DeAngelis, 1996). Exercise may also act to temper the body's response to stress. A chemical produced during exercise, norepinephrine, has been linked to moderating stress responses (Azar, 1996).

Four areas for intervening with physical activity programs for mental health clients have been discussed by Hays (1999). The first is for coping with depression, anxiety, and problems with being overweight. Second, is the use of physical activity to help clients increase their sense of internal locus of control and to enhance feelings of self-efficacy and mastery. The third area is the provision of opportunities for increasing social support. The final area is a general one of assisting clients to experience improved health and well-being.

The obvious value that participation in physical activity can have on physical and mental health and well-being has not been missed by the field of parks and recreation. There have been calls for park and recreation professionals to engage citizens in more active lifestyles that involve physical activity. For example, O'Sullivan stated:

> We need to engage the attention, the interest and the in-
> volvement of that 80% of the people who aren't running
> up and down the field or even walking through the park.
> (1996, p. 63)

All signs point to a real and immediate need for recreation therapists to focus more on the provision of physical activities in order to both prevent and combat problems in physical and mental health. Such an emphasis would appear to hold the potential of becoming paramount within the recreation therapy profession as more and more practitioners embrace the need to provide programs for both treatment and high-level wellness, a need reflected in Austin's (1998, 1999) Health Protection/Health Promotion Model of practice.

New Ways of Viewing Physical Activity

When considering the impact of physical activities on health, it is important to note that recent research findings have indicated that physical activities do not have to be of high intensity. Phillips, Kiernan, and King in their in-depth literature review on physical activity and health wrote:

> The extensive research base underpinning the recommenda-
> tions of the Surgeon General's Report on Physical Activity
> and Health has provided sufficient initial evidence to assert
> not only that physical and mental health benefits may be
> elicited with physical activity or exercise that is of far lower
> intensity than recommended by previous guidelines, but also
> that such benefits may be elicited by accumulating shorter
> bouts of physical activity or exercise throughout the day. This
> has resulted in what has been termed a "paradigm shift" from
> an "exercise training–fitness model" to a "physical activity–
> health paradigm." (2001, p. 649)

Such a paradigm shift has direct implications for recreation participa-tion. The new paradigm calls for involving individuals in any number of common leisure pursuits (e.g., walking, gardening, swimming, cycling) rather than the stereotypes one might think about when considering physical activities (e.g., calisthenics, gym workouts, jogging, running, jumping rope, cross-country skiing).

Tied to this new way of thinking are changes in the use of terms related to physical activity. The term *physical activity* has been adopted as the broad term to encompass exercise, sport, or other "bodily movement produced by the contraction of skeletal muscle that increases energy expenditure above the basal level" (Phillips, Kiernan & King, 2001, p. 628). Therefore, the terms exercise and physical activity are often used interchangeably in the literature (Hays, 1999). Technically, however, *exercise* is a subset of physical activity "that is planned structured, repetitive, and purposeful with the objective of improving one or more aspects of physical fitness" (Phillips, Kiernan & King, 2001, p. 628). Following popular convention, the term physical activity can be employed as an encompassing term.

Yet, even with the very apparent need to provide physical activities as interventions and a paradigm shift that has lead to a broadening of the term physical activity the need for proper training of recreation therapists to conduct physical activities has not been widely recognized within the profession. Therapeutic recreation educators at universities need to champion curriculum reform to assure the adequate training of therapeutic recreation students in the theory and practice of delivering interventions that involve physical activity.

The Need to Require Understandings of Exercise, Fitness, and Physical Activities

Assuming the major periodical of the therapeutic recreation profession, *Therapeutic Recreation Journal,* would contain references to the need for therapeutic recreation curricula to require training in physical activity programs if articles on the topic were being written, a review of *TRJ* was conducted for the decades of the 1980s and 1990s. Several articles appeared on the topic of university professional preparation programs. In 1981, Peterson and Connolly authored an article calling for greater standardization of curricula. In 1983, Mobily suggested a need for quality control in therapeutic recreation education. In 1984, Carter argued the necessity for recreation therapists to engage in continuing education following their university training in order to stay up-to-date in practice skills. In 1986, Coffey wrote about training needs for therapists in psychiatric settings. In 1999, Stumbo and Carter examined the state-of-the-art of therapeutic recreation curricula. In none of these articles, however, was the need for professional preparation programs to provide training in the theory and practice of using physical activity programs as interventions mentioned.

The seeming lack of awareness of the need to prepare recreation therapists to employ physical activities as interventions is alarming. Is the area of physical activity being largely ignored by practitioners and, therefore, practitioners are not urging universities to train students in it? Are therapeutic recreation professionals and educators uninformed about the significant impact physical activities can have on physical and mental health? Are universities simply slow to react to an obvious need to offer students training in the use of physical activities as interventions?

Conclusion

It is difficult to comprehend why physical activity has not been widely embraced by recreation therapists as an intervention within clinical programs. It is clear that physical activities have the potential to take a significant place in health promotion, as well as in treatment and rehabilitation. Perhaps it is time to return to our roots. Since many early recreation therapists held degrees in physical education, they were well-prepared to employ physical activities and regularly conducted exercise, fitness, sport, and other physical activity programs for their clients. Thus within the early years of the profession, recreation therapists had a great deal of interest in using physical activities as interventions. Now is the time for the recreation therapy profession to renew its interest in employing physical activities to intervene in the lives of clients to protect and promote their health. Of course, it will be up to universities to provide emerging recreation therapists with the skills and competencies needed to deliver therapeutic physical activities.

Reading Comprehension Questions

1. In what area were many recreation therapists trained back in the 1960s?

2. Do you understand the author's reasons why there may have been a decline in the employment of physical activities as interventions? Do you agree or disagree?

3. Is there evidence that participating in physical activities will help to protect and promote health?

4. What is the "paradigm shift" as discussed by Phillips, Kiernan, and King (2001)?

5. Has your own professional preparation included coursework about the theory and practice of using physical activities as interventions? Why or why not?

6. Do you agree with the author that greater attention needs to be given to physical activities both in therapeutic recreation practice and within university therapeutic recreation curricula?

References

Austin, D. R. (1999). *Therapeutic recreation: Processes and techniques* (4th ed.). Champaign, IL: Sagamore.

Austin, D. R. (1998). The Health Protection/Health Promotion Model. *Therapeutic Recreation Journal, 32*(2), 109–117.

Azar, B. (1996). Exercise fuels the brain's stress buffers. *Monitor, 27*(7), 18.

Batavia, A. I. (1988). Needed: Active therapeutic recreation for high-level quadriplegics. *Therapeutic Recreation Journal, 17*(2), 8–11.

Broach, E. and Dattilo, J. (1996). Aquatic therapy: A viable therapeutic recreation intervention. *Therapeutic Recreation Journal, 15*(3), 213–229.

Broach, E., Groff, D., and Dattilo, J. (1997). Effects of an aquatic therapy swimming program on adults with spinal cord injuries. *Therapeutic Recreation Journal, 16*(3), 159–172.

Carter, M. (1984). Issues in continuing professional competence of therapeutic recreators. *Therapeutic Recreation Journal, 18*(3), 7–10.

Centers for Disease Control and Prevention. (1991). Prevalence of sedentary lifestyle—Behavioral risk factor surveillance system, United States, 1991. *Morbidity and Mortality Weekly Reports, 42*, 576–579.

Coffey, F. (1986). Continuing professional development. *Therapeutic Recreation Journal, 20*(3), 11–20.

DeAngelis, T. (1996). Exercise gives a lift to psychotherapy. *Monitor, 27*(7), 24.

Fowler, R. D. (1996). Exercise: A life-changing habit. *Monitor, 27*(7), 3.

Hays, K. F. (1999). *Working it out: Using exercise in psychotherapy.* Washington, DC: American Psychological Association.

Karper, W. B. and Goldfarb, A. H. (1994). Effects of exercise on acute upper and lower respiratory track infections in older adults. *Therapeutic Recreation Journal, 18*(1), 8–17.

Lee, Y. and Yang, H. (2000). A review of therapeutic recreation outcomes in physical medicine and rehabilitation between 1991–2000. *Annual in Therapeutic Recreation, 9*, 21–33.

Leslie, D. K. (1980). Prescriptive exercise for the aged. *Therapeutic Recreation Journal, 14*(2), 39–42.

Mobily, K. E. (1983). Quality analysis in therapeutic recreation curriculum. *Therapeutic Recreation Journal, 17*(1), 18–25.

Mobily, K. E. (1981). Attitudes of institutionalized, elderly Iowans toward physical activity. *Therapeutic Recreation Journal, 15*(3), 30–40.

Mobily, K. E., Mobily, P. R., Lane, B. K., and Semerjian, T. Z. (1998). Using progressive resistance training as an intervention with older adults. *Therapeutic Recreation Journal, 17*(1), 13–27.

O'Sullivan, E. (1996). The four Es. *Parks & Recreation, 31*(10), 60–66.

Patrick, G. D. (1986). The effects of wheelchair competition on self-concept and acceptance of disability in novice athletes. *Therapeutic Recreation Journal, 20*(4), 61–71.

Peterson, C. A. and Connolly, P. (1981). Professional preparation in therapeutic recreation. *Therapeutic Recreation Journal, 15*(2), 39–45.

Phillips, W. T., Kierman, M., and King, A. C. (2001). The effects of physical activity on physical and psychological health. In A. Baum, T. A. Revenson, and J. E. Singer (Eds.), *Handbook of health psychology* (pp. 627–657). Mahwah, NJ: Lawrence Erlbaum.

Stumbo, N. J. and Carter, M. J. (1999). National therapeutic recreation curriculum study part A: Accreditation, curriculum, and internship characteristics. *Therapeutic Recreation Journal, 23*(1), 46–60.

U.S. Department of Health and Human Services. (2000). *Healthy people 2010* (Conference Edition in Two Volumes). Washington, DC: Author.

Chapter 13

Making Presentations Related to Therapeutic Recreation

Richard Williams, Ed.D., CTRS
John Dattilo, Ph.D., FALS

People learn in a variety of ways (Claxton & Murrell, 1987). Some people learn best by reading, others by listening to presentations and taking notes, others through discussion, and still others learn experientially. McKeachie (1999) recommended that instructors not rely on one style of instruction, but instead offer participants the opportunity to approach material in a variety of formats.

The lecture is a traditional and time-honored method of instruction. While some instructors consistently deliver engaging lectures that capture the attention of those in attendance, too often people describe this form of instruction as boring and ineffective. Inspired by an increased understanding of the learning process, other methods of instruction are being explored to help people learn from more interactive methods of teaching, such as the use of guided discussions and experiential learning activities (Bonwell, 1996). Although the lecture may not be used as pervasively as it once was, when it is done well, it remains a helpful tool for facilitating learning. This chapter presents some information to help the reader learn more about making presentations and hopefully to enhance the preparation and delivery of effective presentations. The chapter consists of four main parts: Be Prepared, Be Clear, Be Interesting, and Evaluate Yourself.

Be Prepared

Thorough preparation is the foundation of an effective presentation. Preparation includes learning the material to have an extensive understanding of it. Another aspect of preparation is developing effective presentation notes. Developing teaching aids, such as work sheets, increases confidence that the presentation will go well. Selection of appropriate audiovisual materials, including video clips, graphic images for overhead transparencies, slides or computer-generated programs, and web sites can help create a classroom environment conducive to learning.

Know the Content

One way to gain confidence when preparing a presentation is to have a thorough understanding of the material being presented. Contrarily, once an audience begins to doubt an instructor's understanding of the material, they are less likely to learn what the instructor had hoped to teach them. The more one knows about a topic, the more likely he or she is to project confidence and to connect with people attending their educational program.

For instance, during leisure education sessions, therapeutic recreation specialists often discuss sophisticated and complicated constructs, such as self-determination, choice, freedom, and intrinsic motivation. It is vital for specialists to have a thorough understanding of leisure prior to attempting to teach others this material. A particularly deep understanding of such ideas is required to present them so that they are both comprehensible and relevant to therapeutic recreation clients. One tool that can help instructors develop an understanding of their material is to prepare notes.

Develop Presentation Notes

Presentation notes can help instructors organize a presentation, stay on task during a presentation, and maintain a logical flow that is easy to follow. Additionally, presentation notes help to increase the chance that information will not be accidentally omitted from a presentation. Since presentation notes are just that, "notes," and not a verbatim transcript of a talk, it is also important not to rely too heavily on presentation notes.

To illustrate the importance of presentation notes, Kelly and Kelly (1982) studied in-class performance of nine professors who had won teaching awards and reported that these effective teachers made little use of notes during an actual lecture; rather, the effective teachers viewed teaching as a theatrical performance. Reading presentation notes can result in a detachment of the audience from the speaker. If eye contact is not maintained, it can reduce participants' confidence in the speaker's grasp of the material being presented, and it can limit the projection of the speaker's enthusiasm for the topic. Preparing presentation notes is vital to organizing and planning a presentation; however, overreliance on notes during a presentation can be detrimental.

Develop an Outline

Ross (1989) studied perceptions of 181 students about characteristics of effective teaching. According to Ross, people value presentations that are organized, clear, and easy to outline. Developing an outline that contains a hierarchy of main categories and subcategories can help organize a presentation. Once a hierarchical outline is generated, it is helpful to ask such questions as: "Does one idea logically flow into the next?" and "Will this material be easy for participants to outline?" Weiss, Weaver, and Cotrell (1988) suggested that providing outlines of presentations helps students record their notes and improves their learning. Contrarily, presentations that lack a clear outline or organization may confuse and frustrate participants.

Outlines can be provided in different ways, such as being recorded on a chalk or dry erase board, easel, slides, overheads, or computer-generated projections. Distributing an outline of the presentation at the beginning of a class can be helpful as well. These outlines allow participants to concentrate more on what the presenter is saying without struggling to write each word.

Providing an outline can help participants understand the organization and the logical flow of material being presented. Outlines can be referred to at the beginning of a presentation, throughout the course of a presentation to help participants keep track of the material being presented, and at the end of a presentation to help summarize the main points and bring closure to a session.

Construct Written Material for Use in Class

Work sheets prepared before class can be valuable teaching aids because they can provide visual and experiential supplements to presentations and can promote active learning (McKeachie, 1999). Supplementary material (e.g., photocopied newspaper article) can also be used to facilitate brief in-class discussions of issues contained in a lecture. Such discussions provide a different learning approach to the material and can facilitate social interaction between participants that contributes to a more engaging learning atmosphere.

One approach to instruction is to spark audience interest with a lecture and then use a work sheet that requires participants to apply the information and concepts to their personal or professional lives. For instance, after lecturing for half of an education session on a particular theory relevant to therapeutic recreation, such as optimal experience (Csikszentmihalyi, 1988), an instructor might use a work sheet that requires participants to apply the theory to previous experiences. Such a work sheet might consist of brief descriptions of the attributes of optimal experience (e.g., merging of action and awareness, alteration in perception of time) followed by blank spaces for participants to use to describe their own qualitative experiences during one of their favorite activities. By relating theoretical constructs to their own experiences, participants are more likely to perceive the content of a presentation as being relevant to their own lives.

Be Clear

Although a person may work diligently to prepare a presentation, extensive preparation will not salvage a presentation that is confusing or unclear to participants. Additionally, when preparing a presentation, it is important to keep the audience in mind. A presentation for professional therapeutic recreation specialists is going to differ immensely from a presentation for students. Numerous strategies can be used to enhance the clarity of a presentation, such as devising and sticking to a plan while delivering a presentation, defining terms that may be unfamiliar to participants, limiting the amount of new material to present, and allowing time to summarize the main points in a presentation.

Have a Plan and Stay with It

Although it can be tempting at times to wander off on a tangent, it is probably best to avoid doing so without a compelling reason. The organization of a presentation and creation of a logical structure for participants to follow is impaired if too much digression occurs. Also, a tangent can confuse participants, and they may perceive tangents as a sign of disorganization. For instance, 1,249 university students who responded to a survey administered by Clarke (1994) reported that lack of structure was one of the most disliked characteristics of presentations while clarity was among the most valued ones.

If a tangent occurs in a presentation, the instructor can make it clear that a brief divergence from the plan is occurring that is followed by a description of how this unplanned new material relates to the objectives of this presentation. For instance, during therapeutic recreation group sessions, participants will share stories about their lives. Often these stories are related to the topic at hand, but occasionally a participant will share a story that is unrelated to the material being presented. Often with a little work and cleverness, therapeutic recreation specialists can find a connection (no matter how tenuous) between the participant's story and the topic being discussed. It is important not to discourage active participation, but it is equally important to keep presentations focused.

Define Terms

Having a thorough understanding of a topic is accompanied by having a command of a vocabulary unique to the topic. Numerous terms in professional vocabularies may be unfamiliar (or their meanings may be unclear) to people listening to a presentation. As an example, the word *leisure* has proved devilishly difficult to define in a way that encompasses all of the meanings different people attach to the word. Thus, if a speaker uses the word *leisure*, it would add clarity to the presentation to define the word *as it is being used*. Without guidance, different participants could associate leisure with time (e.g., so called "free time") or activity, while the speaker might be using the word to mean a kind of experience. Likewise, the concept of *flow* (Csikszentmihalyi, 1988) is quite familiar to people in recreation and leisure studies, but it may be completely unfamiliar to others.

Use of acronyms may create confusion and make some participants feel ignorant (Dattilo, 2002). This breakdown in the communication process hurts the ability of an instructor to present information in a clear and understandable way. For example:

> On the first day of an introductory therapeutic recreation course, an instructor repeatedly used the "common" abbreviation "TR" for therapeutic recreation without first explaining the abbreviation to the students. Twenty minutes into the presentation, one person raised her hand and said, "Excuse me. How do you spell that word you keep saying and what is it?" When the instructor explained, an instant look of relief and understanding appeared on the majority of the students' faces.

Many people in an audience are more likely to remain confused during such experiences rather than ask a potentially embarrassing question. Thus, in the interest of clarity, it is important to define any terms and acronyms that might be unfamiliar to participants.

Limit the Amount of New Material

An abundance of new material can overwhelm participants, inhibit learning and dampen enthusiasm for a subject. For example, in a study of 123 medical students, Russell, Hendricson, and Herbert (1984) reported that (a) lectures contributed more to learning when they were restricted to only the most essential points, and (b) lectures with too much information did not contribute as much to learning. Instructors are often intimately familiar with material to which participants have had little or no exposure. While it is important to challenge an audience and to have high expectations of them, it is equally important to insure that they understand the material presented.

One way to promote understanding of new material is to place new material in the context of familiar information (Weiss, Weaver & Cotrell, 1988). For instance, presenters at professional conferences can take advantage of the fact that much of the training received by therapeutic recreation specialists is fairly standardized. While differences exist between undergraduate therapeutic recreation programs, the presence of the national certification exam insures that nearly all therapeutic recreation specialists will have a great deal of shared professional knowledge. Thus, presentations about an innovative and new therapeutic recreation program could begin with a presentation of the elements of the program that are familiar to most specialists, such as program goals and objectives, the population for which the program is designed, evaluation tools, and expected outcomes.

In addition, referring to ideas that have been presented in the popular press may help participants connect with the material, pique their interest, and encourage them to see its relevance. For instance, a therapeutic recreation specialist conducting exercise programs in a retirement facility could keep a file of clippings from popular magazines (e.g., *Time*, *Newsweek*) and newspapers (e.g., *USA Today*) that discuss the benefits of exercise for older adults. Often these popular publications provide concise and easily understood explanations of scientific and medical information that many people find trustworthy and reliable. These clippings could be used to encourage participation in the exercise program.

A brief review of previously discussed information conducted at the beginning of each session can help facilitate learning. Also, if the presentation is a part of a more extensive course or workshop, then reference to the purpose and objectives of the broader course or workshop can help participants make connections between the material covered during a particular session and the bigger picture.

Summarize Major Points

While taking notes, participants may lose track of the big picture. Thus, an effective presentation includes time to summarize the main points and to describe how each element of a presentation relates to the others. Not only is it helpful for instructors to summarize major points, but after studying a novel notetaking technique, Davis and Hult (1997) also found that people who were given time during lectures to write brief summaries demonstrated significantly more understanding of the presented material than people listening to a lecture without the opportunity to summarize. Similarly, Ruhl and colleagues (1987) reported that people experienced better recall of material when they were given several short breaks during a lecture to re-read and summarize information in their notes. Therefore, opportunities to summarize major points throughout a presentation can be one approach for the instructor to clarify material with participants.

Providing time for participants to collect their thoughts and summarize the main points may be particularly beneficial for many people who receive therapeutic recreation services. People with attention deficit hyperactivity disorder, people with brain injuries, people with cognitive limitations and others could benefit from periodic summaries of the principle points of a lecture or presentation. A therapeutic recreation specialist can build these summaries into a presentation through the use of brief handouts or visual aids. For instance, if a therapeutic recreation specialist has the goal of presenting three benefits of leisure during a leisure education session, she may stop after describing each benefit and distribute a piece of paper with each of the main points about that benefit. Alternately, the therapeutic recreation specialist might use a flip chart and have participants describe the main points of each benefit as it is discussed. Whatever method is employed, participants can benefit from the added focus provided by periodic summaries and from the additional time to process new information.

Be Interesting

Any presentation can be thought of as having two parts: content and process. The *content* of a presentation includes information such as facts, theories, and concepts to be communicated. The *process* can be thought of as the methods (or vehicle) in which the content is delivered. Although the content of a presentation is critical, to ignore the process may result in participants either missing the point of a presentation or not being interested enough to obtain the content. Conversely, if a presentation is delivered in an interesting manner (excellent process) but lacks substance, then participants may be interested and entertained but learning objectives will not be achieved. Effective presentations typically result from close attention being paid to both process and content. As a result, participants are likely to have an enjoyable learning experience. While the process in which a presentation is delivered will vary greatly from person to person, a number of broad suggestions are offered in this section to help improve the content of presentations despite individual styles and personalities.

Be Enthusiastic

An important characteristic of effective presentations is the instructor's enthusiasm about a particular topic. Participants perceive an instructor's enthusiasm, and are more likely to feel excited about a topic when instructors are passionate and interested. In a study of award-winning university instructors, Kelly and Kelly (1982) reported that two of the common characteristics of successful teachers were their enjoyment of teaching and their enthusiasm for the subject being taught. Similarly, after surveying 1,006 students attending a community college, Hilgemann and Blodget (1991) reported that enthusiasm was an important characteristic of good teaching.

In another example, Wood (1999) investigated effects of teacher enthusiasm on student learning and reported that teachers rated as enthusiastic had students who were more motivated and paid more attention than students of teachers rated as being unenthusiastic. Additionally, students of enthusiastic teachers were more likely to remember class material when compared to students of teachers characterized as unenthusiastic. While projecting enthusiasm about a topic can help instructors arouse and maintain the interest of participants, numerous other techniques can be used to the same end.

Integrate Stories and Relevant Examples

A simple recitation of facts by an instructor is unlikely to help participants learn; rather, it would appear that memory is aided by placing new information in the context of a demonstration or story. It appears that without the benefit of techniques, such as stories and examples, people have a difficult time remembering information that is presented verbally. For example, when reporting on the results of 497 college students, Cravens (1996) concluded that the use of stories and relevant examples was one of the most helpful methods employed by college instructors.

Stories can help participants understand practical applications and implications. Instructors can share stories about their lives (within appropriate interpersonal boundaries), about famous people, and even about fictional characters. Over time, instructors can gather a library of stories that can be used to illustrate points in presentations. The following story involves a visit to leisure skills class conducted in an elementary school. It illustrates the importance of teaching participants sufficient skills so that they will be free to make choices.

> The instructor had allocated a half-an-hour for "leisure learning." When asked to describe what happened during this time the instructor said that since she wanted the children to have free choice, she let them choose any table game to play.

I noticed that the children were playing UNO. Since it was Friday, I asked what they played on Monday and she said "UNO." Tuesday? "UNO." And, what game do you think they played on Wednesday and Thursday? You guessed it… UNO. As the instructor spoke she was standing in front of an open cabinet that contained many different games. Unfortunately, the children had not yet learned to play them, so I struck a compromise with the instructor. For the first fifteen minutes of "leisure learning" she would teach them to play a new game, and for the last fifteen minutes the children could choose to play any game. A few weeks later I returned to visit the class during the last portion of the leisure learning time and found the children happily playing a variety of games.

Stories can help bring information to life, and can help participants see the application of material discussed. People often remember interesting and meaningful stories and thus, retain some of the lessons associated with the stories.

Demonstrate Ideas

Demonstrations can help participants bridge the gap between the purely theoretical and objective reality. By demonstrating rather than describing, instructors can help participants understand how concepts apply in the real world. Demonstrations can supply a point of reference for further discussion, and can attract and maintain participant interest. Some lessons are almost impossible to teach without the benefit of a demonstration. For example, to introduce transferring skills to a group of camp counselors, an instructor borrowed several wheelchairs from a local hospital and demonstrated the basics of helping people transfer from wheelchairs to cots, chairs, and cars. Following several demonstrations, the counselors practiced with each other. While the counselors could have learned about transferring abstractly, the hands-on experience proved to be an effective teaching method.

Use Visual Aids

Visual aids can promote learning. As way to illustrate, Scerbo, Warm, Dember, and Grasha (1992) studied effects of verbal and written cues on the information retention of 160 college students. Results indicated that students were more likely to write down and remember visually cued statements than they were to write down or recall verbally cued statements.

Some presenters have replaced overhead transparencies and slides with more flexible and less costly computer-generated graphic presentations, such as those created with Microsoft's PowerPoint software. Cassady (1998) investigated perception of effectiveness of instruction using computer-generated graphics and reported that presentations that used computer-generated graphics were perceived as more organized, easier to follow, and more interesting than the traditional presentations. Additionally, PowerPoint and similar programs are relatively simple to learn and to use.

One benefit of computer-based presentations is that graphics, such as photographs or clip art, can be scanned or obtained from the World Wide Web and are easily manipulated and incorporated into a presentation. Another advantage of the use of such programs is that, over the long term, it reduces expenses because a presentation can be modified without production of additional material. The fact that no hard copy of the presentation is required provides flexibility and allows for modifications to a presentation up to the time immediately prior to a session and even can be modified during a presentation. It is advisable, however, to have the material available in an alternative format in case technological problems arise.

Include Various Learning Techniques

Bonwell (1996) and McKeachie (1999) suggest that instructors incorporate a variety of teaching techniques into any presentation. For instance, to help participants get involved in a presentation, instructors can ask relevant questions of participants and have them provide examples related to the material. For example, a therapeutic recreation specialist discussing the importance of friendship and the actions needed to maintain friendships might ask participants to discuss their best friends from different periods of their lives. The examples offered by participants could be integrated into the discussion, helping to maintain their interest.

McDougall and Granby (1996) investigated thirty students' expectations of oral questioning during class. Results indicated that students who expected to be called on during class were more likely to complete assigned reading prior to class and were more likely to recall information from the readings than students who expected voluntary questioning. In many facilities, therapeutic recreation specialists are asked to conduct patient education sessions to help promote compliance with treatment, particularly related to lifestyle changes such as prescribed exercise and progressive relaxation. Participants are often given a packet of information to learn, and specialists can explain to participants that they will be asked to recall material from the packet during the next patient education session.

Bonwell (1996) suggested that if instructors want to increase active learning, they could intersperse their lecture with other learning strategies.

These strategies include brief writing assignments, paired discussions, and short quizzes.

Brief writing assignments can be used to help participants reflect on and process information from a session. For instance, many adventure programs provide diaries for participants to record their thoughts during their experiences with the program. Participants can benefit from the opportunity to reflect on their experiences, and the task of writing appears to help many people sort out their thoughts.

Paired discussions can help participants check their understanding and to gain a different perspective on information being presented. For instance, after a presentation to adolescents about the personal and social consequences of violence, a therapeutic recreation specialist might group participants into pairs to discuss how violence has affected them personally.

In classroom settings, *short quizzes* can help participants check their understanding of the material. For example, during a series of in-service training sessions related to the Americans with Disabilities Act, a therapeutic recreation specialist finished each session with a quiz that helped participants determine what parts of the material they misunderstood. While using such techniques takes time, when used effectively these strategies can promote participant interest and learning.

Use Humor

While humorous anecdotes and stories can improve presentations, humor can be a double-edged sword. Sarcasm and humor that belittles people is almost universally perceived as negative. It is important to remember that the Greek root for sarcasm means "to tear flesh." A sarcastic comment directed toward a participant might cause severe damage to the participant's self-esteem and can damage the relationship between specialist and client. However, an appropriate use of humor can have many beneficial effects.

Kaupins (1991) investigated the use of humor in college classrooms and in corporate training and reported that humor is used most effectively when participants understand the humor and the humor is relevant to the material being discussed. For humor to be understood, indeed for a comment to be humorous at all, it must be grounded in truth (McGhee, 1979). More to the point, an audience must be able to recognize the element of truth in a humorous statement. To illustrate the point that the use of acronyms can confuse people unless people hearing them are clearly aware of the meaning of the acronym, the following possibly humorous statement can be made:

> When I was in my first TR class, the instructor mentioned
> in her first lecture that NTRS was a branch of NRPA that

collaborated with ATRA to give input to NCTRC into obtaining CEUs needed for becoming a CTRS.

In this example, knowledge of these acronyms can help someone better appreciate the humor in the story. Attempts at humor that assume participants have knowledge of a topic, when in reality they do not, can tend to alienate and confuse individuals.

Equally important is to be sure that participants understand the context and particulars of a humorous comment. For example, while instructing a group of older adults, humorous comments that reference popular culture, such as mention of a current band, may not be understood. Similarly, an instructor may be disappointed by the blank looks on young participants' faces in response to a reference to comedian who was popular years ago.

The use of examples and comparisons to popular culture is a simple way to incorporate humorous elements into a presentation. Although it is challenging to remain current with popular culture, there are a number of references to popular culture that almost all people will recognize. For instance, since a significant part of two generations of American children spent hours watching Sesame Street and similar programs, humorous references to Sesame Street might be effective with members of these generations. Additionally, many news stories, such as elections and celebrity scandals, become part of a national consciousness. Obviously, a certain amount of discretion is needed when deciding upon the appropriateness of discussing certain topics.

While the use of completely antiquated references to popular culture may lead to mild ridicule, many participants appreciate an effort to use humor. Perhaps as importantly, a positive social climate can be facilitated if participants perceive that instructors are at least open to and appreciative of appropriate humor.

Evaluate Yourself

Quantitative evaluations of instructors are used to evaluate one-time presentations, workshops, or ongoing courses. Often participants are presented with an additional opportunity to make qualitative comments. These evaluations will likely serve as the sole indication of the quality of teaching. Instructors interested in improving their teaching can use a number of different methods to evaluate their teaching. Three of these methods are presented in this section.

Videotape Yourself

It can be useful to review a videotape of oneself teaching. Often we have images of ourselves that are not totally accurate. Viewing a twenty-minute videotape of oneself making a presentation can permit identification of strengths and can be the catalyst for improvement.

When facilitating a teaching seminar, the authors of this chapter noted the discomfort evoked in participants when it was revealed that each of them would be videotaped delivering a brief presentation. Participants stated to us that it was not so much the videotaping that was distasteful to them, but it was the watching of the videotape that caused participants consternation. Each participant admitted to watching the videotape alone, often in a locked room. As one exasperated participant in the teaching seminar asked, "When did 'uh' become such an important word in my vocabulary?" Just as treatment for some ailment can be both uncomfortable and beneficial, watching a videotape of our own presentations can be a challenging yet valuable way to improve our teaching ability.

Qualitative Formative Evaluations

Asking participants to provide written feedback about aspects of instruction throughout a course, workshop or series of presentations can be helpful. Systematic solicitation of comments and suggestions can supply insight into ways to improve lecturing and teaching in general. This form of evaluation creates an opportunity for instructors to respond to participants and to create a learning environment that suits their learning needs. Although not all suggestions can be met such as "Can we move the class an hour later?" some comments can identify aspects of instruction that may not have been considered by the instructor such as "I like your lectures, but the words on your slides are too small for me to see in the back of the room."

Solicit Peer Evaluations

While it is important to obtain feedback from participants through formative and summative evaluations, it can be very instructive to have peers evaluate our teaching abilities. If there is no formal peer evaluation system in place, an instructor may simply invite a colleague to sit-in on a class, and feedback can be provided in as simple a form as a casual conversation. Additionally, it may be beneficial to solicit input from a colleague from a different area of expertise. Teaching practices and approaches to instruction can be quite different across disciplines, and a peer with a different perspective can supply valuable insights for improvement.

Summary and Conclusions

This chapter is a resource for people interested in improving the quality of their teaching skills and in becoming more confident and effective as instructors. Thorough preparation helps insure the quality of a presentation and will contribute to the confidence of instructors. Well-organized and clear presentations can contribute to the ability of participants to learn. Incorporating techniques to make a presentation interesting contributes to the enjoyment of participants and to the learning experience. Self-evaluation and evaluations of others are important avenues to improving instruction.

A rare few people were born to teach, innately possessing many of the skills needed to deliver consistently informative and engaging presentations. The rest have to work at it. Almost anyone can learn to teach well, and the best instructors are constantly working to improve their teaching abilities.

Reading Comprehension Questions

1. Identify topics that you could comfortably present in a leisure education class. What topics would require you to develop greater knowledge?

2. Select a topic you might present in a community reentry session for participants in an inpatient physical rehabilitation hospital. Develop a logical outline of topics and activities.

3. Develop a handout or work sheet that you could use in the session noted in question 2.

4. Identify terms commonly used by therapeutic recreation specialists that would need to be defined for clients.

5. Identify a personal experience that you could use to demonstrate the concept of social support (Chapter 3), self-determination (Chapter 4), or control (Chapter 5).

6. Based on what you know about your own presentation abilities, what do you need to improve? What are your strengths?

References

Bonwell, C. C. (1996). Enhancing the lecture: Revitalizing the traditional format. *New Directions for Teaching and Learning, 67*(4), 31–44.

Cassady, J. C. (1998). Student and instructor perceptions of the efficacy of computer-aided lectures in undergraduate university courses. *Journal of Educational Computing Research, 19*(2), 175–189.

Clarke, J. A. (1994). *Tertiary students' perceptions of important events that occur in their learning environments.* Paper presented at the Annual Meeting of the American Educational Research Association, New Orleans, LA.

Claxton, C. S. and Murrell, P. H. (1987). Learning styles: Implications for improving educational practices. *ASHE-ERIC Higher Education Report, 4.* Washington, DC: Association for the Study of Higher Education.

Cravens, T. F. (1996). *Students' perceptions of the characteristics of teaching excellence.* Paper presented at the Annual Meeting of the National Social Science Conference, Reno, NV.

Csikszentmihalyi, M. (1988). Introduction. In M. Csikszentmihalyi and I. S. Csikszentmihalyi (Eds.), *Optimal experience: Psychological studies of flow in consciousness* (pp. 3–14). New York, NY: Cambridge University Press.

Dattilo, J. (2002). *Inclusive leisure services: Responding to the rights of people with disabilities* (2nd ed.). State College, PA: Venture Publishing, Inc.

Davis, M. and Hult, R. E. (1997). Effects of writing summaries as a generative learning activity during note taking. *Teaching of Psychology, 24*(1), 47–49.

Hilgemann, V. and Blodget, J. (1991). Profile of an excellent teacher: Summary of research. Salem, OR: Chemeketa Community College. (ERIC Document Reproduction Service No. ED 353 017).

Kaupins, G. E. (1991). Humour in university and corporate training: A comparison of trainer perceptions. *Journal of Management Development, 10*(1), 33–41.

Kelly, N. and Kelly, B. (1982). *Backgrounds, education, and teaching styles of teaching award winning professors.* Paper presented at the Annual Meeting of the Rocky Mountain Educational Research Association, Albuquerque, NM.

McDougall, D. and Granby, C. (1996). How expectation of questioning method affects undergraduates' preparation for class. *Journal of Experimental Education, 65*(1), 43–54.

McGhee, P. E. (1979). *Humor: Its origin and development.* San Francisco, CA: W. H. Freeman and Co.

McKeachie, W. J. (1999). *Teaching tips: Strategies, research, and theory for college and university teachers.* Boston, MA: Houghton Mifflin.

Ross, J. M. (1989, March). *Critical teaching behaviors as perceived by adult undergraduates.* Paper presented at the Annual Meeting of the American Educational Research Association. San Francisco, CA.

Ruhl, K. L., Hughes, C., and Schloss, P. (1987). Using the pause procedure to enhance lecture recall. *Teacher Education and Special Education, 10*(1), 14–18.

Russell, I. J., Hendricson, W. D., and Herbert, R. J. (1984). Effects of lecture information density on medical student achievement. *Journal of Medical Information, 59*(11), 881–889.

Scerbo, M. W., Warm, J. S., Dember, W. N., and Grasha, A. F. (1992). The role of time and cueing in a college lecture. *Contemporary Educational Psychology, 17*(4), 312–328.

Weiss, P. E., Weaver, R. L., and Cotrell, H. W. (1988). *Using public-speaking skills for teaching improvement in the classroom.* Bowling Green, OH: Bowling Green State University. (ERIC Document Reproduction Service No. ED 294 259)

Wood, A. M. (1999). The effects of teacher enthusiasm on student motivation, selective attention, and text memory. *Dissertation Abstracts International, 59*(9a).

Chapter 14

Some Tips for Students about Attending Conferences

Youngkhill Lee, Ph.D., CTRS
Janet A. Funderburk, M.S., CTRS
David R. Austin, Ph.D., CTRS, FALS

I am a student who has just completed my undergraduate degree, and realize that a great deal of learning can and does take place outside of the classroom. I was encouraged to attend, and did attend conferences and meetings throughout my studies. I discovered the great value of attending meetings and conferences: from hearing "experts" talk about their work, to meeting other people interested in research and learning, to being able to view posters on a variety of topics. These extras added value to my education that I couldn't get from reading textbooks and articles. Conferences also give me an opportunity to contribute my own thoughts during discussions, and expose me to a wide variety of approaches to the same topic that I wouldn't necessarily get from my own instructors. Attending meetings and conferences has been an integral part of my learning experience and I encourage other students to use this valuable avenue for expanding their learning experience. (J. Folder, personal communication, 2001)

For most things that we do in life, giving them some amount of prior thought is apt to enhance the experience. This is true for all who participate in a professional conference. If you are a student about to embark on your first professional conference, the need for thinking about the experience and what you hope to achieve from it is particularly important. This chapter focuses on providing students with a conceptualization of conferences and strategies to employ before, during, and after attending a professional conference to get the most out of it.

Conceptualizing Conferences

Attending conferences is an integral and important part of your therapeutic recreation professional preparation. Universities and agencies are not the only places where learning occurs. While classroom-based learning is a cornerstone of professional preparation, attending conferences is an important arena that should not be overlooked as a part of professional preparation. Conference participation can be a powerful learning opportunity, and can help prepare you to be a competent and more active professional.

Meaning of the Term *Conference*

The term *conference* may be defined as a structured event for professionals to formally discuss specified topics. While this definition describes the general nature of conferences, it limits the actual scope of these meetings. This traditional concept of a conference includes practitioners and, perhaps educators, but not students. In fact, the professional conference is not exclusively designed for the formal discussion of certain topics. Rather the meaning of the term conference varies between individuals. For many participants, it means sharing their expertise and research findings with other professionals as well as obtaining knowledge and research findings from others. For some, it may mean networking. For yet other participants, a conference may mean serving the profession through leadership. While similar meanings may be embraced by some graduate students, many undergraduate and graduate students prefer to focus on listening to talks and learning from others.

Although these meanings provide a general introduction, an attempt should be made to conceptualize conferences from a student's perspective. For you as a student, a conference can provide more than an opportunity to be a mere consumer of knowledge. There are other important ways students can take an active role during a conference. First of all, conferences provide opportunities to talk openly with instructors from other universities without any of the potential power-relationship difficulties that can arise between students and instructors. Further, you may want the chance to discuss some of the stresses and struggles of the profession. You also can engage in informal "chats" with professors from other universities, and practitioners from many different locations and sometimes even from other countries. You can also prepare copies of your resumé to distribute to practitioners to secure an internship or a job. If you plan to pursue a graduate degree, conferences can be a good way to obtaining information about various schools and meet with professors and students from other universities.

Attending the conference itself can become a leisure experience, since you freely select any topic that you want to learn more about (i.e., freedom of choice and intrinsic motivation). Also, it can be nice to get away from the regular classroom setting with your instructor standing at the head of the classroom and rows of classmates seated at desks. Finally, participating in a conference may be perceived as your first step toward continuing education.

Benefits of Attending Conferences

According to Stumbo and Carter (1999), adjunct faculty make up over 40% of faculty teaching therapeutic recreation, 40% of faculty have only a master's degree, and one third do not even belong to a professional organization (e.g., NTRS, ATRA). Further, students typically are exposed to only one or two therapeutic recreation instructors within their program, and work with only one or two practitioners during their internship. Considering these facts, while instructors and internship supervisors may share a variety of opinions and ideas, as a student attending a conference, you are exposed to different perspectives from *numerous* educators and practitioners.

One benefit of attending a conference is that it can help you keep abreast of new trends in therapeutic recreation practice. It is important to keep up-to-date because service settings change so rapidly. New trends range from developments in legislation that directly effect therapeutic recreation, to changes in national certification policies, or new techniques in service delivery. Who knows, maybe you will come back to class with "one up" on your professor!

According to a recent study, "networking" was rated *and* ranked as the second most important benefit of professional therapeutic recreation membership—right behind "attending conferences" (Funderburk, 2000). Because networking, for the most part, occurs during conferences or workshops, it is important that students attend conferences to begin making these connections early in their careers. As mentioned before, networking can take the form of interacting with students from other universities, with professors, and with practitioners.

Attending conferences as a student marks the beginning of your early socialization into professional involvement. This concept cannot be stressed enough. If you wait until you become a practitioner, it may be more difficult to socialize and feel comfortable when attending conferences. Attending conferences as a student allows you to form habits that will hopefully become ingrained. Unfortunately, students often do not realize the importance of professional involvement and the potential impact they, as individuals, can have on the field.

The second author of this chapter would like to share a personal experience with you:

> I first became professionally involved with the field of therapeutic recreation when an undergraduate professor urged me to run for the board of directors as a student representative for the North Carolina Recreation Therapy Association. After I was elected, I experienced my first conference. It was a wonderfully overwhelming experience and one I will never forget. The next year at the conference, I was recognized as the "Student of the Year." As a result of early involvement and socialization in the profession, I was honored to serve several years later as the President of one of the leading state ATRA chapter affiliates in the country, served as a Chair on national committees, and found myself presenting at state, regional, and national conferences as well as coordinating national legislative efforts.

While this example may not be the norm, it is an example of how, with just a little effort and willingness, you can make a difference through professional involvement. Attending at least one conference as a student is a step in the right direction.

Langsner (1994) identified benefits associated with participation in continuing education. The following may well summarize potential benefits associated with attending conferences. These include:

- Stay abreast of new developments in the field
- Develop professional knowledge and skills
- Help become more competent in current work
- Further match knowledge or skills with the demands of work situations
- Consider changing the emphasis of present professional responsibilities
- Learn from interactions with other professionals
- Mutually exchange thoughts with professional colleagues
- Sharpen perspectives of professional role or practice
- Maintain personal identity with the profession
- Assess the directions in which the profession is going

- Help obtain leadership capabilities for the profession
- Enhance the image of the profession
- Reflect on the value of professional responsibilities
- Relate ideas to professional peers

Before the Conference

Which Conference to Attend?

The first thing that you need to considered is which type of conference would be best to attend. Should you start with a state conference? a regional conference? a national conference?

In order to learn conference behaviors, it is probably wise to first attend a state conference. First of all, state conferences generally are the closest. Thus, they involve less cost in terms of time and, usually, money. Typically you can drive to state conferences with other students or one of your professors. Also, state conferences usually last only two days as compared to regional or national conferences that may run three to five days in length.

Occasionally, however, a regional or national conference will be held in a city near your university. If a regional or national conference is nearby, it may be a wise choice even as an initial conference experience. Regional and national conferences generally charge a higher registration fee than state conferences, but are worth the extra expense because they typically offer more variety and "experts."

To select wisely, you will need to obtain information about each conference you are considering. Most conference organizers distribute printed information about their events. Another means of gathering conference information is from web sites. Charlie Dixon's Therapeutic Recreation/ Recreation Therapy web site (i.e., http://www.recreationtherapy.com) regularly posts information about professional conferences. National professional organizations, such as the American Therapeutic Recreation Association (ATRA) and the National Therapeutic Recreation Society (NTRS) also maintain web sites that contain conference information. Perhaps the best source of information on conferences, however, can be obtained from your professors. Professors regularly attend professional conferences and are often involved in presentations, so they typically have a great deal of first-hand experience about conferences to share with students.

What information should students look for when assessing conferences? A key factor is when the conference is to be held. Is it at a time that will not unduly interfere with your academic program? If it is a conference within an easy driving distance, is there a "student day" identified in the program so you can day-trip?

Another factor is cost. Does the conference organizer offer a special student rate? If the conference is run by a professional organization, do they offer members a discount? Some conferences permit students to serve as room hosts for part of the day in order to receive a complementary registration or offer student "working scholarships" that often cover expenses.

A third factor is housing. Typically, conferences are held at hotels. Most hotels hosting conferences provide special rates for those attending. Check rates at neighboring hotels anyway to see if they can "beat" the rate at the conference hotel. Other housing possibilities include staying at the home of a fellow student whose family lives in the area, or even staying with students at universities located near the conference. Again, professors often have "local knowledge," and can be a good source of advice on housing.

All of these considerations assume, of course, that the conference is one that will interest you and offer the potential for obtaining professional information. Be assured that this is the case, most therapeutic recreation conferences will meet the basic criteria of providing interesting programs and valuable information.

Getting Organized to Attend

Once the conference is selected, the next step is to prepare to get the most out of your attendance. It is wise to review the program prior to going to the conference. Because most conference programs offer multiple educational sessions at the same time (known as *concurrent sessions*), you will want to examine the program closely to determine how you will want to spend your time. You will not be able to do everything, so it is important to consider to your choices. There will likely be topics or speakers that will be of particular interest to you and thus affect your choices.

The next step may be checking with others about appropriate conference attire. Most participants at professional conferences do not "dress up," nor do they "dress down." Typical school clothing is often seen as a bit too informal for attending conferences. On the other hand, it is not expected that students wear their "Sunday best." Probably somewhere in between is the wisest choice—a "professional casual." Keep in mind that you never know who you may run into. Perhaps you will encounter a future internship supervisor. Remember, you only get "one chance to make a first impression." It may be wiser to overdress rather than underdress. A good rule of thumb is to check with your professors who have probably attended the conference before, and will be able to offer advice about what is best to wear.

Conference organizers will often provide a packet of materials which includes paper for notetaking during sessions. Nevertheless, it is usually a good idea to take your own pen and paper to the conference with you. Usually organizers will give you a folder or inexpensive bag in which to carry your program, pen, and paper.

Another suggestion is to bring copies of your resumé and to create some "student business cards." This will allow you to conveniently give personal information to those you meet so you can keep in contact.

A final tip is for you to make certain that your professors know that you will be attending the conference. Tell them that you look forward to seeing them there. Once at the conference location, do not be bashful about talking with your instructors. They will want to know which students attended, and will likely wish to help you feel comfortable at the conference.

At the Conference

When attending your first conference, it may be a good idea to have at least one buddy with whom to attend. Having another person with you can make you feel more comfortable, and give you someone to confer with when making decisions about which sessions to attend and where to eat. If you do go by yourself, try to make a new friend at the conference so you don't feel lost in the crowd. In order to facilitate the socialization of students into conference behavior and help students feel comfortable, some conference organizers have established mentor programs in which students are taken to lunch by a professional so a mentoring relationship can develop.

Occasionally, students attending their first conference will lack a point of orientation. Experiencing that feeling of "not being anchored" can be troubling for some individuals. Thus it may be wise to identify a place to which you can return to meet others or just "hang out." Some conferences designate a "meeting point" where those attending can mingle with others. The lobby of the meeting center may also serve this function. Occasionally, conference organizers will establish a student room or resource room where students may go to meet students from other universities. At any rate, it may be smart to establish a place where you will return to meet or talk with other attendees.

Interacting with Others at the Conference

First, understand it is natural for students to be a bit anxious, or even intimidated, when attending a conference. Yet, one of the major things you should get out of the conference experience is to interact with others you would not otherwise encounter. Others with whom you will want to interact will include students and professors from other universities, professionals from the field, and speakers providing conference sessions.

Students should realize that students from other universities are probably a little nervous about being "out of their element" as well, and will welcome the friendly face of another student—even one from a rival school. Professors from other schools usually understand that students are often uncomfortable in the conference environment, and therefore, will be happy to chat with students from universities other than their own.

All professionals were students once, so they know the importance of helping students feel comfortable. Besides, recreation therapists are helping professionals who have a natural tendency to want to help others. Take advantage of this nature by initiating interaction with them.

Finally, do not be intimated by "big names" who are speaking at the conference. They usually enjoy the opportunity to interact with students. Most will welcome your interest in their research or area of expertise.

Strategies to Get to Know Others

A good way to introduce yourself to a speaker is to tell him or her that you enjoyed their presentation. Even big shots like to hear nice things about themselves. Following your compliment, introduce yourself and tell them about your personal interest in their research or presentation.

A good way to meet other students and professionals is to introduce yourself to the person or persons sitting next to you at each session you attend. Find out their names, where they are employed and what they do, or where they go to school. You will usually have a few minutes to talk before the session starts.

Other places to meet people are at meals, social events, in poster sessions, exhibit areas, or even in the hallways. Many friendships have been developed while sitting at a table during a meal. During meals is a good time to sit with individuals who are not fellow students. Instead of sitting with a table full of students, sit with conference participants who you do not know. Attend conference social events. These are good times to meet others because they are natural social events, and conference participants usually attend to interact with others. Force yourself to introduce yourself to professionals and speakers. (Speakers are often identified by speakers' ribbons on their nametags.) Schedule time to spend outside of educational sessions and social events. Poster sessions and exhibit areas are excellent places to strike up conversations. Even consider occasionally "hanging out" in the hallways of the conference center if you tire of attending sessions. You may be surprised to find some of the most seasoned conference participants in the halls having conversations during sessions. This may be an excellent time to talk with one of the big shots.

Conference organizers almost always provide attendees with a nametag. Make sure you wear your nametag so others will know your name and university. Scan others' nametags for names and affiliations. You may recall a name of a professional who has spoken at your university or is an alumnus. Perhaps you will identify someone who has written an article or book that you read for a course. You may be able to find someone who works at an agency or university that you have knowledge about, or want to learn more about. You may even spot someone from your hometown or, at a regional or national conference, someone from your home state.

After the Conference

Hopefully the trip home can serve as a "debriefing session" to discuss your conference experience with fellow students or professors. The hours traveling back to school can be a great time to share stories about the sessions you attended and the people you met. You may also be able to share valuable information about potential internship sites or professional positions. Occasionally, professors will devote a portion of a class session to postconference discussions. This is often a good means to share information.

Another postconference activity may be to follow up with someone that you met at the conference by contacting them. After returning to school, you may wish to drop a note or send an e-mail to someone you met at the conference. Contact people within a few days of returning from the conference so it is fresh on your mind, and the person who you are contacting will recall you.

Conclusion

One common misperception associated with attending professional conferences is that it is only for professors and practitioners. This chapter attempted to dispel this myth by reconceptualizing the term conference itself. Conferences are a viable learning tool for students as well as educators and practitioners. This conceptualization further emphasizes some active roles that students can play during the conference, and some important benefits associated with attending conferences. In addition, this chapter offered specific strategies and tips that are useful when planning to attending a conference. Attending conferences is an important way to develop a commitment to lifelong learning and to begin your commitment to ongoing professional development. Experience a conference—you will agree with many points introduced here.

Conference Checklist

Before the Conference:
- ☐ Gather conference information
- ☐ Decide which conference to attend
- ☐ Find a buddy to go with you
- ☐ Make housing and travel arrangements
- ☐ Review the conference program
- ☐ Determine which sessions to attend
- ☐ Prepare and Pack:
  - ___ appropriate conference attire
  - ___ a notepad and pen to take notes during sessions
  - ___ copies of your resumé
  - ___ student business cards to network
- ☐ Tell professors that you will be attending the conference

During the Conference:
- ☐ Wear your nametag
- ☐ Find someone to "hang out with"
- ☐ Designate a meeting point or place to meet others
- ☐ Be assertive—Introduce yourself to professionals and other students
- ☐ Attend social events
- ☐ Gather materials in the resource room
- ☐ Distribute your resumé and student business cards

After the Conference:
- ☐ Debrief about your experience(s) with fellow students and professors
- ☐ Follow-up with someone you met at the conference (e.g., call, e-mail)

Notes:

Figure 14.1 Conference Preparation Checklist

Reading Comprehension Questions

1. What are the benefits associated with attending conferences?
2. Do you agree that attending conferences is not only for practitioners and educators? Why or why not?
3. How does early socialization impact future professional involvement?
4. What actions can you take to become more professionally involved?
5. What are some strategies for networking and getting to know others during a professional conference?
6. Why is it important to "debrief" after a conference?
7. What kinds of things should you take with you to a conference?

References

Funderburk, J. A. (2000). *The perceived benefits and barriers to membership in state professional therapeutic recreation associations in North Carolina: A comparison of members vs. nonmembers.* Unpublished master's thesis, East Carolina University, Greenville, NC.

Langsner, S. J. (1994). Deterrents to participating in continuing professional education: A survey of the NTRS. *Therapeutic Recreation Journal, 28*(3), 147–162.

Stumbo, N. J. and Carter, M. J. (1999). National therapeutic recreation curriculum study part A: Accreditation, curriculum, and internship characteristics. *Therapeutic Recreation Journal, 33*(1), 46–60.

Chapter 15

Professionalism

David R. Austin, Ph.D., CTRS, FALS

In the complex world of healthcare, some therapeutic recreation professionals are thriving while others are not. Why is this? What is the difference between them? The capacity to exhibit professionalism is a key to thriving as a professional. A sense of professionalism helps to define ourselves and our work.

But just what is this thing termed professionalism? *Professionalism* can be viewed as exhibiting professional qualities in one's thoughts and behaviors. Those who exhibit professionalism openly embrace their profession. They are proud of their profession and, therefore, attempt to live up to the high standards important for those who claim to be professionals in their discipline.

> In my mind, a professional's degree of professionalism has to do with the qualities exhibited by an individual. A "true professional" is one who exhibits the highest degree of professionalism. (Austin, 1997, p. 6)

Therapeutic recreation professionals help their clients define their values, strengths and goals, and then facilitate client planning so that clients can focus on achieving their goals. Similarly, therapeutic recreation professionals need to examine their values, strengths and goals so that they may focus on how to achieve their own life and professional goals. A clear vision of what is possible moves us toward developing ourselves and achieving a sense of self-fulfillment. In spite of being in a demanding, often underpaid, and sometimes stressful profession, therapeutic recreation can be one of the most rewarding professions for those who understand what it means to be a professional. It is never too early to develop personal and professional awareness and to begin to evolve as a professional. A very good time to start this process is as a student in a professional preparation program.

Nine qualities of professional thought and behavior that help define professionalism are:

1. Gaining an appropriate educational background;
2. Having a professional organization as a major reference;
3. Believing in autonomy and self regulation;
4. Holding a belief in the value of therapeutic recreation to the public;
5. Having a sense of calling;
6. Contributing to the body of knowledge;
7. Actively engaging in professional and community service;
8. Taking part in continuing and advanced development; and
9. Employing theory-based practice. (Austin, 1997)

The sections that follow review each of these qualities. As you read, begin to assess yourself in terms of your own values, strengths, and goals in order to determine your personal path to professionalism. Of course, you will value certain qualities more than others, and have personal strengths that allow you to develop some qualities further than others. This is to be expected. Reviewing these qualities, however, will hopefully help you define your own personal and professional goals.

Educational Background

Are you currently receiving, or have you already received, a professional preparation that equips you to perform adequately as a therapeutic recreation professional? As a student or emerging professional it may be difficult for you to assess the quality of your professional preparation. One approach to assess your level of professional preparation is to complete a self-evaluation using the checklist in ATRA's *Guidelines for Competency Assessment and Curriculum Planning in Therapeutic Recreation: A Tool for Self-Evaluation* (Kinney & Witman, 1997). The *Guidelines* publication provides an instrument for self-assessment of competencies needed to practice as a therapeutic recreation professional. Of course, those who want to perform at an advanced level of practice will require the additional educational background to perform their functions.

Professional Organization as a Major Reference

Are you a member of your state therapeutic recreation professional organization? Do you hold a membership in either the American Therapeutic Recreation Association (ATRA) or the National Therapeutic Recreation Society (NTRS)? Do you regularly read newsletters and other literature published by the professional organizations to which you belong? A minimum level of professionalism is to belong to at least one professional society. This professional organization should be a place for you to turn to for information and assistance to keep up with trends and issues in professional practice. Professional organizations also offer the therapeutic recreation practitioner a sense of belonging to a discipline that has the agenda of advancing practice within the profession.

Autonomy and Belief in Self-Regulation

Being a professional involves assuming a level of independent functioning. Are you able to exercise an appropriate level of professional judgment as a practicum student, intern, or professional? Are you familiar with the professional codes of ethics and standards of practice?

Belief in the Value of Therapeutic Recreation to the Public

Professionals believe in the value of their profession to clients and the public at large. Behaviors reflecting this belief include the ability to communicate with policymakers regarding therapeutic recreation, expressing to others how essential therapeutic recreation is within an agency (or for society in general), writing articles or news stories about the value of therapeutic recreation, and gaining media coverage for therapeutic recreation. If we do not believe in the value of our profession, it is difficult to believe in ourselves as agents of change.

Sense of Calling

For helping professionals, their work is more than just a job. They have been drawn to a profession which serves others. Ways to reflect this sense of calling include expressing to others your dedication to the profession, and contributing financially to causes that support your profession.

Contributions to the Body of Knowledge

It is important for therapeutic recreation, like any profession, to grow in terms of expanding its body of knowledge. Both students and professionals can make contributions to the literature. Activities include conducting research; collaborating with others on research; or authoring a newsletter, journal article, or book chapter.

Professional and Community Service

Professional service activities include assuming leadership roles in professional organizations, such as state or national therapeutic recreation societies. Opportunities for leadership include becoming a committee chair, board member, or officer. Other professional service functions include serving as a lecturer for a university therapeutic recreation class, providing in-service training sessions, and presenting at a workshop or conference. Community services include volunteer activities such as serving on a local accessibility committee or assisting with inclusive recreation services for persons with disabilities.

Continuing and Advanced Development

All professionals are responsible to keep up with the latest developments in their profession. To do so, professionals attend workshops and conferences provided by local, state, or national professional societies. A second means for continuing development is to systematically read professional journals or books related to your specialty. A third means is locating and using web-based resources. A fourth means is to receive clinical supervision at the workplace (or help establish such a program). A well-designed clinical supervision program should be a required for every therapeutic recreation professional. A final means for advancing professional development is taking graduate-level courses or completing a master's degree in therapeutic recreation to develop skills for more advanced practice.

Theory-Based Practice

It is important for professionals to have a basis for practice. Every therapeutic recreation professional should employ the therapeutic recreation process (i.e., assessment, planning, implementation, evaluation) in his or her practice. Each therapeutic recreation student and professional should also adopt, adapt, or design a therapeutic recreation practice model to guide his or her practice. The Health Protection/Health Promotion Model (Austin, 1999), the Self-Determination and Enjoyment Enhancement Model (Dattilo, Kleiber & Williams, 1998), and the Leisure Ability Model (Peterson & Stumbo, 2000) are examples of practice models that may be adopted or adapted.

Conclusion

It is critical for each of us to reach a high degree of professionalism if we wish for others to respect us and our profession (Austin, 1997, p. 6). In order to have self-respect, therapeutic recreation practitioners must exhibit professionalism. What is your sense of professionalism? This question demands a serious answer for those who wish to be true professionals.

Reading Comprehension Questions

1. Define the term *professionalism*.

2. Why might it be important for therapeutic recreation professionals to exhibit professionalism?

3. What are qualities of "true professionals?"

4. Have you identified the values, strengths, or goals that can impact your degree of professionalism?

5. Do you feel that your educational background has prepared you well for therapeutic recreation practice?

6. Have you adopted, adapted, or designed a therapeutic recreation practice model? Which one? Why?

7. Is there room for improvement in your own level of professionalism?

References

Austin, D. R. (1999). *Therapeutic recreation processes and techniques* (4th ed.). Champaign, IL: Sagamore.

Austin, D. R. (1997). Professionalism: Exhibiting professional qualities. *ATRA Newsletter, 13*(3), 6.

Dattilo, J., Kleiber, D., and Williams, R. (1998). Self-determination and enjoyment enhancement: A psychologically-based service delivery model for therapeutic recreation. *Therapeutic Recreation Journal, 32*(4), 258–271.

Kinney, T. and Witman, J. (1997). *Guidelines for competency assessment and curriculum planning in therapeutic recreation: A tool for self-evaluation.* Hattiesburg, MS: American Therapeutic Recreation Association.

Peterson, C. A. and Stumbo, N. J. (2000). *Therapeutic recreation program design: Principles and procedures* (3rd ed.). Boston, MA: Allyn & Bacon.

Chapter 16

A Third Revolution in Therapeutic Recreation?

David R. Austin, Ph.D., CTRS, FALS

Why should students preparing for the profession of therapeutic recreation or those professionals practicing therapeutic recreation spend time thinking about the history of their profession? Low (1995) explained that "philosophers and historians advocate the study of history for the understanding of the present." She further states that:

> Knowledge gleaned from appreciation of the past does not come from a dry recital of the chronological sequence of events. It is found in examining relationships between significant events within social, cultural, and political contexts. (p. 3)

Thus to understand where the therapeutic recreation profession is now and where it may be going, it helps to know where it has been. Understanding the historical evolution of therapeutic recreation is gained not from the recitation of dates and events, but from understanding the "story" of the development of the profession. Within this chapter, the evolution of therapeutic recreation will be reviewed to trace where it has been as a profession. Naturally arising from the sketch of the historical development of therapeutic recreation are understandings that can show where the therapeutic recreation profession is today, and where it may be headed.

Early Precursors of the Therapeutic Recreation Profession

The story of the therapeutic use of recreation began thousands of years prior to the first development of therapeutic recreation as an organized profession. Precursors of therapeutic recreation have been found among the ancient Egyptians and Greeks as well as other early societies, according to Frye (1962) and Frye and Peters (1972). Priests in ancient Egypt employed a form of milieu therapy, which included the performance of songs and dances, to create a positive atmosphere in which people could overcome mood disorders. The Greeks established health temples with "ample provisions for instructions, bathing, exercise, and entertainment, along with the restful, relaxing regimen and atmosphere" (Frye & Peters, 1972, p. 37). While not formally recorded in history, Frye and Peters indicate that almost all ancient cultures contained some aspects of recreation within their healing practices, at least until the time of the Middle Ages.

In a period that lasted from the Middle Ages until the late eighteenth century, a deterioration in medical care brought about by an emphasis upon the spiritual aspects of human beings occurred at the cost of concern for physical and mental health. Frye (1962) explained that:

> Not until the latter part of the eighteenth century is there evidence of a renewal of interest in the potentialities of work and recreational activities as aids in helping those suffering from nervous disorders. (p. 41)

With the conclusion of the 1700s and beginning of the 1800s came reformers, such as Dr. Phillipe Pinel in France and Quaker William Tuke in England, who lead humanitarian efforts in the treatment of mental illness. The greatest reformer of the day was probably Florence Nightingale whose mid-nineteenth century crusades in England led to not only the founding of the nursing profession but also to establishing the need for recreation as an aspect in the treatment of soldiers in the military hospitals of her day. Around the same time in the United States, Dr. Benjamin Rush championed efforts to reform the treatment of patients in psychiatric institutions. Rush specifically emphasized the need for recreation as a part of the treatment program (Frye & Peters, 1972; James, 1997/98; Punwar, 1994). Pinel's concept of "moral treatment" was also imported into the United States. Moral treatment emphasized opportunities for physical activity, gardening, and productive work in a home-like environment in which patients were accorded kindness and respect. In short, moral treatment provided an organized series of daily activities very similar to those of healthy individuals (Punwar, 1994).

Moral treatment appears to have had an impact on the philosophy of practice in therapeutic recreation that continues in hospitals today. A number of years, however, would pass before the establishment of the therapeutic recreation profession as we now know it. The formal idea of recreation as a part of a therapeutic enterprise would not emerge in the United States until early in the twentieth century. On the heels of this period of improvements brought on by the nineteenth century reformers came the Civil War followed by an inauspicious period in which America's attention shifted toward more "scientific" approaches to mental illness in large mental hospitals (known as *insane asylums*) which were poorly suited for moral treatment. At the same time, America was attempting to deal with the large number of immigrants from Europe who arrived in crowded cities to obtain factory jobs produced by the industrial revolution. Resulting social concerns ensued. Immigrants who found themselves in inhospitable urban environments often experienced mental health problems, became alcoholics, or turned to lives of crime (James, 1997/98; Punwar, 1994).

Roots of the Therapeutic Recreation Profession

It was this environment that provided the impetus for developments that would ultimately produce the therapeutic recreation profession. Three main developments led to the formation of the therapeutic recreation profession. First was the employment of recreation as an instrument for social change. Second was the use of recreation in military hospitals during World War I. Third was the emergence of recreation as therapy in settings outside military and Veterans' Administration (VA) hospitals.

Recreation was used as a vehicle for social reform to improve conditions brought about in inhospitable cities during the time many emigrated from Europe to America. Boston's Joseph Lee began the "play and recreation movement" which spread throughout America in the late nineteenth century and early twentieth century. To Lee, recreation was a means to self-development. Neva Boyd joined Lee's play and recreation movement, ultimately arriving at Jane Addams' Hull House in Chicago. At this noted settlement house, Boyd used recreation as a medium to help the children of recent immigrants adjust within what had to be a hostile environment, and develop themselves as individuals. Hull House eventually became the site of a training program that Boyd initiated for group workers—a program she later moved to Northwestern University. Boyd has been credited as being the originator of theory and techniques that offered a foundation for the practice of Red Cross hospital recreation workers employed in military hospitals during World War I. Social programs, games, gardening, music, dance, drama, and community outings were among activities led by Red Cross recreation workers for hospitalized military personnel. Following

World War I, in 1921 the VA took control of many military hospitals and in 1931 hired 49 Red Cross hospital recreation workers to establish its own recreation services within the VA (James, 1997/98). Around this time, other types of settings were also beginning to use recreation as therapy. For instance, in 1929 the Lincoln State School and Colony in Illinois established recreation services for children with mental retardation. This program was closely monitored through an evaluative research study for two years, then a report was published. This report deemed the program a success, remarking on the value of recreation in social skills training (Frye & Peters, 1972).

In sum, the play and recreation movement, the establishment of recreation services in military and VA hospitals, and the emerging acceptance of recreation in facilities, such as state schools and state psychiatric hospitals, provided a foundation for what was to follow. Therapeutic recreation was poised for its first revolution—the "great acceleration" in hospital recreation brought on largely by its growth during and immediately after World War II. The tremendous growth in hospital recreation during the 1940s, 1950s, and into the 1960s signaled the beginnings of today's therapeutic recreation profession. Meyer (1980) heralded this time frame as therapeutic recreation's "beginning professionalization period" (p. 6).

The First Revolution:
The Great Acceleration and the
Beginnings of Professionalization

With World War II came great acceleration in the use of recreation in military hospitals, which later expanded into what are termed today Department of Veterans Affairs (VA) hospitals, and, finally, into most state psychiatric hospitals and state institutions for people with mental retardation. This rapid growth in therapeutic recreation (usually called *hospital recreation*) marked the first revolution in therapeutic recreation. To meet the great demand for hospital recreation workers the Red Cross recruited young women from established fields, such as group work and education. Recruits attended a four-week Basic Recreation course at American University in Washington, DC. By the end of the World War II, Red Cross hospital recreator ranks had risen to a total of 1,809. After the war, hospital recreation services from the Red Cross continued within military hospitals. Likewise, medically approved recreation programs were established within all VA hospitals following the war (Frye & Peters, 1972). A benefit of having recreation in military and VA hospitals was that it exposed a great number of physicians and psychologists to the concept of recreation as a part of the treatment milieu (James, 1997/98). James observed, "As the war ended and physicians returned to civilian practice, the demand for recreation therapy programs grew across the country" (p. 89).

As therapeutic recreation grew, two streams of thought formed. One stream was that of "recreation for all." This perspective believed that the right to recreation was something that all should enjoy, including those who were institutionalized, ill, or disabled. They believed that organized recreation participation was beneficial, and recreation during times of illness or disability would help in the general recovery of the patient or client by providing a healthy daily activity. Provision of a satisfying and enjoyable recreation experience was the central goal under this approach. This was the view of those in the "recreation movement" represented by the old Hospital Recreation Section of the American Recreation Society founded in the late 1940s.

Meyer (1980) summed up the position taken by the Hospital Recreation Section by writing:

> Hospital recreation (perceived by the Hospital Section) was not considered to be essentially different from community recreation. The therapeutic value of the recreative experience was present irrespective of setting. Hospital recreation was considered a setting specialization within the organized recreation field. The practitioner who provided hospital recreation was perceived as a *recreator* (no modifying adjective used such as "hospital" recreator). (p. 8)

The second stream of thought was the use of recreation as a therapy. Recreation was seen to be more than a wholesome activity. It was a tool or modality to treat illness and to rehabilitate clients. The primary aim of the individuals who termed themselves *recreational therapists* was not the provision of a recreation experience, but the use of activities to ameliorate pathology and, ultimately, to rehabilitate the individual.

Those subscribing to the recreation as therapy approach were not a part of the "recreation movement" of their day, but instead saw themselves as therapists who assisted medical staff in ameliorating symptoms of illness. Recreation therapy was an adjunctive therapy to medicine. This was the view of the old National Association of Recreational Therapists (NART) that formed early in the 1950s. Most of the founding members of NART were practicing recreational therapists at state psychiatric hospital and state schools serving persons with mental retardation (Austin, 1997; Meyer, 1980; Sessoms, 1982).

A third group of practitioners formed a Recreation Therapy Section within the American Association for Health, Physical Education, and Recreation (RT-AAHPER) in 1952. The Recreation Therapy Section membership remained small throughout its existence and the organization did not have a strong national voice. RT-AAHPER was nevertheless invited to participate with the Hospital Recreation Section and the National Association of Recreational Therapists in the Council for Advancement of Hospital Recreation. In 1953, the Council formed to allow the three professional societies to meet on matters of mutual concern (Crawford, 2001). While seemingly little progress was made by the Council to unite the organizations into one professional society, the Council may have had some effect on bringing the organizations together since unification did become a reality in the 1960s when the two major professional societies merged.

The Hospital Recreation Section of the American Recreation Society (ARS) and the National Association of Recreational Therapists (NART) continued to champion their respective positions (i.e., ARS the "recreation for all" position, NART the "therapy" position) until 1966 when the two societies merged into a branch of the National Recreation and Park Association—the National Therapeutic Recreation Society (NTRS). At the time, *therapeutic recreation* was adopted as an umbrella term to encompass both positions (Austin, 1997).

Beatrice Hill has been credited by Meyer (1980) as the "principal early advocate" (p. 11) of the then new concept of therapeutic recreation. Hill was the driving force behind Comeback, Inc., an advocacy organization to promote therapeutic recreation. A 1961 Comeback, Inc. publication on therapeutic recreation curriculum, she stated:

> The term *therapeutic recreation* is used to describe the recreation services given to people who are ill, disabled, or handicapped and consequently, unable to participate in the recreation programs provided by the community unless special provisions are made in community settings for their inclusion. (p. 1)

While Hill's Comeback, Inc. definition obviously focused on community settings, the then new term of therapeutic recreation:

> ...came to be broadly interpreted as including any recreational service to individuals with mental or physical disabilities, in either the hospital or community, whether for the purpose of providing treatment or for a recreation experience. (Smith, Austin & Kennedy, 1999, p. 7)

The founding of the National Therapeutic Recreation Society ushered in the use of a new term to describe the neophyte profession.

In summary, the first revolution in therapeutic recreation was marked by a vast expansion in therapeutic recreation, and the beginnings of professionalization reflected by the establishment of the first professional therapeutic recreation societies. These professional societies began in the late 1940s and early 1950s, and culminated in the 1960s with the establishment of the National Therapeutic Recreation Society (NTRS). By the end of the first revolution, a full-time occupation of therapeutic recreation existed in numerous healthcare facilities throughout America, and this occupational group had organized within a single professional society, bearing the then new term therapeutic recreation as its title. Therapeutic recreation was in a position to emerge as a profession.

The Second Revolution: Professionalization Occurs

Professionalization has been described by Meyer (1980) as:

> the process by which an occupational group seeks to achieve the characteristics or attributes of a profession, and thereby attempts to demonstrate to the general public and other professions that it is highly competent, the sole master of its craft, and able to regulate itself. (p. 34)

Structural attributes of professionalization applied in studies by Meyer (1980) and Navar (1979) include full-time occupation by the profession's members, a body of knowledge, university training programs, political advocacy to earn legal sanctions, a professional association, and a code of ethics. Attitudinal attributes identified by Meyer and Navar included: a sense of colleagueship; a belief in service to the public; belief in self-regulation; having a dedication, or sense of calling, to the field; and possessing a sense of automony by being able to exercise independent decisions. The desire of therapeutic recreation to become an accepted profession became paramount during its second revolution.

For almost twenty years, the National Therapeutic Recreation Society (NTRS) singly advocated for the professionalization of therapeutic recreation in the United States. During these years a number of advances were made by NTRS toward professionalization. For example, the *Therapeutic Recreation Journal* began publication in 1966. Guidelines were published for community-based programs for special populations in 1978, as well as for clinical standards of practice in 1979. Other indicators of a growing field were also evident during this period. University curricula in therapeutic recreation expanded, and accreditation standards were established. Increasing numbers of therapeutic recreation textbooks and other types of literature appeared. Regional therapeutic recreation training symposia began across the United States. Finally in 1981, the National Council on Therapeutic Recreation Certification was instituted (Crawford, 2001). Such accomplishments quickly bore fruit. As the profession entered the 1980s, a scholarly study by Navar (1979) assessed the professionalization of therapeutic recreation, and found that therapeutic recreation had developed into an "emerging profession."

Yet the National Therapeutic Recreation Society (NTRS) found itself in a philosophical dilemma because it attempted to represent the broadest spectrum of practice by including the "recreation as therapy" position of NART, which viewed recreation as a tool of treatment, and the "recreation for all" position of HRS/ARS, which emphasized that people with disabilities should have access to recreation services whether in a community or hospital setting. The implications the situation were stated by Meyer (1980) who wrote:

> The dual representation of therapists and special recreators by NTRS seems to present some ideological as well as practical difficulties. Ideologically, this position suggests that therapeutic recreation is not an occupation, per se, but rather it is made up of two or more occupational specialties which seems to imply that therapeutic recreation is a "field." This same position also seems to suggest that the uniqueness of therapeutic recreation is not so much in what it provides or how it is provided, but rather to whom it is provided. (p. 41)

Meyer went on to state:

> From a practical and realistic viewpoint, should NTRS (therapeutic recreation) attempt to represent two cadres of practitioners, each with a different immediate service purpose and each practicing their specialty in quite disparate agencies? Can NTRS fulfill its role as a professional association to both of these subspecializations? Which group will set NTRS priorities? How will the energies and resources of NTRS be divided?

> Some might argue that there are not two cadres of practi-
> tioners, only one—therapeutic recreators. To reason in this
> fashion is to ignore the obvious differences between these
> two subspecializations in regard to purpose, work setting,
> accountability structure, etc. Therapists and special recreators
> function in different worlds. Given such significant differ-
> ences it is only a matter of time…when one or the other of
> these specializations seeks their independence from the
> other. (pp. 40–41)

Meyer's (1980) words proved to be prophetic. In 1984, the American
Therapeutic Recreation Association (ATRA) was founded by a grassroots
movement led by clinicians who believed that a new professional organization was needed to more precisely define and advance therapeutic recreation as an area of clinical practice, and to provide the autonomy therapeutic
recreation needed to create a professional identity. Many national leaders,
including a number of NTRS past presidents and board members, believed
that in NTRS's attempt to be "all things to all people" it had not provided
the clear boundaries for the field needed to interpret it to others and to direct clinical practice (Austin, 1997). Also, by being a branch or special
interest group under the National Recreation and Park Association, many
felt that NTRS lacked the ability to advance therapeutic recreation as a
profession separate from parks and recreation.

The American Therapeutic Recreation Association (ATRA) has grown
to become the largest professional society for those in therapeutic recreation.
Today there are over 3,200 members of ATRA (Ann Huston, personal communication, September, 2000). ATRA has captured the professional hearts
and minds of the vast majority of those who choose to be professionally
active in therapeutic recreation.

Most observers would probably agree that by providing a focus on
clinical practice and creating an autonomous professional society, ATRA
has done much to advance therapeutic recreation. At the same time, ATRA
seems to have limited its focus to health protection (i.e., treatment and rehabilitation) with little concern for health promotion. Due in part to this lack
of concern for the total continuum of service that includes health promotion,
Austin (1999) developed the Health Protection/Health Promotion Model.
In this model health promotion joins health protection as a major concern
for therapeutic recreation.

Nor has ATRA taken major strides toward defining explicitly what is
meant by the term therapeutic recreation. This is highly unfortunate because
there is a great deal of confusion regarding the definition of therapeutic

recreation, both by the public in general and within therapeutic recreation. Anyone who has attempted to explain to friends, acquaintances, other professionals, or legislators what Certified Therapeutic Recreation Specialists (CTRSs) do realizes the difficulty in interpreting the profession to others.

It is of little surprise that the general public is often confused about what therapeutic recreation represents because the profession has not clearly and consistently defined itself. This confusion is a significant impediment to the further development of the therapeutic recreation profession. There seems to be a need to provide an accepted definition of therapeutic recreation which will lead to uniform university curricula for professional preparation and to unify practice within the field.

Summary

To this point, there have been two revolutions in therapeutic recreation. The first revolution saw the large-scale arrival of recreation in hospitals and institutions, and the beginnings of the professionalization of therapeutic recreation. This first revolution established therapeutic recreation in the health sector. The second revolution occurred with advances in the professionalization of therapeutic recreation. With professionalization has come professional organizations, university professional preparation programs, the accreditation of university curricula, a growing body of literature, standards and guidelines for practice, and credentialing. At the same time these meaningful strides were being made, the National Therapeutic Recreation Society was perceived by many as lacking both the focus needed to advance clinical practice and the autonomy required for the therapeutic recreation profession. A grassroots movement formed the American Therapeutic Recreation Association (ATRA) to champion the cause of recreation as therapy. Still ATRA can be criticized for a lack of attention to health promotion and the failure to develop a through definition for clinically based therapeutic recreation.

A Third Revolution on the Horizon?

Is there a third revolution for therapeutic recreation on the horizon? An argument can be made that therapeutic recreation is poised to move toward a third revolution in which it declares its independence. To do so therapeutic recreation needs to acknowledge its former stepchild status within parks and recreation, yet proclaim itself to be a separate profession with a primary concern for clinical practice. The formation of ATRA may be viewed as a first step toward revolution.

Separating therapeutic recreation from parks and recreation will not be easy from a philosophical perspective. Philosophically, therapeutic recreation was originally influenced by Joseph Lee's play and recreation movement— a movement that emphasized the instrumental value of recreation. It was this movement that was influential in establishing public park and recreation departments in cities across America to bring about self-development of the citizenry. Followers of the movement, such as Neva Boyd, were the founders of the first hospital recreation programs. While park and recreation agencies have migrated from their original social welfare beginnings toward more of a recreational sports model (James, 1997/98), parks and recreation and therapeutic recreation share roots. Many therapeutic recreation specialists still cling to those roots. These practitioners retain the nonclinical philosophy of the members of the old Hospital Recreation Section of the American Recreation Society, and will be very reluctant to adopt the clinical philosophy of ATRA.

This stance became apparent when, in 1992, Hamilton and Austin surveyed national leaders in therapeutic recreation to examine trends and issues for the decade that was approaching. A burning issue was whether special recreation should be distinguished from therapeutic recreation. In presenting their results these researchers wrote:

> Echoing the discord that has existed since the Hospital
> Recreation Section of the American Recreation Society and
> the National Association of Recreational Therapists first
> appeared, the current leaders could not agree on the issue.
> Those who believed that therapeutic recreation was "the
> application of the therapeutic recreation process, individual-
> ized and goal directed" desired to see the two separated....
> On the other hand, those who viewed therapeutic recreation...
> as the provision of services to persons with illnesses or dis-
> abilities were inclined to include the two under one label.
> There seemed very little room for compromise. (p. 76)

On a related issue, experts were asked about separating therapeutic recreation from university park and recreation curricula. Three trains of thought emerged. One group thought that therapeutic recreation should be more closely aligned with other healthcare professions. They believed that students could not be properly prepared in park and recreation professional preparation programs due to the limited number of therapeutic recreation courses students could take. A second group held the view that "we are recreators first, and therapeutic recreators second" and that separation was not advisable because "our roots are in recreation and play" (p. 76). A third group believed that therapeutic recreation should logically separate from parks and recreation but currently this was not practical because of the relatively small size of therapeutic recreation student bodies. Once again, the clinical versus nonclinical viewpoints of the experts seemed to dominate their views.

Following a discussion of their findings Hamilton and Austin concluded:

> After reviewing all our data, we believe the pivotal issue facing therapeutic recreation in the future will be the resolution of the existing tension between clinical and nonclinical forces within the field. Our interviews lead us to conclude that the distinct philosophical positions will continue due to the deeply entrenched beliefs held by those representing these positions. Both sides of the clinical/nonclinical issue are extremely passionate regarding their positions and there is no reason to anticipate that either side will not energetically pursue their separate agenda. (p. 78)

It seems likely that the lack of agreement found among Hamilton and Austin's national experts is reflective of the profession as a whole in which the clinical versus nonclinical gulf remains a major point of contention. Therefore, on philosophical grounds alone, there seems to be little prospect for the occurrence of a third revolution in therapeutic recreation involving the separation of therapeutic recreation from parks and recreation in order for it to become an independent and autonomous profession.

In fact, a third revolution in therapeutic recreation will not likely take place for some time. A much more likely scenario for the near future would seem to be one reflected by one of Hamilton and Austin's (1992) experts who projected:

> ...that clinical therapeutic recreation will be championed by ATRA, while NTRS will employ its close relationship with

community parks and recreation in order to promote the provision of public recreation services for persons with special
needs. These two separate entities, ATRA representing recreation therapy and NTRS representing special recreation
services, will have continuing jurisdictional disputes but will
learn to exist cooperatively in order to further their respective causes. (p. 78)

Reading Comprehension Questions

1. Why should therapeutic recreation practitioners and students care about the history of therapeutic recreation?

2. Why might it be said that therapeutic recreation has had a long past but a short history?

3. What three major developments may be perceived to have led to the formation of the therapeutic recreation profession?

4. Please identify the following, and their places in the roots of therapeutic recreation: Joseph Lee, Neva Boyd, Red Cross, Veterans Administration, and Lincoln State School and Colony.

5. Describe the two streams of thought in therapeutic recreation. Which one was favored by the Hospital Recreation Section of ARS? which by NART?

6. What organization formed in 1966?

7. When did the term *therapeutic recreation* emerge? Who has been associated with being an early advocate for the term?

8. What events marked the "first revolution" in therapeutic recreation?

9. What is professionalization? What are the criteria or structural attributes of professionalization?

10. How far has therapeutic recreation progressed toward professionalization?

11. What events marked the "second revolution" in therapeutic recreation?

12. Do you see a third revolution on the horizon for therapeutic recreation? Why or why not?

References

Austin, D. R. (1999). *Therapeutic recreation processes and techniques* (4th ed.). Champaign, IL: Sagamore.

Austin, D. R. (1997). Recreation therapy education: A call for reform. In D. M. Compton (Ed.), *Issues in therapeutic recreation: Toward the new millennium* (2nd ed., pp. 193–209). Champaign, IL: Sagamore.

Comeback, Inc. (1961). *Therapeutic recreation curriculum development conference.* New York, NY: Author.

Crawford, M. E. (2001). Organization and formation of the profession. In D. R. Austin and M. E. Crawford (Eds.), *Therapeutic recreation: An introduction* (3rd ed.). Boston, MA: Allyn & Bacon.

Frye, V. (1962). Historical sketch of recreation in the medical setting. *Recreation in Treatment Center, 1,* 40–43.

Frye, V. and Peters, M. (1972). *Therapeutic recreation: Its theory, philosophy, and practice.* Harrisburg, PA: Stackpole Books.

Hamilton, E. J. and Austin, D. R. (1992). Future perspectives of therapeutic recreation. *Annual in Therapeutic Recreation, 3,* 72–79.

James, A. (1997/98). Recreation therapy: A history of concern part I, 1855–1946. *Annual in Therapeutic Recreation, 7,* 83–90

Low, J. F. (1995). *Occupational therapy for physical dysfunction* (4th ed.). Baltimore, MD: Williams & Wilkins.

Meyer, L. E. (1980). *Philosophical alternatives and the professionalization of therapeutic recreation.* Arlington, VA: National Recreation and Park Association.

Navar, N. H. (1979). *The professionalization of therapeutic recreation in the State of Michigan.* Unpublished doctoral dissertation, Indiana University, Bloomington.

Punwar, A. J. (1994). *Occupational therapy: Principles and practice* (2nd ed.). Baltimore, MD: Williams & Wilkins.

Sessoms, H. D. (1982). Therapeutic recreation service: The past and challenging present. In L. L. Neal and C. R. Edginton (Eds.), *Extra perspectives: Concepts in therapeutic recreation* (pp. 1–14). Eugene, OR: Center of Leisure Studies, University of Oregon.

Smith, R. W., Austin, D. R,. and Kennedy, D. W. (1999). *Inclusive and special recreation: Opportunities for persons with disabilities* (4th ed.). Madison, WI: Brown & Benchmark.

Chapter 17

This I Believe...
About Therapeutic Recreation

This chapter is a collection of short statements by current leaders in therapeutic recreation. Its purpose is to provide an indication of the beliefs held by today's leaders in therapeutic recreation. Unfortunately, only a limited number of leaders could be included within this chapter. The editors hope to include views from additional therapeutic recreation leaders in future editions of this book.

This I Believe...

Morris W. (Mick) Stewart, Ph.D., CTRS

Rarely does one get the opportunity to consider what he or she "believes" is important enough for publication. I welcome this opportunity to share some thoughts and experiences that have shaped my understanding and passion for therapeutic recreation service.

While reviewing my experiences as an undergraduate, I was unable to recall any deep conversations about professional philosophy in therapeutic recreation. However, shortly after graduation, I became employed in the field while continuing to pursue a master's degree. A unique opportunity presented itself when forty of the best-known and best-informed leaders in therapeutic recreation gathered on the Indiana State University campus for a discussion about their philosophies and perspectives. I was in awe of the discussion and felt privileged to be a part of the conversation. Elliot Avedon, Gerald O'Morrow, Fred Humphrey, David Park, and Doris Berryman were a few of the attendees that I recall. I wish that I had kept the list I made, but as a student, I underestimated the value of this experience and how it would shape my beliefs. Defining moments are rarely recognized as they happen.

Certainly other classes in my educational experience developed my thoughts and concerns about service delivery, but questions posed in practice were the ones that I found most critical. These questions made me look at how I delivered recreation services. Once, as a new professional at LaRue Carter Psychiatric Hospital in Indianapolis, I announced to a psychiatrist that I had scheduled a basketball game between our hospital and another state mental health facility. Instead of complimenting me on my willingness to take this programming risk, he instead asked me why I hadn't scheduled our children to compete against elementary schools in the area. That was the last interhospital game I ever scheduled. Over thirty years ago, that psychiatrist taught me that inclusion and community-based leisure services would be the approach to program delivery that would make the most significant difference in my clients' lives. Now the Americans with Disabilities Act supports this notion, as does P.L. 94-142, the Education for All Handicapped Children Act (and the Individuals with Disabilities Education Act of 1990). However, these legislative mandates came years after I had already learned the lesson of how inclusion and public awareness can change attitudes and laws.

Historically, the roots of recreation were firmly grounded in social consciousness. Hull House introduced recreation services as a mechanism to deal with disadvantaged youth and to provide them with more wholesome opportunities. We are only beginning to move back to our roots and rediscover how recreation can help fill the void left by broken homes, drug addiction, long work hours, child abuse, and other social and economic ills that can be solved through more comprehensive programs. Social services must include a new (and an old) perspective on leisure. It is within this context that I believe therapeutic recreation must, and should, move closer to general recreation programming services instead of distancing ourselves further.

While therapeutic recreation seems to be striving for more recognition within the medical model, most (if not all) other therapeutic modalities are trying to understand how they can become more closely allied with a holistic approach to treatment. Therapeutic recreation has the inherent connection that can bridge the gap between clinical services and community inclusion while providing an exemplary model for holistic medicine. For instance, as a public service, parks and recreation departments serve many small, medium, and large cities and counties across the country, but those children most often left behind in the schools are also left behind in our programs. We warn a child about behaviors and then eventually, when he or she has crossed the line too many times, we exclude the child from the very service that has the greatest potential to help. As a profession, we must do better. Therapeutic recreation must avoid the pitfalls of the medical model and become more focused on inclusive services. Noninstitutional alternatives for treatment and inclusion will eventually lead to the most successful client interventions, and as a profession, we have the best and most extensive network of associated professionals. Public parks and recreation can provide more of the answers to societal ills and therapeutic recreation has the opportunity to guide the majority of these professionals through the process. Territorial concerns must be set aside, institutional politics must be understood, and administrative weaknesses must be overcome. As we approach our new roles, therapeutic recreation cannot ignore nor neglect clinical services; however, as medical care continues to move toward shorter hospitalization periods our role can and should be enhanced through public park and recreation entities.

These beliefs have been shared with several thousand students and professionals as I have advocated for therapeutic recreation over the past three decades. I would not be so presumptuous as to assume that my beliefs are the only way to visualize the past, present, or future, but that is what makes each of us unique. It is up to our respective audiences to integrate and evaluate these positions and to determine how therapeutic recreation services will best serve clients' needs in the future.

This I Believe...

Ralph Smith, Ph.D.

Although my undergraduate and master's degrees were in another field, my love for working with people with disabilities at camp led me to therapeutic recreation. I began my career in therapeutic recreation in the late 1960s, as a Director of Camping and Recreation for a community-based agency. The term therapeutic recreation was new, having been adopted only a few years prior. In fact, I was so unfamiliar with therapeutic recreation that I spelled it "therapuetic" the first time I wrote the word (I suppose I thought *e* comes before *u* except after *p*). Regardless, I was excited to have my first full-time job, and thrilled to be part of an emerging profession.

In an academic sense, I knew very little about the field of therapeutic recreation; however, experientially I knew a great deal. I knew that the campers I worked with were healthier and happier as a result of recreation participation. I knew that recreation enhanced their social skills, and helped them feel better about themselves. I also knew that functional skills improved as a result of participation in recreation. In short, I knew that the profession I had chosen was important because it made a positive difference in people's lives. I believed that then; and now, more than thirty years later, I believe it more than ever. The therapeutic recreation profession *is* important.

I am acutely aware, however, that my belief in the importance of therapeutic recreation is not universally shared. Some administrators, when faced with budget difficulties, disproportionately reduce the therapeutic recreation staff. Some allied health professionals from other disciplines question the quality of therapeutic recreation services. Some people from the general population express surprise that "fun and games" (their words, not mine) are part of clinical services. I once even worked for a person who jokingly referred to me as the agency's "play-boy."

These reactions from others are disappointing, but not necessarily surprising to me. What does surprise me, however, is that some therapeutic recreation practitioners do not seem to value their own profession. A number of years ago, some colleagues at Penn State and I conducted a study of interprofessional perceptions between therapeutic recreation and occupational therapy practitioners (Smith, Perry, Neumayer, Potter & Smeal, 1992). With respect to professional competence, therapeutic recreation respondents held *less* favorable views of therapeutic recreation than the occupational therapists. Among occupational therapists, 94% stated that therapeutic recreation specialists (TRSs) are competent; however, only 89% of TRSs stated that TRSs are competent. As my coauthors and I noted, these results "suggest therapeutic recreation practitioners need to reflect upon their own opinion of themselves as professionals" (p. 40).

Perhaps the constant barrage of devaluing statements from others has caused us to question our own professional legitimacy. Or, maybe the absence of definitive, methodologically sound efficacy studies has convinced us that our services are not worthwhile. Whatever the reason, I believe it is time for therapeutic recreation professionals to purge such negative thoughts, and recognize that therapeutic recreation has as much, if not more, to offer than other allied health professions. It is time to listen to the many clients who, after discharge, call or write to thank their therapeutic recreation staff for helping them readjust to community life. These clients recognize that therapeutic recreation, no matter how you spell it, changes people's lives for the better. It is time for us to take pride in a profession that matters.

This I Believe...

Thomas K. Skalko, Ph.D., TRS/CTRS

It seems that a statement of what I believe must begin with an understanding of my personal belief system regarding humankind. This personal belief system interfaces with my perspectives of the mission of recreation therapy services. My beliefs about humankind are based upon several assumptions:

- individuals are motivated to meet personal needs (i.e., both the therapist and the consumer of services);
- individuals have a right to make choices that help them perform as effectively as possible in life activities;
- individuals desire to perform as effectively as possible in life activities; and
- the service provider's (recreation therapist/therapeutic recreation specialist) role (obligation) is to create the conditions under which an individual can grow physically, cognitively, and psychosocially in a manner that is consistent with the complex facets of their lives.

The role of recreational therapy, therefore, is to offer quality intervention services that assist others in becoming as effective and successful as possible. The specific services to accomplish this, however, can be as varied as the providers.

Today, contemporary healthcare practice embraces the full continuum of services from active treatment through disease prevention and health promotion—including quality of life issues. In turn, normal life activities are included as an aspect of quality healthcare and should be addressed by the healthcare team. The implications for our field are evident. If contemporary medical and health practice (e.g., treatment services) includes a full continuum of services, then it is the responsibility of every allied health provider to work together to design and deliver a full spectrum of services that address the health and quality of life needs of the consumer. This more comprehensive interpretation of healthcare has implications for the primary mission for the field.

Current practice in the field indicates that recreation therapists are involved in addressing the functional performance of the individual. I, for instance, embrace the World Health Organization's model for addressing health and functioning. In this model, recreational therapy utilizes a full range of interventions to address the various levels of functioning and overcome disability, as well as contextual factors. The interventions respond to the functional performance of the individual and include quality of life issues with recreation and leisure as one of the components (not our only mission). In such a model, the recreation therapist utilizes a wide range of services to impact functioning and disability. These services are not confined to a mission of independent leisure functioning but instead address the functional needs of the individual in context, ultimately to promote the fullest capability of the person. Contemporary practice is not restricted by setting, clinical versus nonclinical, or to the delivery of treatment versus recreation services. Instead, the recreation therapist responds to the needs of the consumer, based on an assessment, in promoting functional ability, health promotion, and disease prevention. Services may include prescribed activity, physical activity for health, social skill training, friendship development, fitness and tolerance for daily activities, education, and recreation opportunity. Within such an approach, no specific service or area of development has any more value than another, but instead they are based on the needs of the individual. The recreation therapist may or may not provide each of the services. The provider most appropriate to deliver these services (e.g., social skill training) is dictated by the individual needs of the consumer, the setting, the mission of the agency, and the skill of the therapist. The service provided at an agency is separate and distinct from the mission of the profession. This means that a CTRS may be hired and charged with the responsibility of ensuring that disadvantaged individuals are provided equal access and opportunity in recreation, or they may be hired to offer specific treatment interventions (e.g., stress management, autogenic training, community integration). Ultimately, however, our collective must separate job function from the mission of the profession. For instance, my position as an administrator and educator is distinctly different than the mission of the profession (i.e., to provide interventions services to improve functional performance).

The mission (and philosophical position) of the profession should not be the monster we have created. The assumption of an intervention-oriented mission embraces the historical moral and ethical convictions of the field with regard to ensuring that persons with illness and/or disability are provided the means (i.e., tools) and opportunities to improve functional limitations, to access their strengths, and to pursue those quality of life activities they deem most rewarding.

As practicing and developing professionals, it is our individual responsibility to protect the interests of the consumers we serve, to provide the highest quality of service based upon the needs of the consumer, and to ensure the consumer has access to all of life's activities to the greatest extent possible. To restrict our services to "special recreation," "independent leisure functioning," or "fitness" for that matter, violates our ethical obligation.

In closing, it seems that the key is to acknowledge that the profession is engaged in healthcare and we are obligated as educators, practitioners, students, and administrators to ensure that we provide services of the highest quality. Whether these services are distinct treatment services to improve functional capacity, services to enhance quality of life, or services to promote health and fitness, we are obligated to prepare ourselves to ensure that we cause no harm and deliver the best possible service. The acknowledgment of this alone will drive our educational preparation and the roles we fulfill as recreation therapists.

This I Believe...

Bob Riley, Ph.D., CTRS

As a veteran of the therapeutic recreation profession for the past 25 years, I have been exposed to a multitude of opinions, philosophies, and models of therapeutic recreation services. From my early involvement in the provision of "recreation for special populations," through the growth and acceptance of the Leisure Ability Model, to the development of the more recently established healthcare models, I have witnessed the ongoing struggle to unite the field under one common view. Proponents of this effort claim that for therapeutic recreation to be accepted and valued by society, it must be represented as one profession, united under one organization and guided by one philosophical mission statement. I don't believe such a strategy is possible or even necessary.

The purpose and goal of therapeutic recreation is to assist individuals to maintain or improve their level of functional independence. Functional independence can be defined as one's ability to determine and accomplish life activities in as unrestrictive a manner as possible. Such activities, depending upon the scope and nature of the disability, may range from initiating basic life functions (e.g., ambulation, preparing a meal, socialization) to achieving higher order goals (e.g., obtaining employment, earning a degree, achieving a sense of self-satisfaction). Life activities that contribute to one's functional independence are heavily influenced by social and cultural norms but are ultimately prioritized by the individual. Thus, functional independence is a highly subjective value that each individual determines for oneself. A prioritized goal for one individual might be to return to work, yet for another person it may be to self-initiate a recreational activity. The attainment of optimal functional independence is the goal of most individuals with or without disabilities. Most individuals with disabilities, however, are restricted in their efforts to achieve functional independence due either to the nature of their disability or to the "handicaps" that society places upon them. It is through the process of therapeutic recreation that individuals might successfully improve their level of independent functioning.

The process of therapeutic recreation involves the selective use of specific activities to restore and (re)habilitate individuals to an independent level of functioning. The specific use of recreation activities, offered in a carefully designed and therapeutic manner, can assist individuals to achieve their goals while participating in healthy and enjoyable activities. The use of recreational activities and programs as treatment modalities provide for a unique opportunity for participants to engage in nonintrusive, enjoyable activities while attempting to increase their level of functional independence. The degree to which such activities are viewed as therapy as opposed to diversionary is determined, in part, by the level of demonstrated achievement of specific outcomes associated with the activities. Identified outcomes of a specific activity must be successfully demonstrated on a predictable and consistent basis for the activity program to be considered a treatment modality. In essence, the concept of therapy is as much linked to the ability to achieve positive change on a reliable basis, as it is related to the context of the applied methodological approach.

The importance of recreational activities cannot be underscored enough. Throughout life and through early learning opportunities most individuals gain an appreciation for the value of recreation activities. Although encompassed under the generic emotional label of "fun," recreation-based activities contain inherent qualities that contribute to our physical, emotional, and cognitive development. Broadly speaking, within youth and carried throughout life, recreation-based activities provide essential opportunities for socialization, physical maintenance, and psychological adjustment—all essential elements for living a healthy and enjoyable life. Ultimately, we all need to possess a sense of goodness in life. This is what often is meant by, achieving a life balance or maintaining quality of life. Recreation activities, as well as our perceived sense of independence, are critical factors that contribute to our subjective quality of life. Therapeutic recreation is a process that enables individuals who possess low levels of independent functioning to improve and to do so through the use of select recreational activities which, when viewed as a whole, have the potential to improve their subjective quality of life.

Much like the process of learning has been linked to the profession of education, or the process of health attached to the profession of medicine, various professional groups have adopted the process of therapeutic recreation. The professionalization of the process of therapeutic recreation is a necessary priority in an effort to protect the public and insure that therapeutic recreation services are conducted in a quality and safe manner. Unfortunately, these professional groups have not kept pace with the research necessary to demonstrate predictable outcomes of service, as they have with other components of the professionalization process (e.g., credentialing, educational preparation). It is toward this end that sincere efforts must be made if the therapeutic recreation process is to be valued as a viable service in the future.

This I Believe...
Nancy Navar, Re.D., CTRS

Therapeutic recreation is a wonderfully effective means for improving the human condition. Additionally, there are structures, processes, and outcomes that help describe the therapeutic recreation profession.

Structures

- Therapeutic recreation is a *profession*. As a profession, it combines both theory from various disciplines and technical information.
- *Certified therapeutic recreation specialist* is the credential that identifies the professional who practices therapeutic recreation.
- The profession is small enough, that *each individual practitioner's* behaviors and attitudes reflect upon the reputation and effectiveness of the profession.
- *Professional preparation* in therapeutic recreation is most credible when the curriculum is comprehensive, accredited, complies with professional standards, and is taught by properly credentialed faculty.
- *Professional organizations*, although imperfect, are the mechanisms for advancing the profession; each practitioner demonstrates professionalism through their membership and active participation.
- Different *models* of therapeutic recreation practice enable different clients with different needs in different settings to benefit from a model that has meaning in that context. Just as different schools of thought exist in other professions (e.g., psychology), various schools of thought can coexist within the profession of therapeutic recreation.
- *Professionalism* in therapeutic recreation involves both the practitioner's attitudes and behaviors, and also the collective membership of an organized group of professional therapeutic recreation specialists.

Processes

- The three main types of therapeutic recreation *services* are functional improvement, leisure education and recreation participation. Each of these types of services is selected based on client needs.
- Therapeutic recreation *programs* are most effectively conducted when each program has a *single focus or purpose* (e.g., functional

improvement, leisure education *or* recreation participation) for which they are accountable.

- Therapeutic recreation programs should be documented, indicating their goals, content and process. Such documentation assists in reliable replication of programs.

- A *systematic process* for placing clients into programs includes client assessment, individualized planning, program implementation, and evaluation.

- Recreation activities are only one modality used in therapeutic recreation. Other processes include discussion, educational experiences, and homework to name a few.

- The most powerful intervention tool used in therapeutic recreation is the therapeutic recreation specialist and her or his meaningful relationship with the client receiving services.

- Therapeutic recreation services are needed in healthcare, human services, recreational, educational, rehabilitation, prevention, treatment, and habilitation *settings*.

- Therapeutic recreation is an exciting, meaningful profession that contributes to the welfare of individual clients and the improvement of society as a whole.

Outcomes

- Improved functioning, improved quality of life, and an improved leisure lifestyle are legitimate outcomes of therapeutic recreation services.

- Some of the outcomes of therapeutic recreation services are clearly and immediately measurable; others are not.

- Following are some examples from thank-you notes written by clients. These sentiments may not be easily realized by the CTRS on a day-to-day basis:

  Thank you for helping me learn how to ride the bus to the swimming pool. (community integration)

  Thank you for playing my favorite music and holding my hand before I die. (palliative care)

  Thank you for treating me with respect and dignity even though I no longer can care for myself and am not fun to be around. (sensory stimulation)

Thank you for giving me the opportunity to be safe, to explore and to travel beyond my neighborhood. (community recreation program)

Thank you for helping me find activities and people that may help me stay sober; and for reminding me that there are many ways to enjoy life. (leisure awareness group)

Thank you for motivating me to keep up with my daily exercises. (rehabilitation planning)

Thank you for helping me find activities my entire family can do—we were growing apart and you helped keep us together. (family leisure education group)

Thank you for helping me adjust to the major changes in my lifestyle and to realize that asking for help doesn't mean I'm helpless. (chronic pain group)

Thank you for keeping me out of trouble; and for helping me feel good about myself. (adolescent leadership group)

Thanks for helping me practice my thinking skills and regain my desire to live; I sure like that Internet. (brain injury program)

Thank you for helping me learn how to make and keep friends; I'm much less lonely now. (social skills training)

Thank you for helping me express my emotions in a way that is OK. (mental health group)

Thank you for treating me like a normal kid, and not just a dying patient; those fish tanks, dog visits, and game times are awesome. (oncology)

Thank you for helping me learn how to make some good decisions; I feel a lot more independent these days. (decision-making skills group)

I believe that the therapeutic recreation specialist, together with the client and the greater professional community, make this a better world. There is value in helping people smell the roses.

This I Believe...
Youngkhill Lee, Ph.D., CTRS

One day I read Aesop's fables to my kids. One story made me stop and think the therapeutic recreation profession. The story went like this:

> A fox had by some means gotten into the storeroom of a theater. Suddenly he spotted a face glaring down on him, and began to be very frightened; but looking more closely he found it was a only a Mask, such as actors use to put over their face. "Ah," said the Fox, "you look very fine; it is a pity you have not got any brains" (Sturrock, 1988, p. 29).

Whatever the face we as therapeutic recreation professionals have now, whether it depicts a very important or less important figure in the popular drama called "Healthcare," the face may just appear to be a powerless mask that outsiders might pity if the face does not seem to have a brain. Our knowledge base is our brain. This means that the therapeutic recreation profession indeed has a brain. Then, one crucial question is: *Is our brain healthy?* I recall reading papers expressing the concern that "not enough" research has been done in therapeutic recreation. Perhaps, therapeutic recreation professionals are skating cautiously on very thin ice when it comes to making significant claims as to efficacy of our services. In this short essay, I share what I believe needs to be provided in order to claim that we have a healthy knowledge base.

Increase Efforts to Demonstrate Ends of Our Service

We live in the era of demonstrating outcome and accountability. The current healthcare environment demands research evidence associated with our services. However, the therapeutic recreation profession lacks sufficient empirical evidence to fully support the efficacy of our services. A colleague and I recently reviewed all possible research articles purported to demonstrate outcomes of recreation in physical medicine and rehabilitation between 1991–2000. We found a very small number of research papers developed by therapeutic recreation researchers. My colleagues at Indiana University also observed lack of research evidence associated with therapeutic recreation outcomes in mental health settings. What is the message here? It is clear that therapeutic recreation falls short of the contemporary requirement for evidence-based practice. It seems we may be skating on very thin ice. Unless we make significant improvements in demonstrating therapeutic recreation outcomes, we will likely continue to worry about the poor ice condition.

Hold a Deeper Understanding Our Means of Services

We need serious efforts to investigate the experiential nature of recreation. If we don't have a clear understanding of it, we are unsure of the process that intends to create ends (i.e., outcomes). We need to understand the richness of recreation as a powerful tool. What distinguishes therapeutic recreation from other allied health professions resides in the richness of recreation. While clinical knowledge and skills are important, the lack of knowledge about the recreation experience is hampering the development of a strong foundation for our profession. The recreation experience provides a sense of purpose and context necessary for creating meaningful lives. This is something that no other profession can do better than us. We need a deeper understanding of the recreation experience to support therapeutic recreation practice. This type of study is valuable to refute the "fun and games" image of the therapeutic recreation profession often perceived by the public.

Share Our Ends and Means with Others

We need to improve communicating our body of knowledge with those outside of our profession. We should not talk only among ourselves. Our research needs to be connected with the allied health profession. While conducting research, we might need to consider using some useful theoretical frameworks developed by allied health profession (e.g., disablement models by World Health Organization and National Center for Medical Rehabilitation and Research). In terms of disseminating our research, scholars in therapeutic recreation need to publish their studies in journals outside therapeutic recreation. Further, while our primary journals (i.e., *Therapeutic Recreation Journal*, *Annual in Therapeutic Recreation*) are listed in PsychInfo, they have not yet appeared in Medline. Without these efforts, we may well experience intellectual and professional isolation.

✳ ✳ ✳ ✳ ✳

In conclusion, the brain is behavior's command post, and all body parts are governed by the brain. The brain has the ability to monitor surroundings and respond with behaviors to manipulate the environment. If the brain is not healthy, our body parts get weak and face difficulty functioning. While there are other important needs in our profession, above-mentioned needs are vital in my belief.

This I Believe...
Gerald Hitzhusen, M.S., CTRS

As therapeutic recreation professionals we do make a difference in the lives of people with disabilities in clinical and community settings. I have personally seen the results of carefully planned therapeutic recreation programs in mental health settings. Utilizing the therapeutic recreation process of assessment, planning, implementation and evaluation, we are able to see the benefits to clients in the therapeutic recreation program. The most difficult area is the transition to the community from clinical setting, and coordinating the continuum of services.

Creativity and Imagination

You must be very creative and imaginative as a therapeutic recreation professional, especially when working with limited budgets, limited staff, and so many different types of clients. Teamwork is essential within clinical and community settings. Again that creativity is challenged when assisting clients in continuing their leisure pursuits in the community. It is essential that therapeutic recreation and recreation personnel in the community cooperate in order to have leisure opportunities for people with disabilities who wish to pursue their interests in the community.

Inclusion

Inclusive leisure experiences had its beginnings in mainstreaming and integration. You must believe in inclusion in order for it to succeed in the community. Often as a therapeutic recreation professional you need to become an advocate for clients in order to overcome physical, psychological, and financial barriers. Support and accommodations can make a huge difference in a person's right to leisure and quality of life.

Experience

There is really no substitute for experience in therapeutic recreation. We need to have quality intern and volunteer experiences in our therapeutic recreation education programs. Also there is no real substitute for working and/or volunteering with several different populations with disabilities or who are elderly. Although the therapeutic recreation processes we use should be very similar, you need to know how to work with clients and other staff in order to understand the needs of both. Prior to becoming a professional in therapeutic recreation, I had worked in at least five different positions in the leisure profession.

Continuing Education

Continuing education is a must. If you are to maintain your national therapeutic recreation certification, you either take an examination or maintain a record of continuing education every five years. Initially, many professionals resisted this, but I have always maintained that this would be the best way to keep professionals current about the new concepts of therapeutic recreation. I have seen this personally and professionally through the Midwest and International Symposiums on Therapeutic Recreation that I have been associated with for over thirty years.

Research, Grants, and Contracts

We must maintain research, grants and contracts in therapeutic recreation and related fields to keep pace with new ideas and techniques. We have done a fairly decent job in obtaining grants and contracts, but we have not been as successful in therapeutic recreation research. This lack of success in research is due to a variety of reasons: time, finances, motivation, and energy.

Legislation

The legislation arena is crucial to all areas of recreation and leisure, including therapeutic recreation. I have personally seen this from work in Washington, DC and in my own home state of Missouri. Technology has been of great assistance in communicating and advocating for our clients and our profession. One of the greatest successes in legislation was the Americans with Disabilities Act signed in 1990. I believe that this opened up the opportunities for leisure, travel, and work in all communities for people with disabilities.

International Therapeutic Recreation

Opportunities around the world are now opening up for experiences in therapeutic recreation and related professions. Therapeutic recreation professional associations in Canada, England, the Caribbean, Japan, and Korea, to name a few, have been established in the last ten years. Meetings, conferences and symposiums in the areas of therapeutic recreation, leisure, tourism, outdoor recreation related to people with disabilities and the elderly have increased significantly. Unfortunately, international internships for therapeutic recreation students have decreased due to national therapeutic recreation certification requirements by the National Council on Therapeutic Recreation Certification. There are just not that many international Certified Therapeutic Recreation Specialists, except in Canada.

Professional Therapeutic Recreation Associations

We must, in the immediate future, work to have a single therapeutic recreation profession association to prosper as a profession. This will provide a needed focus for the profession while reducing membership costs for practitioners. (I am a member of both ATRA and NTRS, and the Canadian Therapeutic Recreation Association.) The financial burden of belonging to two national professional associations, in addition to paying fees to retain national certification, has been too high for many practitioners to bear. The cost of national affiliations often leaves therapeutic recreation practitioners with few financial resources to become active in local, state, or regional associations.

This I Believe...

Jerry G. Dickason, Ph.D., CTRS

Stating one's belief is inseparable from biography. To communicate what I believe about therapeutic recreation requires that I tell you about the influences that brought me to this belief.

My first experience with therapeutic recreation was as a summer worker in 1964 when I was assigned to the therapeutic recreation department at Madison State Hospital in southern Indiana, a state psychiatric hospital. I was a recreation leadership major at Indiana University interested in outdoor recreation. Taking this summer job at Madison between my junior and senior years was fulfilling a requirement of the program. We were encouraged to take a recreation job in an area outside our main vocational interest. Madison State paid well, included room and board, satisfied a curriculum requirement, and was fairly close to home.

Student workers at Madison State were provided opportunities to learn about many aspects of psychiatric care. In the delivery of recreation programs I was amazed at how eager the residents were to participate in activities. In the summertime, we were outside as much as we could be. The psychiatric treatment emphasized engagement in activities and social manipulations to bring about desired behavioral change. Drug therapy was not the primary order of the day. The arsenal of drugs to modify moods and behaviors today was not yet available. Consequently, the hospital staff emphasized that the residents be involved in practically everything possible. When the residents were not at recreation, they were working in many areas of the hospital, such as housekeeping, dietary, and grounds work. These activities were considered vocational therapy. So the power of activity was key to getting better. In other words, one's level of engagement was perceived to be in direct correlation to a level of normality.

It was in this milieu that I began to see the relationship of activity to desired outcomes. In addition to familiarizing myself with diagnostic labels, I learned from the recreation staff how to identify behavioral quirks within a resident and immediately see an activity that could potentially modify that behavior toward normality. The staff was very astute in observations; they intuited remedies. We believed we were in the business of curing people, and belief made it happen. I don't know who was cured, but we sure helped people see the value of activity in their lives and that some activities fostered better mental health than others. It was also an education for me to learn not to be judgmental. If we wanted participation, we had to be willing to accept all levels of responses. Quite surprisingly, these levels of response were accurate baseline performances which the treatment staff used in planning a progression of activities to elicit desired behaviors. I realized we were doing assessments by observation and planning specific activities based on these assessments.

I was fascinated by the power of recreation as a treatment modality, and I thoroughly enjoyed my experience at Madison. After graduation in the summer of 1965, rather than pursuing outdoor recreation, I accepted a recreation position in the activity therapy department at Evansville State Hospital. I now was a professional and was considered a therapist. I attended diagnostic team meetings where I was expected to report initial intake assessments on residents' performance in activities. At these meetings I was also expected to identify specific programs relevant to the diagnostic label and treatment objectives for these new residents. At this time Dr. Paul Haun wrote *Recreation: A Medical Viewpoint*. This book made clear to me that indeed recreation is an effective tool for treatment. Haun's observations that the inability for involvement is evidence of pathology affirmed my experiences in the power of activity, and that fun and joy were vital healers in the wellness process. Haun also helped me see the role of the recreation specialist beyond activity leadership:

> …the recreation specialist has a vitally significant mission as the prophet and guardian of balance—alert to the subtle perversions by which recreation loses it identity; understanding of the institutionalized resistances in our society; and skilled in the tricky field of personal motivation. (p. 48)

From my experiences, recreation specialists have always advocated wholeness and balance and have defended the value of play as the basis of authentic behavior. They have educated and motivated residents to reach their potential in being fulfilled. Having a psychiatrist write this affirmed my professional choice and existence. The recreation staff at Evansville State Hospital put this ideology into practice. Residents, many of whom were from farming families, were taking art and music classes for the first time and discovering their talents. Many residents had incredible life stories to tell and acquired self-confidence and pride in relating these experiences through Toastmasters International, a community-based volunteer program.

After Evansville I spent two years with the American Red Cross in Vietnam (18 months) and Washington, DC (6 months). I was assigned to the 6th Convalescent Center at Cam Ranh Bay. Picture this, my first day as a therapist:

I am a civilian dressed in a new, crispy-clean, drab-olive uniform and walk into a Quonset hut of 28 blue-pajama guys badly shot up and waiting for transfers either to their units, to another in-country hospital, or stateside. I wanted to say, "Hi, I am the recreation therapist," but all I could think of was Herb Shriner, a 1950s TV show host and fellow Hoosier, and simply said "Hello."

I walked around feeling completely out of place among all these injured soldiers. I immediately left, feeling nauseous from the disfigurements. I was angry at my reactions, and then remembered the power of activity, armed myself with a deck of PIT cards, screwed my courage to the sticking place, walked back into that Quonset hut, sat on a guy's bunk in the middle of the hut, and started dealing out the cards to seven GIs in the immediate area.

After the third hand, that hut was jumpin' and noisy like the floor of a stock exchange. These guys were hungry for involvement. I got two more decks, returned and now everybody was playing—regardless of dexterity or vocal ability. The moment was magical. I puffed up with goose bumps from seeing the power of activity and feeling the joy of being a change agent. In the midst of this hellish war, how simple were our joys and satisfactions.

While in Vietnam, I read Josef Pieper's *Leisure: The Basis of Culture*. This had a profound effect on me. For the first time I saw contemporary leisure as capitalistic persuasions. I had been in Vietnam long enough to begin seeing the United States as a foreign county. And as such, I saw people buying their pleasures and saw self-worth determined by the volume of ownership. Pieper as well as C. Wight Mills, in his *Sociological Imagination*, gave me the ability to see the big picture of marketplace manipulations to consume and the trivializing of leisure. I was ready for graduate studies.

I came to New York University in September 1969 to study with Dr. Edith Ball. Dr. Ball introduced me to the concept of therapeutic recreation as a treatment continuum. This overarching structure helped me make sense and design a framework of my four years of professional experience as a therapist. Dr. Ball's construct, I believe, eventually was foundational for the Gunn-Peterson model of leisure ability that is the defining philosophy of so many recreation therapists today. I believe in this model and praise what

Dr. Norma Stumbo has done to revise and explain along with Dr. Carol Peterson, coprogenitor of the model, the myriad ramifications of this model.

Today I firmly believe that leisure is the basis of all cultures and that the quality of our leisure determines the quality of our culture. For a therapist to use recreation as a treatment tool, that therapist must try to understand the cultures from which their clients evolve. Only then will the therapist be able to help the clients understand the possible significance (or value) of leisure in their life. Understanding encourages clients, regardless of the origin of their disabling condition, to become active participants in their own recovery or development and in pursuing activities that affirm authentic interests. This understanding lingers long after treatment, thus helping clients justify their actions within their cultural constraints.

So, have we cured the patients? Probably not. But, we can surmise that once exposed to the value of leisure in their life, clients will think, and perhaps act, differently to maintaining some semblance of wellness. This is a major contribution to the clients' sense of well-being.

This I Believe...

Charlie Bullock, Ph.D.

Therapeutic recreation is a seldom-understood field. It is misunderstood by other professionals and by the people we serve. It is differentially understood by people who call themselves therapeutic recreators. There are myriad understandings, definitions, philosophies, and nuances, none of which are inaccurate, all of which contribute to a lack of consistent understanding across audiences. For consistent understanding, we must embrace our similarities and sell ourselves!

What are our similarities? We believe in the purposive use of recreation to enhance functioning of people with a wide range of abilities. Our interventions are intended to ameliorate dysfunction, as well as to make lifestyle changes to optimize health, wellness, and quality of life. We believe that the people we serve (and not our services) are what matter.

How do we sell ourselves? We sell ourselves not through the explication of definitions and philosophies, but through the telling of stories about therapeutic recreation. Regardless of the specific perspective from which a professional comes, there are countless stories that can be told to explain the uniqueness and viability of our profession. We must tell these stories tirelessly to our colleagues, families, friends and most importantly, the people whom we serve. As I tell these stories, I try to keep in mind these key thoughts.

I believe that leisure education encapsulates the essence of therapeutic recreation. Recreation is a powerful force in everyone's life. It has curative value. It provides pleasure, gives balance, and rejuvenates. If this is the basis of therapeutic recreation interventions, then the goal of any therapeutic recreation service must be help people to develop an individual and contextual understanding of self and leisure, and identify and learn the cluster of skills necessary to participate in freely chosen activities which lead to an optimally satisfying life.

As a field, I believe that we are too provincial. Like so many other related disciplines, we assume that we are the only ones who can provide what we call therapeutic recreation services. I believe that we have to break out of this territorial mode and look for areas of overlap among related disciplines. If we truly believe that the people we serve are what is most important, will not only look for, but also embrace those similarities with other disciplines as a way to provide the most effective and comprehensive services. That means that some things that we think that only we can do, we must allow, even encourage, other professionals to do. By the same token, we must expand the areas of our practice (overlap with other disciplines) so that we can be most effective as well. Such a position is anathema to the tenets of professional organizations. However, we must serve people, not professions, and this transdisciplinary ideology must pervade our education and service delivery.

Therapeutic recreation as a clinical process is not dependent on location. It is, however, dependent on the therapeutic recreation process that includes establishing a therapeutic relationship, conducting an individual and contextual assessment, setting goals, designing treatment or program plans, implementing or coordinating the plan, evaluating progress toward the plan, and documenting outcomes of services. This process can be implemented in a variety of settings and agencies among a variety of people with differing abilities. Use of phrases like "community" or "clinical" therapeutic recreation creates an artificial distinction and lack of understanding among the many audiences whom we want to understand and value us. When telling stories, we must not insert these inaccurate distinctions, rather we must tell how peoples' lives have changed through the provision of therapeutic recreation services.

This I believe...

This I Believe...
David R. Austin, Ph.D., CTRS, FALS

I believe that:

1. *Therapeutic recreation is a profession.* Therapeutic recreation is more than a specialization within recreation and leisure studies. Therapeutic recreation is a true profession that meets, to some degree, all of the criteria that define a profession. It is a unique profession with one foot firmly planted in allied health with the other foot solidly in recreation and leisure studies.

2. *Therapeutic recreation is defined by the therapeutic recreation process.* What defines therapeutic recreation is that the therapeutic recreation (or recreation therapy) process is followed by a trained professional who employs prescribed activities, recreation experiences, and leisure pursuits as modalities. The therapeutic recreation (or recreation therapy) process is the cyclical "APIE" process of assessment, planning, implementation, and evaluation. The term special recreation may be used to describe recreation services for people with disabilities. The term inclusive recreation may be employed to indicate the full inclusion of people with disabilities into the recreation mainstream that allows for joint participation of people with and without disabilities.

3. *Therapeutic recreation is purposeful and goal-directed.* Two important characteristics of therapeutic recreation is that is purposeful and goal-directed. Its outcomes are not random, but are planned. Such planning implies choice making on the part of clients. Because choice is involved, clients perceive their actions to be self-determined. This leads clients to feelings of competence.

4. *The mission of therapeutic recreation is to protect and promote health.* Therapeutic recreation uses activities, recreation, and leisure to assist clients to overcome health problems and to grow toward the highest level of health and wellness possible for each individual.

5. *At the heart of therapeutic recreation is the therapeutic relationship between the therapist and client.* A therapeutic alliance between the client and recreation therapist is a vital element if interventions are to work. A strong bond is essential to the therapeutic enterprise. Clients generally like recreation therapists, see them as supportive,

and associate them with enjoyable experiences. This perception of recreation therapists helps create a positive atmosphere in which each therapist can apply his or her skills to meet client needs.

6. *Control is a key component within therapeutic recreation.* The provision of control is a central element in therapeutic recreation practice. The recreation therapist attempts to allow as much control as possible to remain with the client. Clients are encouraged to select therapeutic activities and to take a meaningful part in affecting the outcomes of these activities. All practice models share the aim of decreasing the therapist's control while increasing the client's control.

7. *Therapeutic recreation embraces a humanistic perspective.* Those in the therapeutic recreation profession take a holistic view of each individual. They believe in the dignity and worth of each individual. They hold that individuals do not just react to the world that they encounter but are capable of being in dynamic interaction with their environments. They see both children and adults as being capable of making changes in themselves and their environments. Finally, they believe that humans strive for self-actualization

8. *Fun, enjoyment, and pleasure are key to therapeutic recreation.* People are motivated to participate in activities from which they receive fun, enjoyment, or pleasure. Therapeutic recreation uses enjoyable activities as interventions to bring about therapeutic outcomes. To paraphrase a popular song, recreation therapy activities are "the honey that makes the medicine taste good" (i.e., therapeutic intervention is something enjoyable).

9. *Intervention strategies are based on client strengths.* As a part of the therapeutic recreation process, both client problems and strengths are assessed. Assessment of problems results in a needs list. These needs are then translated to treatment or rehabilitation goals. Interventions flow from client strengths. Strengths include personal skills, abilities, and talents, as well as resources, such as social support from family, friends, and the community.

10. *Therapeutic recreation will continue to emerge as a valued profession.* Therapeutic recreation is still an emerging profession and will remain so in the near future. Therapeutic recreation practice is becoming increasingly evidence-based as more protocols are developed, and more theory-based as greater numbers of practice models provide guidelines for practitioners. It will be up to today's

students to move therapeutic recreation toward the status of being viewed as an established profession.

Reading Comprehension Questions

1. Which *This I Believe...* statement do you like best? Analyze that statement to determine which specific elements appeal to you.

2. Would you categorize some authors as being more clinical than others? Which ones? What makes these statements more clinical in nature to you?

3. Choose two *This I Believe...* statements that seem to differ. Compare and contrast them.

4. Can you draw on elements found in these statements to construct your own *This I Believe...* statement?

References

Haun, P. (1965). *Recreation: A medical viewpoint*. New York, NY: Teachers College, Columbia University.

Mills, C. W. (1959) *The sociological imagination*. New York, NY: Oxford University Press.

Pieper, J. (1965). *Leisure: The basis of culture*. London, UK: Collins. (First published in Great Britain, Faber & Faber, 1952)

Smith, R. W., Perry, T. L., Neumayer, R. J., Potter, J. S., and Smeal, T. M. (1992). Interprofessional perceptions between therapeutic recreation and occupational therapy practitioners: Barriers to effective interdisciplinary team functioning. *Therapeutic Recreation Journal, 26*(4), 31–42.

Sturrock, W. (1988). *Aesop's fables*. Morris Plains, NJ: Unicorn Publishing House.

Chapter 18

Leaders in Therapeutic Recreation

This chapter presents some of the individuals who have laid the foundation for therapeutic recreation in America. Most of the therapeutic recreation vanguard featured in this chapter were previously identified by *Palaestra* magazine as being leaders of the profession. Special thanks is extended to the staff of *Palaestra* for allowing authors of those tributes that appeared in their magazine to include material from those features in this chapter.

In an effort to include more therapeutic recreation leaders, the editors surveyed those identified by *Palaestra* and asked them to list additional individuals they believe should be included in a chapter about leaders in therapeutic recreation. Individuals who appeared on several lists were selected for this chapter. For a variety of reasons, the editors were not able to obtain tributes for some therapeutic recreation leaders they identified. The editors hope to expand this chapter in the future editions to include those not featured here. Finally, thanks to each of the contributors of these essays about these featured leaders.

David R. Austin
Ralph Smith, Ph.D.

Born in 1941, David R. Austin was two years old when his family moved from Pittsburgh, Pennsylvania, to Indiana where he was raised. Following high school, Austin studied health and physical education at Union College in Kentucky, and received his bachelor's degree in 1963. After one year as a recreational therapist at Madison (Indiana) State Hospital, Austin left to pursue his master's degree in recreation at Indiana University. In 1965, master's degree in hand, he took a position as a recreation therapy supervisor at Evansville (Indiana) State Hospital. There, he worked under Al Grubb, part-time Executive Director of the National Association of Recreational Therapists (NART). Grubb perceived recreational therapy to be "a tool for treatment"—a position that significantly influenced Austin's own philosophy of practice.

Before long Austin was promoted to Director of Recreation Therapy at Evansville State Hospital. He held this position until 1969, when he began his Ph.D. studies at the University of Illinois while acting as a visiting instructor. A colleague at Illinois, Jerry Kelley, shared Austin's practitioner background in mental health. Kelley's highly clinical and theory-based approach to therapeutic recreation helped Austin build upon his early philosophical foundation. Kelley, who was president of the National Therapeutic Recreation Society (NTRS), also socialized Austin into the profession. Following Kelley's lead, Austin began what was to become a lifetime of involvement in professional societies, which included helping to establish the Midwest Therapeutic Recreation Symposium in 1971.

In addition to Kelley's influence, Professor Mary Virginia Frye had a great impact upon Austin. Frye, a prominent figure in therapeutic recreation, perceived recreation to be a purposeful intervention to assist in health restoration. Austin quickly embraced this view. Two other Illinois professors, Doyle Bishop and Rainer Martins, also influenced Austin. Their research on the social psychology of leisure inspired him, and led to his completion of a minor in social psychology. Throughout his academic career, Austin's thinking, writing, and research have been strongly influenced by social psychology.

Upon receiving his Ph.D., Austin assumed a post at North Texas State University in 1973. Three years later, he accepted a faculty position at Indiana University (IU) where he has since remained. The high quality of his teaching and advising is evidenced by his receiving IU's Frederic

Bachman Lieber Memorial Award for Distinguished Teaching in 1988, and the Society of Park and Recreation Educators' (SPRE) Teaching Excellence Award in 1994.

Austin has been a prolific author having published more than 100 journal articles, numerous abstracts and book chapters. He is also the author or coauthor of three highly influential textbooks in the field: *Therapeutic Recreation: Processes and Techniques* and *Therapeutic Recreation: An Introduction* (with Michael Crawford) are invaluable resources for clinically based practitioners; *Inclusive and Special Recreation* (with Ralph Smith and Dan Kennedy) focuses upon delivering nonclinical recreation services for people with disabilities. Austin's work, including his development of the Health Protection/Health Promotion practice model for therapeutic recreation, has provided inspiration for therapeutic recreation students throughout the world.

Austin has received many awards for his writing and research efforts, including the Holis Fait Scholar Award (1993) and the American Association for Leisure and Recreation's J. B. Nash Scholar Award (1995). He has been a Fellow in the Academy of Leisure Sciences since 1988. In 1998, Austin received the National Recreation and Park Association's prestigious National Literary Award for his contributions to recreation-related literature.

Austin's service contributions include being a founding member of the American Therapeutic Recreation Association (ATRA), serving as its president from 1994–1995. He has also been president of the Society of Park and Recreation Educators (SPRE), and the Academy of Leisure Sciences. He has served on the boards of ATRA, SPRE, NTRS, and the National Recreation and Park Association (NRPA). Because of his outstanding service, Austin received Distinguished Fellow Awards from NTRS, SPRE, and ATRA. He holds the distinction of being the only individual to receive the highest honor given by all three national societies.

Throughout his career, David Austin has dedicated himself to the field of therapeutic recreation, and his many contributions continue to enrich the profession.

Edith L. Ball

Jerry G. Dickason, Ph.D., CTRS

Edith L. Ball (1905–1996) believed that recreation participation contributes greatly to the overall worth and wellness of an individual. This woman of conviction expressed her views in the right place and at the right time. The Grand Dame of the recreation profession, ever so proper yet humble and kind, never missed an opportunity for a teachable moment.

Born in New York City on September 4, 1905, Ball graduated from Columbia University's Teachers College in 1927. Shortly after graduation, she started her professional career as the Director of Physical Education for Women at the University of Maryland. In 1931 she moved to Cleveland, Ohio, to be the Director of Physical Education and Recreation for the School of Nursing at what is now Case Western Reserve University. While there, the university hospital staff asked her to set up recreation programs for the patients. This was Ball's first endeavor in developing hospital recreation programs.

In 1937, at the height of the Great Depression, Ball returned to Maryland and took a position with the federal government as the supervisor of recreation for the Works Progress Administration. She stayed in government recreation services until after World War II. In 1947, she returned to New York City to work at Stuyvesant Neighborhood House and began her graduate studies at New York University (NYU). The university invited her to teach a course on social recreation. While teaching college courses, she became interested in how academic instruction addressed the professional preparation of recreation personnel which became her dissertation topic. She completed her doctorate of education in recreation administration in 1953 and began teaching at NYU.

As a new professor of the rapidly growing recreation profession, Ball gave impetus to several professional developments. She was a member of the American Recreation Society (ARS), where she provided leadership in curriculum development. This eventually led to the formation of national curriculum standards and the Council on Accreditation to oversee academic standards for the preparation of professional recreation personnel. As a member of ARS, she served on the Executive Committee of the Hospital Section of the Society. Her activities with the Hospital Section eventually led to cooperation with the National Association of Recreational Therapists (NART) to form the National Therapeutic Recreation Society (NTRS) in 1966–1967. Between 1953 and 1973, Ball was either chairing committees that were shaping the future of the recreation profession, or was instrumental in selecting people who would provide the leadership to bring about professional developments. Even after retiring in 1973, Ball was involved in a host of professional activities until 1986, when she chaired the accreditation visitation team for Western Washington University.

Ball died on December 31, 1996 in Tucson, Arizona. One can read about Ball's professional story in Catherine Eilenberger's (1992) dissertation "The Contributions of Edith L. Ball to the Professional Field of Recreation 1930–1985."

Ball was a teacher. She professed that therapeutic recreation professionals should always deal with the whole person when thinking of needs and services. This whole-person philosophy was the basis of her therapeutic recreation continuum model. Ball explained that people find themselves in different health conditions at different times in their lives. It is important to identify, on a continuous scale of recreation engagement, where a person may be functioning. This theoretical construct was presented at the Ninth Southern Regional Institute of Therapeutic Recreation held in Chapel Hill, North Carolina, in May 1969. The presenters and the participants hammered out a philosophy of therapeutic recreation at the conference. Ball's recreation continuum model brought together the two contentious philosophies of therapeutic recreation: recreation as an end unto itself (as supported by professionals affiliated with the Hospital Section of ARS) and recreation as a tool of treatment (as supported by members of NART). The gradation of steps and the degrees of freedom for the client in this model form the basis of several current therapeutic recreation practice models.

In Dr. Ball's recreation administration course, she stated that it was important to know on any job where you hang your hat. At the time, students thought it was a funny comment. Only later did I myself realize the wisdom of this statement. Ball picked her issues and focused intently on every one until she had achieved her goal. She always knew where she was hanging her hat, and if not, she didn't stay around.

Neva Leona Boyd

Ann James, Ph.D., CTRS

Neva Boyd (1876–1963) was born in Sanborn, Iowa, on February 25, 1876. After graduating from high school, she went to Chicago where she studied at the Chicago Kindergarten Institute, a school that specialized in preparing people to work with children and young adults. Her studies brought her into contact with Hull House, the settlement house founded by Jane Addams. Through her work with immigrant youth at Hull House, Boyd discovered the power of play in the social and emotional development of young people.

Prior to this time, most scholarly literature on play focused on the benefits to physical health and development. As Boyd's experience working with at-risk youth grew, so did her conviction that scholars had missed much of the impact that recreation experiences could have on the socialization and personal development of youth. She began to develop her own theories, and began to test them at Hull House.

Boyd's work drew the attention of the Chicago Women's Club (advocates of the play movement that was growing at the turn of the century). The Club persuaded the Chicago Park Commission to hire Boyd to organize recreation programs for one of its parks. This demonstration proved successful, and the Commission voted to hire social workers for developing programs at each of its playgrounds.

As the playground movement continued to grow, so did the demand for trained leadership. In 1911 Boyd established the Chicago Training School for Playground Workers through which she shared her knowledge, theories, and experience on the use of recreation for the "personal and social development of children" (Simon, 1971, p. 257). After several years Boyd's program was incorporated into the Chicago School of Civics and Philanthropy, and eventually into the Sociology Department at Northwestern University. Throughout its existence, the curriculum focused on the psychology of play, small group dynamics, and the ability to meet the developmental needs of youth through recreation experiences. Field work, much of it done at Hull House, was always an integral part of the program.

Although Boyd pioneered the field of group work and remained allied to social work, many of her students went on to work with physically disabled, developmentally disabled, psychiatric, and incarcerated populations. She referred to their work as recreational therapy. In 1919 she compiled a booklet of activities titled *Hospital and Bedside Games*. In the foreword, Boyd said that she produced the booklet at the request of workers in civilian and military hospitals. She wrote, "The work that they have done has convinced them that such games have curative value" (Boyd, 1919, p. 4).

In 1929 Boyd joined a former student in a three-year project to uncover the potentials of recreational therapy with mentally retarded clients. The report concluded that:

> By selecting those activities which hold the greatest possibilities for growth and directing them in such a way that the potentialities of the individual, however limited, are called into action, a fuller utilization of the individual's powers may be accomplished and a more harmonious, constructive social life achieved. (Simon, 1971, p. 59)

Paul Simon of the University of Illinois cited Boyd's work as contributing to the development of game theory, problem-solving methodology, play theory, and to our knowledge of group dynamics, leadership principles, and psychodrama (Simon, 1971). In this writer's opinion, she is the leading contender for the title Mother of Recreation Therapy.

Neva Boyd retired from teaching in 1947 and continued to live at Hull House until it closed in 1961. She died in 1963. Students who would like to learn more about this pioneer in our field can find her papers in the Archives of Jane Addams' Hull House on the Chicago Circle campus of the University of Illinois.

Marcia Jean Carter

Karen C. Wenzel, M.S., CTRS
Jane K. Broida, Ed.D., CTRS

For students and professionals in therapeutic recreation, the name of Marcia Jean Carter is synonymous with the highest standards of professionalism. Carter's rich legacy includes numerous textbooks, professional presentations, teaching, practitioner experience, and professional leadership.

Carter was born in Great Barrington, Massachusetts, in 1946. Her involvement with people with disabilities began in the 1970s when she worked in camp settings providing recreation programs. Carter's academic training reflects her interest in people with disabilities. She earned her doctorate at Indiana University in recreation and adapted physical education.

Carter's commitment to individuals with disabilities is demonstrated by her ongoing work in the field. She worked in clinical rehabilitation at the Roger C. Peace Rehabilitation Hospital and has extensive experience in community-based therapeutic recreation programs including the Cincinnati Recreation Commission, Dallas Park and Recreation Department, and the Northern Suburban Special Recreation Association.

Sharing knowledge with others is a large part of Carter's career. She has taught for almost three decades at numerous universities throughout the country. Her philosophy of teaching includes encouraging students to achieve the highest professional standards. Currently, Carter is an associate professor and coordinator of the Recreation Program at the University of Northern Colorado, Greeley, Colorado.

Carter's passion for working with people with special needs stems from the influences of both her family and key leaders in the field. Of note is the influence of Drs. Carol Ann Peterson and Gerald O'Morrow, who provided Carter with guidance and support as she navigated her career path into therapeutic recreation.

Some of Carter's strongest professional influences in therapeutic recreation have been within the areas of certification, accreditation, and standards. Carter initiated the process to create the National Council on Therapeutic Recreation Certification (NCTRC) and was its first president. She was also instrumental in the development of the NRPA certification examination for leisure professionals. Carter has served as the Chair of the Council on Accreditation of the National Recreation and Park Association/American Association for Leisure and Recreation, and most currently, conducted research to update therapeutic recreation accreditation standards. Carter has served on the editorial boards of the *Journal of Physical Education, Recreation and Dance*, *SCHOLE*, and *Leisure Today*. From 1998–1999, Carter provided leadership to the National Therapeutic Recreation Society as president of that organization.

Carter has coauthored an introductory textbook and a management textbook in therapeutic recreation, and has published numerous articles on aging, aquatics, and therapeutic recreation practice. With over 150 presentations on similar themes, she continues to share her knowledge and experience with fellow professionals and students around the world.

Carter has been honored as a Senior Fellow for the American Leisure Academy, American Association for Leisure and Recreation; and has received a Merit Service Award, Honor Award, and Outstanding Achievement Award. The National Therapeutic Recreation Society recognized Carter's achievements by bestowing its highest awards to her—Distinguished Service Award, and Member of the Year.

Even with all the accolades, Carter is best known for her warmth and compassion to both consumers and students of therapeutic recreation. Her profound impact on the professionalism of therapeutic recreation and her influence will be everlasting.

David M. Compton
Gerald Hitzhusen, M.S., CTRS

David M. Compton has been a leader in therapeutic recreation for over thirty years. His contributions include leadership, preparation of future professionals, and scholarship. More specifically, his early work on assessment is a valuable contribution to the field.

Compton is Professor and Executive Director of the Western Laboratory for Leisure Research at the University of Utah. Earlier appointments include Chair of Parks, Recreation, and Tourism at the University of Missouri and University of North Texas. He is a past Director of Research of the National Recreation and Park Association. He is a Fellow of the Academy of Leisure Science and a past President of the National Therapeutic Recreation Society. Compton has secured over two million dollars in grants for research related to therapeutic recreation, including one grant which lead to the development of the Leisure Diagnostic Battery. Compton currently directs a variety of projects related to at-risk youth under the EXCELS Youth Innovative Project.

Compton has been an editor, associate editor, and reviewer for the *Therapeutic Recreation Journal, Leisure Today, Rehabilitation and Human Development, Adapted Physical Activity Quarterly, Journal of Park and Recreation Administration*, and *Journal of Therapy and Design*. He has published numerous articles in the above publications as well as *Expanding Horizons in Therapeutic Recreation* and the *Journal of Sports Medicine*. Compton is the author and editor of key textbooks in therapeutic recreation including *A Profession in Transition* and *Issues in Therapeutic Recreation: Toward the New Millennium*.

The mark of a truly outstanding professional is the ability to sustain a passion and commitment to the field. Compton is widely recognized for his enthusiasm and unwavering belief in the value of leisure and recreation to the welfare and benefit of all. His most recent work is focused on at-risk youth, and has developed some exemplary models for conducting activities and programs. Compton's work is based on a philosophical approach that recognizes the dignity of each human being, and is grounded in a personal belief that words, desire, and advocacy are not enough. To this end, he interacts personally with clients. His hands-on approach to program implementation has endeared Compton to students, peers, families, and clients. Compton's contributions have enriched the field and, most importantly, have made a difference in the lives of others.

Peg Connolly

Bob Riley, Ph.D., CTRS

While many in the field of therapeutic recreation talk about what needs to be done, others *just do it!* Undoubtedly, Peg Connolly is a member of the latter group. Known to most simply as "Peg," Connolly is widely recognized as a national leader in therapeutic recreation. She has played a vital role in the advancement of therapeutic recreation during the past 25 years. Connolly has demonstrated extraordinary leadership in the critical areas of organizational leadership, professional credentialing, and program accountability.

With family roots based in the Midwest, Connolly attended Southeast Missouri State University and graduated with a degree in Psychology/ Sociology in 1972. She was first introduced to therapeutic recreation upon assuming a supervisory position within hospital recreation with the American Red Cross. Her varied duties and early therapeutic recreation experiences included an assignment to assist the Vietnamese Refugee Evacuation program while stationed in Guam in 1975.

Recognizing the need to further her professional education, Connolly enrolled in the therapeutic recreation master's degree program at the University of Illinois. With guidance from Dr. Carol Peterson, Connolly flourished in the program. Her own blend of insight, motivation, and intelligence, coupled with the dynamic opportunities afforded through the University of Illinois program, provided her with opportunities for professional and scholastic leadership. Her fast-track professional trajectory placed her in the forefront of the emerging therapeutic recreation movement. Connolly remained at the University of Illinois and earned her Ph.D. in 1981.

Among many of her professional accomplishments and contributions to the field, Connolly is best known for her organizational leadership. She served on the National Therapeutic Recreation Society Board of Directors from 1980–1983. Given the robust growth and expansion of therapeutic recreation academic programs across the nation, Connolly assumed a faculty position in therapeutic recreation at Florida State University from 1983–1986. She was elected as the founding President of the American Therapeutic Recreation Association in 1984. In 1986 she left the full-time faculty ranks to assume the Executive Director position at the National Council for Therapeutic Recreation Certification (NCTRC). During her tenure at NCTRC Connolly forged the way for the establishment of the National Certification Exam for Therapeutic Recreation. In her role as Executive Director, she often serves as the recognized spokesperson for therapeutic recreation in discussions with other allied health and human service organizations. During her fifteen-year stewardship, NCTRC has emerged into a nationally recognized credentialing body representing over 17,000 Certified Therapeutic Recreation Specialists.

Connolly is noted for her scholarly contributions to the field as well. Her areas of research include program accountability, evaluation, and professional development. She has published over forty manuscripts, many of which address the applied nature of program evaluation. Connolly is a highly respected speaker, and has delivered over 200 speeches, lectures and workshops to a variety of audiences throughout the United States and Canada.

Considered a "living legend" within the field of therapeutic recreation, Connolly serves as a positive role model to guide therapeutic recreation students and new professionals. The profession has acknowledged her significant contribution by awarding her the ATRA Distinguished Fellow Award and by establishing a national scholarship program in her name.

Gerald L. Hitzhusen
Gary Robb, M.S.

Gerald (Jerry) L. Hitzhusen completed both his bachelor's (B.S. in Education, 1963) and master's degrees (M.S. in Recreation, 1971) at the University of Missouri. He worked as the Director of Sports and Recreation at the St. Cyprians School in Lakewood, California, from 1965–1968. Afterward, he worked as Director of Therapeutic Recreation at the Mid-Missouri Mental Health Center in Columbia, Missouri, from 1968–1972. From there, he became a consultant and therapeutic recreation specialist with the National Recreation and Park Association in Washington, DC. Since 1974 Hitzhusen has been on the faculty of the Department of Parks, Recreation and Tourism at the University of Missouri and is currently an Associate Professor. In addition, he has held an appointment as a Recreation Extension Specialist since 1974. Hitzhusen has also been the Director of Project LIFE (Leisure Is For Everyone) since 1982. Project LIFE is a program contracted with the Missouri Department of Mental Health. From 1985–1987 he chaired the Parks, Recreation and Tourism Department at the University of Missouri.

Hitzhusen's most notable contributions to the field of therapeutic recreation are through his coordination of continuing education programs in therapeutic recreation. Since 1975 Hitzhusen has conducted professional development and continuing education programs for therapeutic recreation students and professionals. He has coordinated the Midwest Therapeutic Recreation Symposium since 1974; the Missouri Therapeutic Recreation Institute since 1975; the Missouri Therapeutic Recreation Workshop since 1987; and the International Symposium on Therapeutic Recreation since 1989. He has been the national leader in introducing therapeutic recreation in the United Kingdom, Puerto Rico, the West Indies, and several European and Asian countries. His work has earned him worldwide recognition by organizations, such as the World Leisure and Recreation Association, Canadian Therapeutic Recreation Association, The Royal Inspectorate (England), the National Therapeutic Recreation Society, and the Latin American and Caribbean Council of Applied Sciences to Physical Education and Sport.

The Midwest Symposium on Therapeutic Recreation has thrived under Hitzhusen's leadership for the past three decades. It is the premier therapeutic recreation continuing education program in the world with an annual attendance of approximately 900 students, practitioners, and educators.

Under Hitzhusen's leadership the Midwest Therapeutic Recreation Symposium provides the forum for the development of countless aspiring professionals and serves as a catharsis and meeting place for therapeutic recreation practitioners and educators throughout the country.

Hitzhusen has contributed heavily to therapeutic recreation literature through his editorship of *Expanding Horizons*, the publication of proceedings from the Midwest Symposium on Therapeutic Recreation. He has also authored, edited, or coedited over forty books or chapters of books.

Fred Humphrey

Jerry Jordan, Ed.D.

Fred Humphrey's (1922–1994) commitment and dedication to therapeutic recreation was not a result of his studies in higher education, but rather from his personal experiences. His interest in sport and recreation began early in life. He was very active in high school athletics and played varsity sports at Tarkio College in Missouri. He joined the army during World War II and was wounded by mortar fire during the Battle of the Bulge in the winter of 1944–1945 (shrapnel in his right shoulder). Humphrey spent almost a year in rehabilitation at a Veterans Administration Hospital in Denver to regain use of his right arm. During his rehabilitation, he found sports participation a more exciting approach to rehabilitation than other traditional therapies.

Humphrey became one of several truly dedicated leaders in the early development of therapeutic recreation who provided the foundation for the profession we enjoy today. He was a member of the Hospital Recreation Section of the American Recreation Society (HRS-ARS), and served as its Chairman from 1965–1966. During his tenure as Chair, the American Recreation Society (ARS) joined with four other national organizations to form the National Recreation and Park Association (NRPA). The Hospital Recreation Society, then a part of ARS, and under Humphrey's leadership, met with the leadership of the National Association of Recreational Therapists. Their discussions resulted in the merger of the two organizations which formed the National Therapeutic Recreation Society (NTRS). Humphrey has the distinction of being the only individual to serve two terms as president of the NTRS (1967–1968, 1988–1989).

In 1965 Humphrey accepted a faculty position at the University of Iowa. He developed both the undergraduate and graduate curricula at that university, a task that he would repeat at two other major universities (Pennsylvania State University, Temple University). In 1973, he earned his Ph.D. from Penn State University. Humphrey spent the last fifteen years of his professional career (1975–1990) as chairperson of the Department of Recreation at the University of Maryland. He was also responsible for the development of the Therapeutic Recreation Management School (1977), and later the Leisure and Aging Management School (1980). Both schools were originally held at Oglebay Park in Wheeling, West Virginia, but later moved to Springmaid Beach Resort in Myrtle Beach, South Carolina.

Humphrey will always be remembered as an advocate of recreation opportunities for people with disabilities. One of his earlier Rehabilitation

Services Administration grants, Community Recreation for Multiply Handicapped Adults (1974–1977) at Temple University, typified his commitment to unserved and underserved special population groups. He continually immersed himself in professional public service as a speaker, author, resource consultant, member of grant review panels, member and/or chair of accreditation teams, and member and/or chair of an extensive number of committees and task forces related to services for people with disabilities.

Humphrey earned many honors such as the Distinguished Service Award of NTRS (1971) and the Award for Outstanding Contribution to Graduate Education of Minorities from the Ethnic Minority Council of AAHPERD (1989). His contributions to therapeutic recreation may best be remembered through the establishment of the NTRS Fred Humphrey Public Policy Fellowship Program initiated in 1996.

For those so honored to have known and worked with Fred Humphrey, most would attest to the strong beliefs that he had in humankind and his chosen profession of therapeutic recreation. He gave freely of his time and expertise, and was always willing to help anyone who asked. He served the profession at a time of both growth and turmoil, and challenged therapeutic recreation professionals to be strong advocates for what they believed. At the annual membership meeting in San Antonio (1989), Humphrey commented about changes in the future and his vision of a dramatic expansion of the therapeutic recreation profession into more nontraditional and community-based settings in the twenty-first century. Challenging the role we would play, he stated:

> The choice is ours. We can bury our heads in the sands of the traditional definition of therapeutic recreation, or we can exercise a dynamic human service leadership role in the decade ahead.

Ira J. Hutchison
David C. Park, M.S.

Ira J. Hutchison began his career as a therapeutic recreation professional in 1950 when he became the Recreation Director of the Topeka (Kansas) State Hospital. Thus commenced a career that has spanned over fifty years and has touched the lives of scores of professionals, as well as thousands of individuals who are disabled or disadvantaged. Hutchison's career has also been characterized by outstanding leadership, a significant impact on the profession of therapeutic recreation, and on the lives of people with disabilities throughout the country.

Webster's Dictionary defines the word *pioneer* as "to open or prepare for others to follow." This word characterizes the career of Ira J. Hutchison. As one of the earliest full-time professionals in therapeutic recreation, he has frequently been in a position of initiating new programs or exploring new ways to enhance and improve services. As the Director of the Recreation Department at Topeka (Kansas) State Hospital in 1950, at a time when the profession was in its infancy, he was responsible for initiating new methods and techniques for meeting the needs of the patient population. While employed there he also established the first therapeutic recreation program on a pediatric ward at Stormont Vail General Hospital. In 1963, he initiated and directed the first tax-supported therapeutic recreation program for narcotic addicts in New York City, and in 1965 organized recreation and rehabilitation programs for emotionally disturbed populations at St. Vincent's Hospital in Harrison, New York.

Hutchison's pioneering work continued at the national level in 1966 when he was elected the first president of the newly created National Therapeutic Recreation Society, and in 1967 became the first full-time executive secretary of that organization. In 1969 he organized and directed the first Urban Affairs program for the National Recreation and Park Association which focused on the role of park and recreation opportunities to meet the unique needs of citizens in the inner cities of our nation. In 1979, as Deputy Director of the U.S. National Park Service, he created a special office to address the issue of equal accessibility for people with disabilities to the many wonders found in our National Parks. This program has over the years emerged as a national and international role model for providing equal opportunity for disabled citizens in the park and recreation environment. In 1983, Hutchison was named Director, Office of Historically Black Colleges and Universities Programs at the U.S. Department of the

Interior. This is the first professionally staffed office established within a cabinet-level department devoted exclusively to the interests of predominately Black educational institutions. Following his retirement from the Department of the Interior, he created Roundtable Associates, Inc., an organization of African American park, recreation, and conservation professionals.

Hutchison's accomplishments made immeasurable contributions to the emergence of therapeutic recreation as a vibrant and viable profession. Much of the success and recognition enjoyed by the therapeutic recreation profession today, as well as the increased opportunities for recreation participation by disabled and disadvantaged populations, is a direct result of the efforts and contributions of Ira J. Hutchison.

Ann James

Mandy B. Harrison, M.S.
Fran McGuire, Ph.D.

Ann James was born in Elmore, Ohio, in January 1942. James attended Bowling Green State University, and in 1964 received her Bachelor of Science in physical education and biology. After teaching physical education and biology in a Michigan high school, James began work as a therapeutic recreation specialist with the American Red Cross, and was assigned to military hospitals in the United States, Vietnam, and Germany. Having found her vocation, James returned to school at the University of North Carolina at Chapel Hill and had the fortune to have Lee Meyer and H. Douglas Sessoms as mentors—both influenced her professional philosophy. Meyer encouraged James to be aware of the changes in behavior rendered by recreation therapy, and Sessoms gave her an appreciation for the people and ideas that laid the foundation for current therapeutic recreation practice. James tries to emulate the keen ability of both Meyer and Sessoms to objectively analyze circumstances and ideas. During her time at Chapel Hill, James attended her first therapeutic recreation conference. Although James' philosophy differs significantly from that of Fred Humphrey, she was greatly influenced by his assertion in the plenary speech of the conference that recreation activities were neutral structures, neither good nor bad, but frameworks for experiences that could be either negative or positive. While she pursued her master's degree, James worked as a recreation therapist with developmentally disabled students in the public school system and assistant director of a day camp for emotionally disturbed youth and mentally retarded children. She received her master's degree in Recreation Administration with a Therapeutic Recreation focus from the University of North Carolina in 1971.

After receiving her master's degree, James worked as the Therapeutic Recreation Supervisor at Wilford Hall U.S. Air Force Medical Center in San Antonio, Texas. In 1974, she began studies toward her Ph.D. at the University of New Mexico. In 1975 James began to teach in the Department of Parks, Recreation, and Tourism Management of Clemson University. In 1980 she became the coordinator of the therapeutic recreation curriculum, and was department chair from 1995–1998. In addition to producing numerous journal articles, writing several chapters, and holding editorial positions, James published an analysis of the conceptual development of recreation therapy from Nightingale through Peterson as well as coauthoring the book,

Finding the Path: Ethics in Action. James' service has spanned both therapeutic recreation professional organizations. She served a term as president of National Therapeutic Recreation Society, as a member of the Board of Directors of ATRA, and on the NCTRC and ATRA Ethics boards. James was instrumental in establishing the Southeast Therapeutic Recreation Symposium. The Ann James Award was named in her honor to recognize the outstanding speaker of that annual symposium. In 2000, James' contributions were recognized by ATRA when she was given the Distinguished Fellow Award. Currently, basking in the glow of upcoming retirement, Ann James can be found at Clemson University, or possibly at her cabin on the lake, planning her next adventure.

Gerald S. O'Morrow

Morris W. Stewart, Ph.D., CTRS

Gerald S. O'Morrow has been a leader in therapeutic recreation for over three decades. His education, experience, teaching, and writing have all contributed to the development of the profession. More specifically, his involvement has been instrumental in enhancing the role of therapeutic recreation in the treatment process.

O'Morrow received each of his degrees in therapeutic recreation. He graduated with his B.A. from Sacramento State College in 1957, where he majored in recreation therapy and obtained a minor in psychology. After graduation, O'Morrow worked for one year as a therapeutic recreation practitioner before pursuing his master's degree in hospital recreation at the University of Minnesota. He completed his M.Ed. in 1959, and in 1969, under the supervision of Dr. Elliott Avedon, O'Morrow completed his Ed.D. in therapeutic recreation service at the Columbia University Teachers' College. His innovative doctoral dissertation entitled, *A Study of Recreation Services to Psychiatric Patients in Relation to Predischarge Planning and Aftercare*, foreshadowed the present emphasis on transitional services in therapeutic recreation. This research documented the first attempt at understanding leisure counseling, and developed a broader basis for therapeutic recreation beyond the walls of institutional settings.

Experience has always been an important aspect of therapeutic recreation. O'Morrow realized this and, as a practitioner, developed and administered numerous programs. His initial service was with clients within the state mental health system in California. He continued to develop his expertise and moved to the Indiana mental health system and worked in several state hospitals there. In 1966 he became the director of educational and activity therapies with the Indiana Department of Mental Health. He assumed responsibility for education and activity therapy service programs for nine psychiatric institutions and three hospitals and training schools for persons with mental retardation. In this position, O'Morrow recruited new professionals in therapeutic recreation to the Indiana mental health system through special training funds. Each student grant required a year of professional service upon graduation and provided incentive and support for these individuals to become therapeutic recreation specialists.

In 1968, O'Morrow began to "profess" therapeutic recreation as an associate professor at Indiana State University. Three years later he attained the rank of full professor. In 1973, became Chairperson of the Department of Recreation at Indiana State University. O'Morrow joined the faculty at the University of Georgia in 1976 where he coordinated the Department of Recreation and Leisure Studies' graduate program. In 1980, he accepted the position of professor and chair for the Department of Recreation and Leisure Services at Radford University in Virginia. Throughout his academic career, O'Morrow demanded that his students meet professional expectations that would prepare them to deal with the future of therapeutic recreation service. One of his goals is to have students understand the role of therapeutic recreation and how to facilitate the rehabilitative process through recreation services. As a teacher, he brings a wealth of experience to the classroom.

As an early leader in therapeutic recreation, O'Morrow edited one of the first textbooks in the field, the *Administration of Activity Therapy Service* (1966). This text became a reference volume for almost every professional in the field. Later he published *Therapeutic Recreation: A Helping Profession* (1976), one of the first textbooks to clearly identify the role and scope of contemporary therapeutic recreation service. This text is now in its third edition (1989) and, as noted by David Park, Chief of the National Park Service's Special Programs and Populations Branch, "adds immeasurably to the profession due to the special qualifications and expertise of the author." O'Morrow continued to expand his writing with *A Study Guide for the National Council for Therapeutic Recreation Certification Examination* (1990) and a more recent text entitled, *Effective Management in Therapeutic Recreation Service* (1997). His involvement in therapeutic recreation through authoring or coauthoring eight books or monographs and over 45 professional journal articles or book chapters has established O'Morrow as one of the most prolific and influential professionals in the history of therapeutic recreation.

During his career, O'Morrow twice served as president of the National Therapeutic Recreation Society, and received twelve special awards and citations for his exemplary service. These numerous awards include two of the highest honors given in the profession. The National Therapeutic Recreation Society acknowledged him with the Distinguished Service Award and with a prestigious Appreciation Award for twenty years of continued contributions—both of which speak clearly of his ongoing and significant commitment to therapeutic recreation. In 1995 the National Recreation and Park Association recognized him with the Distinguished Professional Award for his vision and leadership in the field of parks and recreation. O'Morrow's scholarly and service contributions have had a profound impact on therapeutic recreation service, and have served as a viable force for enhancing the quality of life for clients.

David C. Park

Youngkhill Lee, Ph.D., CTRS

David C. Park is one of the must-remember leaders in therapeutic recreation. Many of his contributions to the profession should be revisited to learn about his leadership and vision for the profession. This short biography describes his life history and highlights this leader's major contributions to the profession.

David Park was born in August 1, 1940. Park attended the University of Kentucky as a history major, and never imagined that he would become part of the history of a profession called therapeutic recreation. His first encounter with therapeutic recreation happened when he faced a financial need to stay in school, and found a part-time job as a recreation aide at the Eastern State Hospital in Lexington, Kentucky, in 1960. Park recalls that significant experience:

> It was this experience that convinced me that there was a "professional career opportunity," so I became quite interested in exploring the long-term possibilities. (D. Park, personal communication, 2001)

Park attended a Kentucky Department of Mental Health Workshop. There he met Dr. Gerald O'Morrow, who inspired him to pursue a master's degree in therapeutic recreation. Following graduation in 1962, he worked as a full-time assistant director for recreation at the Frankfort State Hospital and School for over two years. In 1964, he enrolled the graduate program at the University of North Carolina at Chapel Hill where he worked part-time at Memorial Hospital while completing his master's degree in therapeutic recreation.

When Park finished his master's degree in therapeutic recreation, he became Chief of the Therapeutic Recreation Services in the Department of Psychiatry at North Carolina Memorial Hospital. This administrative experience laid a strong foundation for his career. In his own words:

> The five years that I spent in Chapel Hill really refined my philosophical base of the profession, gave me experience in the pragmatic delivery of the service, and began my involvement in the professional development endeavors (D. Park, personal communication, 2001).

Park well recalls the year 1969, because that is when he became the full-time Executive Secretary of National Therapeutic Recreation Society (NTRS), succeeding Dr. Ira Hutchison. During Park's tenure, he served as managing editor of *Therapeutic Recreation Journal* and other publications by the Society, executive manager of the certification program, as coordinator of the Legislative Network, and chief provider of education and technical assistance for the Society. He further served the Board of Directors in several areas that needed the attention of the Society. Yet Park remains a humble leader who gives credit for his successes to his predecessor. Park has stated "It was Ira who mentored me for several years in that job" (D. Park, personal communication, 2001). Among Park's most important achievements were his efforts in developing a clear definition of therapeutic recreation. Park wanted to see the profession defined with clarity, greater consistency, and precision.

During the 1970s and early 1980s, Park and his NTRS colleagues experienced a lack of support and loss of professional freedom from NRPA. The group felt a burning need for a new professional association with a more focused identity and mission. In 1983 he and a group of colleagues gathered in his hotel room during the NRPA Congress in Kansas City and explored ways to establish a new professional organization. In 1984, the therapeutic recreation profession experienced one of its most significant turning points—the birth of American Therapeutic Recreation Association. This new organization emerged with focused mission and identity: to use recreation as a tool for treatment service. Park united his colleagues for advancement of the profession.

Park is still involved in the delivery of recreation services for people with disabilities as the National Park Service Accessibility Program Manager. While we don't have Park's direct leadership in the profession anymore, some lessons can be learned from David Park. Throughout his career he displayed that therapeutic recreation leaders should be servant leaders who are not promoters of themselves, but instead promoters of others, not administrators but initiators, not takers but givers, and not talkers but listeners and doers. David Park is a wonderful role model for all therapeutic recreation leaders.

Carol Ann Peterson

Janiece J. Sneegas, Ph.D., CTRS

Few people have had greater influence on the profession of therapeutic recreation than Carol Ann Peterson. Peterson's connection to the field began while she pursued a baccalaureate degree in recreation at the University of Illinois where she was mentored by Charles K. Brightbill. This background in leisure studies would serve as a foundation for her conceptualization of therapeutic recreation as a service delivery system with a focus on the leisure lifestyle of individuals with disabilities.

After completing her undergraduate degree, Peterson earned a master's degree in therapeutic recreation from San Jose State University. Upon graduating she worked on a psychiatric unit as a recreation therapist at St. Elizabeth's Hospital in Washington, DC. In 1968 she began her doctorate at Columbia University. Her first teaching job was at Indiana University. She subsequently taught at Michigan State University prior to moving to the University of Illinois where she would spend the next twelve years. She left Illinois in 1989 to assume the position of Department Chair at Virginia Commonwealth University. While at VCU she served as Interim Dean for the School of Community and Public Affairs. In 1994 she left to become Dean of the College of Human Performance and Development at the University of Nevada—Las Vegas where she remained until her retirement in 1997.

Peterson's contribution to therapeutic recreation in the areas of scholarship, teaching and service are remarkable. The influential text *Therapeutic Recreation Program Design: Principals and Procedures* is her most important and recognized work. This text (currently in its third edition, Peterson and Stumbo, 2000) introduced therapeutic recreation outcome programming based upon systems theory, and defined the Leisure Ability Model of therapeutic recreation. This book has received international recognition, and has even been published in Japanese.

Peterson is a consummate educator. Her enthusiasm, creativity, and dedication to the field inspired thousands of students; she entertains and educates simultaneously. While at Illinois she built a highly rated academic program at both the undergraduate and graduate level. Her influence in therapeutic recreation continues through the contributions of her students— many of whom are scholars and leaders in the field today.

Outstanding professional organization leadership highlights Peterson's energy and commitment to service in therapeutic recreation. She was elected to the Board of Directors of the National Therapeutic Recreation Society serving from 1975–1978 and from 1980–1981 as its President. She served on the Council of Accreditation 1982–1985 and was Vice-Chair of the Council in 1984–1985. Peterson was a founding member of the American Therapeutic Recreation Association. She worked extensively as Committee Member (1990–1992, 1993–1994) and chaired the Future Scholars Program for the Academy of Leisure Sciences (1992–1993).

Peterson received several awards throughout her career. She has been inducted as a Fellow of the Academy of Leisure Sciences and as a Fellow of the American Academy of Park and Recreation Administrators. Peterson received the Brightbill Alumni Award from the University of Illinois, the Individual Citation from the Alberta Therapeutic Recreation Association, the Honor Award from the American Association for Leisure and Recreation, and the Distinguished Service Award from the National Therapeutic Recreation Association.

How then to summarize the many contributions of Carol Ann Peterson? Her influence has been profound, far-reaching, and long-lasting. Her brush strokes are bold and clearly identifiable—they have made the canvas of therapeutic recreation more visible, vibrant, affecting, and effective. Numerous colleagues, students, therapeutic recreation practitioners and therapeutic recreation consumers have benefited from her energy, commitment and dedication to the profession of therapeutic recreation.

Gary M. Robb

Gerald Hitzhusen, M.S., CTRS

Gary Robb's leadership in therapeutic recreation spans more than thirty years and includes service as a practitioner, educator, and administrator. Currently Robb is the Executive Director of Bradford Woods Outdoor Education and Leadership Development Center. He also directs the National Center on Accessibility and is an Associate Professor in the Department of Recreation and Park Administration at Indiana University. Robb's educational background includes bachelor's and master's degrees from the University of Utah. After working for two years as a Boys Club director, Robb's career in therapeutic recreation began. In 1967 he became a practitioner at the Children's Psychiatric Center in Salt Lake City, Utah. Three years later, he took a position as an instructor in the Department of Leisure Studies at the University of Massachusetts at Amherst. In 1973, Robb went to the University of Illinois, serving as an Assistant Professor and therapeutic recreation specialist until 1976. As his career progressed, Robb complemented his knowledge of therapeutic recreation with expertise in external funding and outdoor recreation.

These combined skills serve him well. In 1976, Robb became the Executive Director at Camp Allen, a residential camping facility in New Hampshire. His leadership enabled Camp Allen to become one of the most prominent and successful camping programs for people with disabilities in the United States. Robb left Camp Allen in 1979 to accept his current positions at Bradford Woods and Indiana University. During his career, Robb developed federal and state grants and contracts in therapeutic and outdoor recreation for people with disabilities that total over three million dollars.

Robb's commitment to therapeutic recreation, outdoor recreation, and accessibility for people with disabilities is evident in the services he has provided, as well as the awards he has received. For example, Robb is a past President of the National Therapeutic Recreation Society (NTRS), and received its highest honor, the Distinguished Service Award, in 1979. He served on the governing boards for NTRS, the National Recreation and Park Association, the National Coalition on Education in the Outdoors, and the Therapeutic Recreation Management School. He served as a member of the President's Committee on Employment of the Handicapped, as well as the U.S. Access Board's Recreation Advisory Committee. In 1995, Robb received the Distinguished Service Award from the Latin American and Caribbean Council of Applied Sciences to Physical Education and Sports.

Robb has also provided educational and academic leadership to the field of therapeutic recreation. He has conducted more than 160 presentations and workshops in the United States and has lectured and led workshops in the West Indies, Puerto Rico, England, Portugal, Spain, Scotland, and Wales. He has published more than 35 articles in a variety of venues, plus numerous booklets, guides, and educational materials. Robb has been a co-coordinator of the Midwest Symposium on Therapeutic Recreation and is presently co-coordinator of the International Symposium on Therapeutic Recreation. He has served as a coeditor of a special issue of *Therapeutic Recreation Journal*, and is a coauthor of *Therapeutic Recreation: A Practical Approach* with Marcia Carter and Glen Van Andel. Now in its second edition, this text has served as a valuable introduction to the field of therapeutic recreation for university students since 1985. Robb's prolific scholarship earned him the Hollis Fait Scholar Award in 1991.

Robb's professional career is dedicated to removing barriers to recreation participation for people with disabilities. In recent years, this professional drive has merged with one of Robb's avocational interests—golf. He has served as codirector of a series of national forums on accessible golf and is a member of the Association of Disabled American Golfers' Board of Directors. Today, Robb is widely recognized as one of the nation's foremost authorities on making golf accessible to people with disabilities.

The field of therapeutic recreation thanks Gary Robb for his many contributions as well as his continuing efforts on behalf of people with disabilities. Drive on.

References

Ball, E. L. (1970). The meaning of therapeutic recreation. *Therapeutic Recreation Journal*, 4(1), 17–18.

Ball, E. L. (1968). Academic preparation for therapeutic recreation personnel. *Therapeutic Recreation Journal*, 5(2), 13–19.

Boyd, N. L. (1919). *Hospital and bedside games.* Chicago, IL: Author.

Eilenberger, C. (1992). *The contributions of Edith L. Ball to the professional field of recreation 1930–1985.* Doctoral dissertation, Texas Woman's University, Denton, Texas.

Simon, P. (1971). *Play and game theory in group work: A collection of papers by Neva Leona Boyd.* Chicago, IL: University of Illinois at Chicago Circle.

Other Books by Venture Publishing, Inc.

The A•B•Cs of Behavior Change: Skills for Working With Behavior Problems in Nursing Homes
by Margaret D. Cohn, Michael A. Smyer, and Ann L. Horgas

Activity Experiences and Programming Within Long-Term Care
by Ted Tedrick and Elaine R. Green

The Activity Gourmet
by Peggy Powers

Advanced Concepts for Geriatric Nursing Assistants
by Carolyn A. McDonald

Adventure Programming
edited by John C. Miles and Simon Priest

Assessment: The Cornerstone of Activity Programs
by Ruth Perschbacher

Behavior Modification in Therapeutic Recreation: An Introductory Manual
by John Datillo and William D. Murphy

Benefits of Leisure
edited by B. L. Driver, Perry J. Brown, and George L. Peterson

Benefits of Recreation Research Update
by Judy M. Sefton and W. Kerry Mummery

Beyond Bingo: Innovative Programs for the New Senior
by Sal Arrigo, Jr., Ann Lewis, and Hank Mattimore

Beyond Bingo 2: More Innovative Programs for the New Senior
by Sal Arrigo, Jr.

Both Gains and Gaps: Feminist Perspectives on Women's Leisure
by Karla Henderson, M. Deborah Bialeschki, Susan M. Shaw, and Valeria J. Freysinger

Dimensions of Choice: A Qualitative Approach to Recreation, Parks, and Leisure Research
by Karla A. Henderson

Diversity and the Recreation Profession: Organizational Perspectives
edited by Maria T. Allison and Ingrid E. Schneider

Effective Management in Therapeutic Recreation Service
by Gerald S. O'Morrow and Marcia Jean Carter

Everything From A to Y: The Zest Is up to You! Older Adult Activities for Every Day of the Year
by Nancy R. Cheshire and Martha L. Kenney

Evaluating Leisure Services: Making Enlightened Decisions, Second Edition
by Karla A. Henderson and M. Deborah Bialeschki

The Evolution of Leisure: Historical and Philosophical Perspectives
by Thomas Goodale and Geoffrey Godbey

Experience Marketing: Strategies for the New Millennium
by Ellen L. O'Sullivan and Kathy J. Spangler

Facilitation Techniques in Therapeutic Recreation
by John Dattilo

File o' Fun: A Recreation Planner for Games & Activities, Third Edition
by Jane Harris Ericson and Diane Ruth Albright

The Game and Play Leader's Handbook: Facilitating Fun and Positive Interaction
by Bill Michaelis and John M. O'Connell

The Game Finder—A Leader's Guide to Great Activities
by Annette C. Moore

Getting People Involved in Life and Activities: Effective Motivating Techniques
by Jeanne Adams

Glossary of Recreation Therapy and Occupational Therapy
by David R. Austin

Great Special Events and Activities
by Annie Morton, Angie Prosser, and Sue Spangler

Group Games & Activity Leadership
by Kenneth J. Bulik

*Hands on! Children's Activities for Fairs,
Festivals, and Special Events*
by Karen L. Ramey

*Inclusive Leisure Services: Responding to
the Rights of People with Disabilities,
Second Edition*
by John Dattilo

*Innovations: A Recreation Therapy
Approach to Restorative Programs*
by Dawn R. De Vries and Julie M. Lake

*Internships in Recreation and Leisure Ser-
vices: A Practical Guide for Students,
Second Edition*
by Edward E. Seagle, Jr., Ralph W. Smith,
and Lola M. Dalton

*Interpretation of Cultural and Natural
Resources*
by Douglas M. Knudson, Ted T. Cable,
and Larry Beck

Intervention Activities for At-Risk Youth
by Norma J. Stumbo

*Introduction to Recreation and Leisure
Services, 8th Edition*
by Karla A. Henderson, M. Deborah
Bialeschki, John L. Hemingway, Jan
S. Hodges, Beth D. Kivel, and H.
Douglas Sessoms

*Introduction to Writing Goals and Objec-
tives: A Manual for Recreation Therapy
Students and Entry-Level Professionals*
by Suzanne Melcher

*Leadership and Administration of Outdoor
Pursuits, Second Edition*
by Phyllis Ford and James Blanchard

*Leadership in Leisure Services: Making a
Difference, Second Edition*
by Debra J. Jordan

*Leisure and Leisure Services in the 21st
Century*
by Geoffrey Godbey

*The Leisure Diagnostic Battery: Users
Manual and Sample Forms*
by Peter A. Witt and Gary Ellis

*Leisure Education I: A Manual of Activities
and Resources, Second Edition*
by Norma J. Stumbo

*Leisure Education II: More Activities and
Resources, Second Edition*
by Norma J. Stumbo

*Leisure Education III: More Goal-Oriented
Activities*
by Norma J. Stumbo

*Leisure Education IV: Activities for
Individuals with Substance Addictions*
by Norma J. Stumbo

*Leisure Education Program Planning: A
Systematic Approach, Second Edition*
by John Dattilo

Leisure Education Specific Programs
by John Dattilo

*Leisure in Your Life: An Exploration, Fifth
Edition*
by Geoffrey Godbey

*Leisure Services in Canada: An Introduction,
Second Edition*
by Mark S. Searle and Russell E. Brayley

*Leisure Studies: Prospects for the Twenty-
First Century*
edited by Edgar L. Jackson and Thomas
L. Burton

*The Lifestory Re-Play Circle: A Manual of
Activities and Techniques*
by Rosilyn Wilder

*Models of Change in Municipal Parks and
Recreation: A Book of Innovative Case
Studies*
edited by Mark E. Havitz

*More Than a Game: A New Focus on Senior
Activity Services*
by Brenda Corbett

*Nature and the Human Spirit: Toward an
Expanded Land Management Ethic*
edited by B. L. Driver, Daniel Dustin,
Tony Baltic, Gary Elsner, and George
Peterson

*Outdoor Recreation Management: Theory
and Application, Third Edition*
by Alan Jubenville and Ben Twight

Planning Parks for People, Second Edition
by John Hultsman, Richard L. Cottrell,
and Wendy Z. Hultsman

Other Books by Venture Publishing, Inc.

The Process of Recreation Programming Theory and Technique, Third Edition
by Patricia Farrell and Herberta M. Lundegren

Programming for Parks, Recreation, and Leisure Services: A Servant Leadership Approach
by Donald G. DeGraaf, Debra J. Jordan, and Kathy H. DeGraaf

Protocols for Recreation Therapy Programs
edited by Jill Kelland, along with the Recreation Therapy Staff at Alberta Hospital Edmonton

Quality Management: Applications for Therapeutic Recreation
edited by Bob Riley

A Recovery Workbook: The Road Back from Substance Abuse
by April K. Neal and Michael J. Taleff

Recreation and Leisure: Issues in an Era of Change, Third Edition
edited by Thomas Goodale and Peter A. Witt

Recreation Economic Decisions: Comparing Benefits and Costs, Second Edition
by John B. Loomis and Richard G. Walsh

Recreation for Older Adults: Individual and Group Activities
by Judith A. Elliott and Jerold E. Elliott

Recreation Programming and Activities for Older Adults
by Jerold E. Elliott and Judith A. Sorg-Elliott

Reference Manual for Writing Rehabilitation Therapy Treatment Plans
by Penny Hogberg and Mary Johnson

Research in Therapeutic Recreation: Concepts and Methods
edited by Marjorie J. Malkin and Christine Z. Howe

Simple Expressions: Creative and Therapeutic Arts for the Elderly in Long-Term Care Facilities
by Vicki Parsons

A Social History of Leisure Since 1600
by Gary Cross

A Social Psychology of Leisure
by Roger C. Mannell and Douglas A. Kleiber

Steps to Successful Programming: A Student Handbook to Accompany Programming for Parks, Recreation, and Leisure Services
by Donald G. DeGraaf, Debra J. Jordan, and Kathy H. DeGraaf

Stretch Your Mind and Body: Tai Chi as an Adaptive Activity
by Duane A. Crider and William R. Klinger

Therapeutic Activity Intervention with the Elderly: Foundations & Practices
by Barbara A. Hawkins, Marti E. May, and Nancy Brattain Rogers

Therapeutic Recreation and the Nature of Disabilities
by Kenneth E. Mobily and Richard MacNeil

Therapeutic Recreation: Cases and Exercises, Second Edition
by Barbara C. Wilhite and M. Jean Keller

Therapeutic Recreation in the Nursing Home
by Linda Buettner and Shelley L. Martin

Therapeutic Recreation Protocol for Treatment of Substance Addictions
by Rozanne W. Faulkner

Tourism and Society: A Guide to Problems and Issues
by Robert W. Wyllie

A Training Manual for Americans with Disabilities Act Compliance in Parks and Recreation Settings
by Carol Stensrud

 Venture Publishing, Inc.
1999 Cato Avenue
State College, PA 16801
phone: 814–234–4561
fax: 814–234–1651